Roadside Flowers of Texas

NUMBER ONE

The Elma Dill Russell Spencer Foundation Series

The Elma Dill Russell Spencer Foundation Series

With the publication of this volume the University of Texas takes pride in announcing the establishment of the Elma Dill Russell Spencer Foundation Series, made possible by a gift to the University from Mrs. Richard French Spencer of San Antonio through the Foundation which bears her name.

Mrs. Spencer's far-sighted action was inspired by the memory of her father, the late Richard Robertson Russell, himself a great and generous Texan, who taught his daughter not only to know the wildflowers of Texas but to cherish all that is good in the heritage of the State.

Proceeds from the sale of this volume and subsequent books in the Elma Dill Russell Spencer Foundation Series will go into a revolving fund for the publication of other books of importance to Texas. Mrs. Spencer's gift will thus continue to enrich the State which both she and her father have known and served so well.

HARRY H. RANSOM, *President*
The University of Texas

March, 1961

FLUTTER-MILL
Oenothera missouriensis

ROADSIDE
FLOWERS
OF TEXAS

Paintings by Mary Motz Wills

Text by Howard S. Irwin

UNIVERSITY OF TEXAS PRESS · AUSTIN

International Standard Book Number 0-292-77009-X
Library of Congress Catalog Card Number 59-12861

First Paperback Printing, 1975

A Note on the Paintings

IN 1913 Col. W. D. Wills, a U.S. Army officer stationed in the Canal Zone, adopted the practice of bringing home to his wife, who was recuperating from a serious illness, many of the exotic wildflowers of Panama. A skilled painter and an enthusiastic amateur botanist, Mrs. Wills began executing delicate watercolors of the more beautiful species. Soon she became fascinated by the challenge of capturing with her brush the elusive beauty of these flowers.

Some years later, after Colonel Wills' untimely death in Maryland, Mrs. Wills took up her permanent residence in Abilene, Texas. Here she plunged with enthusiasm into the task of making a pictorial record of the wildflowers of Texas, a project which was to engage her attention for most of the next forty-seven years. Constantly on the lookout for species which had not yet come before her easel, she enlisted the aid of friends throughout the state, who sent her many rare flowers. Garden clubs became interested in her work, and she soon found herself in constant demand as a lecturer.

Mrs. Wills' first important recognition came when Ellen Schulz Quillin of the Witte Museum, herself the author of a splendid book on the wildflowers of Texas, brought her paintings to San Antonio for a major exhibit; the Witte later purchased one hundred of them for its permanent collection. During the Texas Centennial celebration, B. C. Tharp, professor of botany at the University of Texas, took a large collection of Mrs. Wills' paintings to Austin; through his agency the Texas Memorial Museum purchased 450 of them. Many additional paintings are in private hands. All in all, Mrs. Wills has produced more than 2,000 paintings of Texas wildflowers.

The watercolors reproduced in this book were selected from the two museum collections mentioned above and from Mrs. Wills' personal store. The publishers are deeply grateful to Ellen Schulz Quillin of the Witte Museum and to W. W. Newcomb, Jr., of the Texas Memorial Museum for their generosity in making paintings from their institutions available for reproduction.

vii

Contents

ix

Introduction

OF THE MORE THAN 5,000 species of flowering plants known to occur naturally in Texas, at least 1,000 fall into the popular category of "wildflower." All Texas plants, of course, in the strictest sense are wildflowers, but for most of us the term is reserved for the more attractive, conspicuous members of our native flora. This book contains keys to and paintings and descriptions of 257 species of the more common wildflowers of the state, together with casual notes on many more. Inevitably, there have been omissions, especially of certain kinds which are plentifully represented in scattered local areas. But our attempt has been to include the most widely distributed *and* common plants, with special attention to those frequenting fields, fence rows, forest borders, roadside shoulders, and other places readily reached by motorists.

Distributional ranges are in most instances outlined by counties. For the reader not familiar with Texas counties these ranges may be worked out with the aid of the map and the legend following the Keys, on page 86. Although a conscientious attempt has been made to employ recent information in determining the distribution of each described species, the reader should remember that plants are more or less migratory and that every year species are found in localities where their presence had not been previously recorded. Unfortunately, it is true also that some are decreasing in frequency and range, largely because of the vast and sudden changes wrought on natural habitats through human activity.

Botanists have long given up attempting to include more than a smattering of common names in floras and manuals. However, for the student of wildflowers common names are not only useful tools of identification but also indexes of utility, history, and folklore. The common names used in the headings of this book are those which are in most general use; invention or modification has been held to a minimum. As a result, one important limitation of common names becomes readily apparent: different species of plants—sometimes close relatives (e.g., the numerous Yuccas and the various Blue-bonnets), sometimes distantly related or unrelated species (e.g., the Buttercups)—often share the same common name. Thus, the reader should become familiar also with the much maligned and misunderstood scientific names. * Several criteria were used in determining the common name in most general use: (1) the geographical extent of its use on a national level, (2) the geographical extent of its use in Texas, and (3) its relative popularity throughout its geographical extent. All common names known to be in use, along with the selected key common name, have been included in the textual discussion of the species and in the index.

The authors firmly believe that a full understanding and appreciation of wildflowers can come only with study. Such study is facilitated by some knowledge of the external structure of plants. For some readers, the descriptions may at first seem "too technical," but through liberal use of the glossaries and with a little practice the relatively few technical terms used will soon become well-understood and helpful tools. Possession of them in one's vocabulary and an appreciation of the concepts they embrace as well as the conciseness they afford will surely increase one's understanding of plants and further his desire to learn more. It should be said here that it is our goal rather to encourage an intelligent interest in Texas wildflowers than to stimulate purely sentimental rapture.

Two means of approach to the identification of an unknown wildflower are possible with this handbook. The first is a hit-or-miss search through the illustrations until the proper one is found. The second, much to be preferred, entails use of the keys, beginning with Key A on page 66, to determine the name, then a comparison of the plant in hand with the illustration referred to by the keys, and finally a closer check by comparison with the appropriate description. The latter approach to identification is better not only because the keys virtually force one to take a good look at the plant but also because they point out the differences among plants. The descriptions, in addition to requiring a closer examination of the plant, fill in the details that cannot always be seen in the illustrations and make one aware of the breadth of variability in that species. This last aspect is important since each illustration is but a single fixed image of what in nearly every instance is a variable species. Variability may sometimes extend beyond the limits given in the descriptions; exceptionally vigorous or extremely unthrifty plants may well exceed or fall below the dimensional information given. Flowering dates will have to be modified according to one's position in the state as

---

*An excellent discussion of this subject appears in L. H. Shinners' *Spring Flora of the Dallas-Fort Worth Area* (1958), Appendix III.

well as by the character of the season—whether cool or warm, wet or dry. It must always be borne in mind that the number of plants included is limited. The reader should not expect from this volume successful identification of rare or exotic kinds.

The keys involve a series of choices, mostly of an "either-or" nature, but in some instances there are three or more alternatives. In any given couplet or larger grouping, one chooses the statement which best fits the material at hand and then proceeds to the next couplet as indicated by the number or letter in the right-hand margin. Eventually a name is reached. If the material to be identified does not match the illustration or description under that name elsewhere in the book, there are two possibilities. Either a mistake has been made in using the key, or else the material at hand is not accounted for in the key. For those unfamiliar with keys, valuable practice may be had by tracing through a wildflower whose name is already known.

The authors wish to express their gratitude and appreciation to the following for their assistance in the preparation of this book: Drs. B. L. Turner, B. C. Tharp, and M. C. Johnston, Department of Botany of the University of Texas, for much incidental information and continued encouragement; Dr. Walter H. Lewis, Department of Biology of Stephen F. Austin State College, Nacogdoches, for help with Texas roses; Dr. Barton H. Warnock, Department of Biology of Sul Ross State College, Alpine, for suggestions regarding Trans-Pecos species; Dr. W. W. Newcomb, Jr., Director of the Texas Memorial Museum, Austin, and Mrs. Ellen Schulz Quillin, Director of the Witte Museum, San Antonio, for the loan of paintings. We also wish to thank Mrs. Marian S. Irwin for typing the manuscript and for her many editorial suggestions.

Roadside Flowers of Texas

Plate numbers are repeated in bold-face type in the margins of the text pages where the flowers depicted in the plates are described. This makes possible easy cross reference between text and pictures.

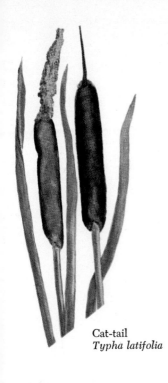

Cat-tail
Typha latifolia

Eastern Arrow-head
Sagittaria latifolia

Spanish-moss
Tillandsia usneoides

Ball-moss
Tillandsia recurvata

1

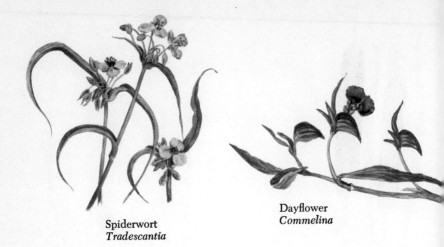

Spiderwort
Tradescantia

Dayflower
Commelina

Green-lily
Schoenocaulon drummondii

Wild Onion
Allium drummondii

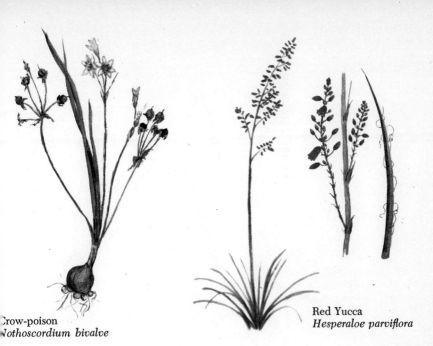

Crow-poison
Nothoscordium bivalve

Red Yucca
Hesperaloe parviflora

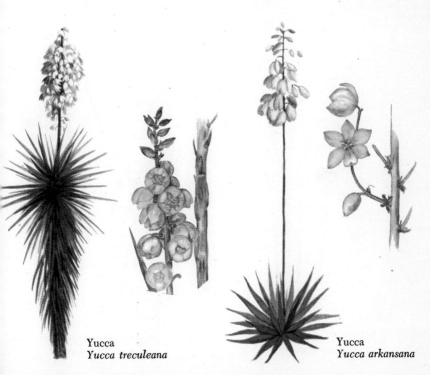

Yucca
Yucca treculeana

Yucca
Yucca arkansana

3

Yellow Star-grass
Hypoxis hirsuta

Sotol
Dasylirion texanum

Rain-lily
Cooperia drummondii

Left: Rain-lily
      Cooperia pedunculata
Right: Atamasco-lily
      Zephyranthes texana

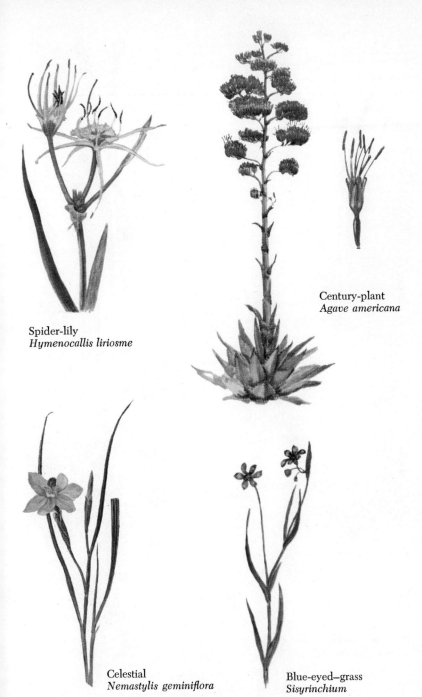

Spider-lily
Hymenocallis liriosme

Century-plant
Agave americana

Celestial
Nemastylis geminiflora

Blue-eyed–grass
Sisyrinchium

5

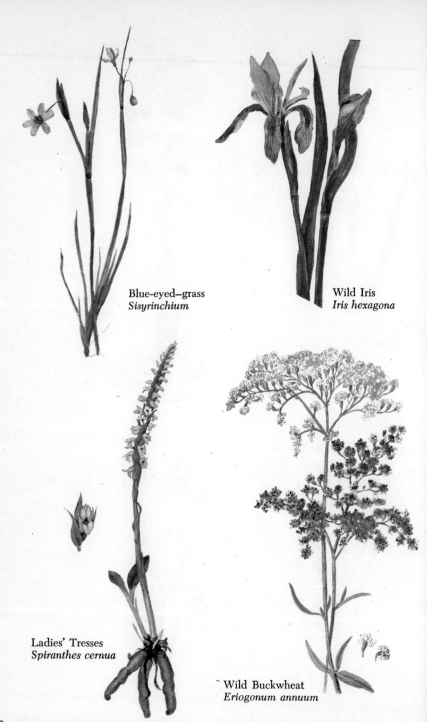

Blue-eyed–grass
Sisyrinchium

Wild Iris
Iris hexagona

Ladies' Tresses
Spiranthes cernua

Wild Buckwheat
Eriogonum annuum

Canaigre
Rumex hymenosepalus

Snake-cotton
Froelichia floridana

Umbrellawort
Mirabilis nyctagineus

Left: Spiderling
     Boerhavia erecta
Right: Wine-flower
     Boerhavia coccinea

7

Sand-verbena
Abronia fragrans

Devil's-bouquet
Nyctaginea capitata

Angel's-trumpet
Acleisanthes longiflora

Small Pokeweed
Rivina humilis

Moss-rose
Portulaca pilosa

Great Pokeweed
Phytolacca americana

Pusley
Portulaca oleracea

Flame-flower
Talinum lineare

9

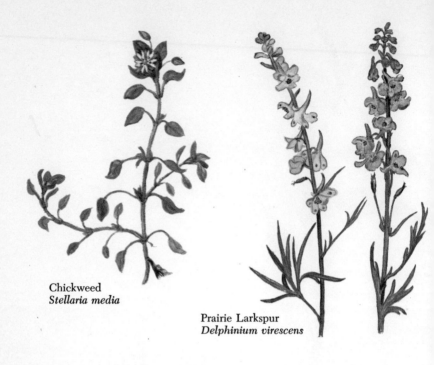

Chickweed
Stellaria media

Prairie Larkspur
Delphinium virescens

Anemone
Anemone decapetala

Old-man's–beard
Clematis drummondii

Large-flowered Buttercup
Ranunculus macranthus

Leather-flower
Clematis reticulata

Water-lily
Nymphaea elegans

Agarita
Berberis trifoliata

11

Texas Prickly-poppy
Argemone albiflora

Yellow Prickly-poppy
Argemone aenea

Red Prickly-poppy
Argemone sanguinea

Virginia Peppergrass
Lepidium virginicum

Large-flowered Peppergrass
Lepidium alyssoides

Wild Mustard
Brassica juncea

Left: Whitlow-grass
       Draba platycarpa
Right: Bladderpod
       Lesquerella gracilis

Left: Large-flowered Clammy-weed
       Polanisia dodecandra var.
         uniglandulosa
Right: Clammy-weed
       Polanisia dodecandra var.
         trachysperma

13

Wild White Rose
Rosa bracteata

Wild Pink Rose
Rosa setigera

Wild Blackberry
Rubus trivialis

Apache-plume
Fallugia paradoxa

Sensitive-briar
Schrankia uncinata

Huisache
Acacia farnesiana

Mesquite
Prosopis juliflora

Redbud
Cercis canadensis

15

Two-leaved Senna
Cassia roemeriana

Lindheimer's Senna
Cassia lindheimeriana

Partridge-pea
Cassia fasciculata

Paloverde
Parkinsonia aculeata

16

Bird-of-paradise
Caesalpinia gilliesii

Wild-indigo
Baptisia leucophaea

Bluebonnet
Lupinus subcarnosus

Bush-pea
Baptisia sphaerocarpa

Bluebonnet
Lupinus texensis

Top: Yellow Sweet-clover
      Melilotus officinalis
Center: White Sweet-clover
      Melilotus albus
Bottom: Alfalfa
      Medicago sativa

Shrubby Dalea
Dalea frutescens

Scurvy-pea
Psoralea cuspidata

Goat's-rue
Tephrosia lindheimeri

Catgut
Tephrosia virginiana

Woolly Loco
Astragalus mollissimus

Bush-clover
Lespedeza virginica

19

Coral-bean
Erythrina herbacea

Storksbill
Erodium texanum

Pin-clover
Erodium cicutarium

Yellow Wood-sorrel
Oxalis dillenii

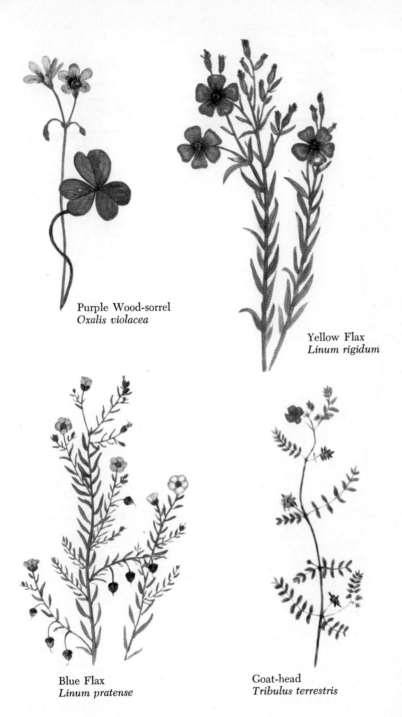

Purple Wood-sorrel
Oxalis violacea

Yellow Flax
Linum rigidum

Blue Flax
Linum pratense

Goat-head
Tribulus terrestris

21

Creosote-bush
Larrea tridentata

Desert-poppy
Kallstroemia grandiflora

White Milkwort
Polygala alba

Pink Milkwort
Polygala polygama

Blue Milkwort
Polygala longa

Bull-nettle
Cnidoscolus texanus

Snow-on-the-mountain
Euphorbia bicolor

Flowering Spurge
Euphorbia corollata

23

Shining Sumac
Rhus copallina

Smooth Sumac
Rhus glabra

Top: Virginia-creeper
    Parthenocissus quinquefolia
Bottom: Poison-ivy; Poison-oak
    Rhus toxicodendron

Red Buckeye
Aesculus pavia

Left: Velvet-leaf
     Wissadula holosericea
Right: Indian Mallow
     Abutilon incanum

Copper-mallow
Sphaeralcea angustifolia

Wine-cups
Left: *Callirhoe involucrata*
Center: *Callirhoe leiocarpa*
Right: *Callirhoe digitata*

Turk's-cap
Malvaviscus drummondii

25

Ocotillo
Fouquieria splendens

Bird's-foot Violet
Viola pedata

Missouri Violet
Viola missouriensis

Wild Pansy
Viola bicolor

May-pop
Passiflora incarnata

Stick-leaf
Mentzelia nuda

Stick-leaf
Mentzelia oligosperma

Texas Prickly-pear
Opuntia lindheimeri

27

Cholla
Opuntia arborescens

Tasajillo
Opuntia leptocaulis

Devil's-head
Echinocactus texensis

Meadow-beauty
Rhexia virginica

Buttercup
Oenothera triloba

Cut-leaved Evening-primrose
Oenothera laciniata

Pink Evening-primrose
Oenothera speciosa

Flutter-mill
Oenothera missouriensis

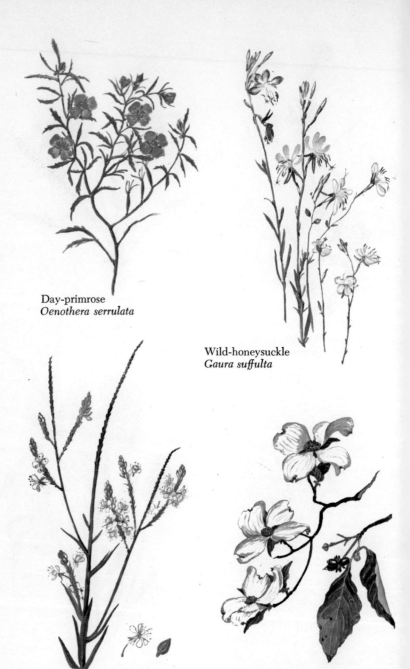

Day-primrose
Oenothera serrulata

Wild-honeysuckle
Gaura suffulta

False-gaura
Stenosiphon linifolium

Eastern Dogwood
Cornus florida

Wild Carrot
Daucus pusillus

Eryngo
Eryngium leavenworthii

Menodora
Menodora longiflora

Redbud
Menodora heterophylla

Meadow-pink
Sabatia campestris

Blue-bell
Eustoma grandiflorum

Butterfly-weed
Asclepias tuberosa

Purple Milkweed
Asclepias brachystephana

Green Milkweed
Asclepias oenotheroides

Shaggy Evolvulus
Evolvulus nuttallianus

Top: Texas Bindweed
       Convolvulus hermannioides
Bottom: Wild Morning-glory
       Ipomoea trichocarpa

Goat-foot—creeper
Ipomoea pes-caprae

Dodder
Cuscuta

Texas Baby-blue-eyes
Nemophila phacelioides

Blue-curls
Phacelia congesta

Phacelia
Phacelia patuliflora

Prairie Phlox
Phlox pilosa

Dwarf Phlox
Phlox nana

Annual Phlox
Left: *Phlox glabriflora*
Right: *Phlox drummondii*

Annual Phlox
Left: *Phlox cuspidata* var. *humilis*
Right: *Phlox cuspidata*

35

White Gilia
Gilia longiflora

Blue Gilia
Gilia rigidula

Standing-cypress
Ipomopsis rubra

Purple Ground-cherry
Quincula lobata

Ground-cherry
Physalis angulata

Ground-cherry
Physalis viscosa var.
cinerascens

Trompillo
Solanum eleagnifolium

White Nightshade
Solanum triquetrum

Left: Horse-nettle
     Solanum dimidiatum
Right: Buffalo-bur
     Solanum rostratum

Mustard-tree
Nicotiana glauca

Smooth Jimson-weed
Datura stramonium

Hairy Jimson-weed
Datura wrightii

Puccoon
Lithospermum incisum

Wide-flowered Heliotrope
Heliotropium convolvulaceum

Prairie Verbena
Verbena bipinnatifida

Low Verbena
Verbena pumila

39

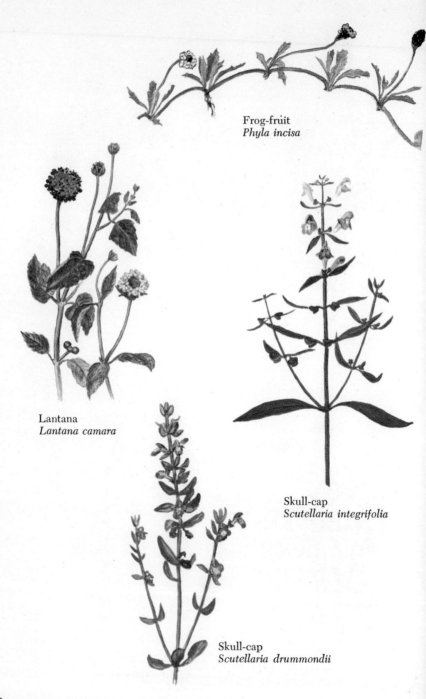

Frog-fruit
Phyla incisa

Lantana
Lantana camara

Skull-cap
Scutellaria integrifolia

Skull-cap
Scutellaria drummondii

Rattlesnake-flower
Brazoria scutellarioides

Lion-heart
Physostegia intermedia

Heal-all
Prunella vulgaris

Henbit
Lamium amplexicaule

41

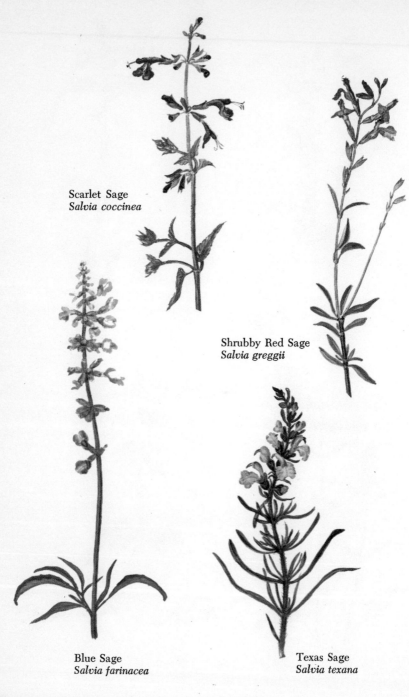

Scarlet Sage
Salvia coccinea

Shrubby Red Sage
Salvia greggii

Blue Sage
Salvia farinacea

Texas Sage
Salvia texana

Pink Horsemint
Monarda fistulosa

Left: Lemon Horsemint
Monarda citriodora
Right: Yellow Horsemint
Monarda punctata

Great Mullein
Verbascum thapsus

Cenizo
Leucophyllum frutescens

43

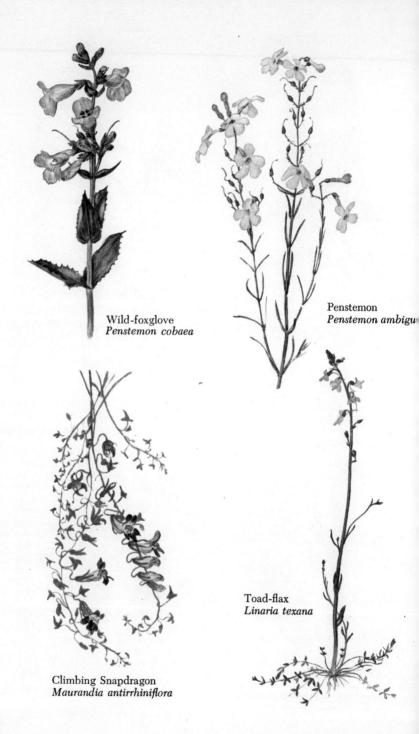

Wild-foxglove
Penstemon cobaea

Penstemon
Penstemon ambigu

Climbing Snapdragon
Maurandia antirrhiniflora

Toad-flax
Linaria texana

Western Paintbrush
Castilleja latebracteata

Purple Paintbrush
Castilleja purpurea

Left: Scarlet Paintbrush
    Castilleja indivisa
Right: Yellow Paintbrush
    Castilleja purpurea var.
      citrina

Snake-herb
Dyschoriste linearis

45

False-mint
Dicliptera brachiata

Wild-petunia
Ruellia occidentalis

Wild-petunia
Ruellia caroliniensis
var. *semicalva*

Trumpet-creeper
Campsis radicans

46

Yellow-elder
Tecoma stans

Cross-vine
Anisostichus capreolatus

Desert-willow
Chilopsis linearis

Devil's-claws
Martynia louisianica

Ribbon-grass
Plantago lanceolata

Heller's Plantain
Plantago helleri

Texas Mistletoe
Phoradendron serotinum

Button-bush
Cephalanthus occidentalis

48

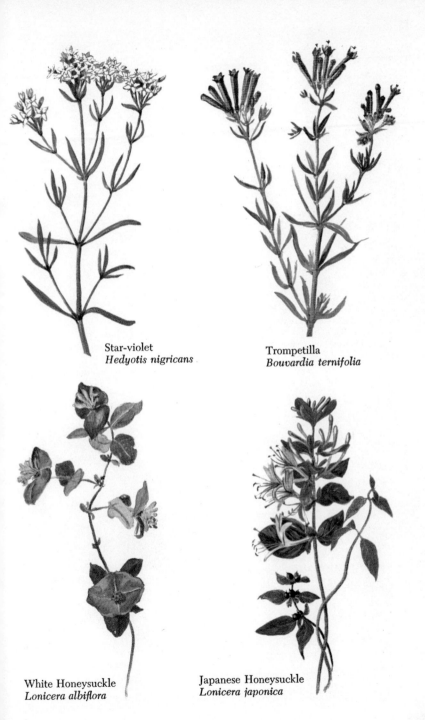

Star-violet
Hedyotis nigricans

Trompetilla
Bouvardia ternifolia

White Honeysuckle
Lonicera albiflora

Japanese Honeysuckle
Lonicera japonica

Coral Honeysuckle
Lonicera sempervirens

Elderberry
Sambucus canadensis

Lamb's-lettuce
Valerianella amarella

Wild Gourd
Cucurbita foetidissima

50

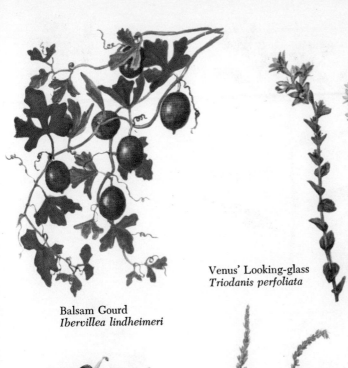

Balsam Gourd
Ibervillea lindheimeri

Venus' Looking-glass
Triodanis perfoliata

Blue Lobelia
Lobelia appendiculata

Cardinal-flower
Lobelia cardinalis

51

Iron-weed
Vernonia texana

Iron-weed
Vernonia lindheimeri

Elephant-foot
Elephantopus carolinianus

Gay-feather
Liatris squarrosa

Gay-feather
Liatris punctata

Broom-weed
Gutierrezia dracunculoides

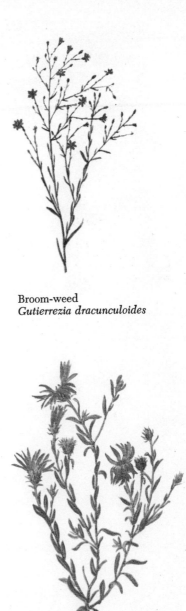

Gum-weed
Grindelia squarrosa

Sleepy Daisy
Xanthisma texanum

53

Saw-leaf Daisy
Prionopsis ciliata

Goldenrod
Solidago radula

Goldenrod
Solidago nemoralis

Goldenrod
Solidago altissima

54

Lazy Daisy
Left: *Aphanostephus ramosissimus*
Right: *Aphanostephus skirrhobasis*

Smooth Aster
Aster laevis

Narrow-leaved Aster
Aster prealtus

Small-leaved Aster
Aster oblongifolius

Annual Aster
Aster sublatus var.
ligulatus

Broad-leaved Aster
Aster sagittifolius

Tansy-aster
Machaeranthera tanacetifolia

Cudweed
Gnaphalium wrightii

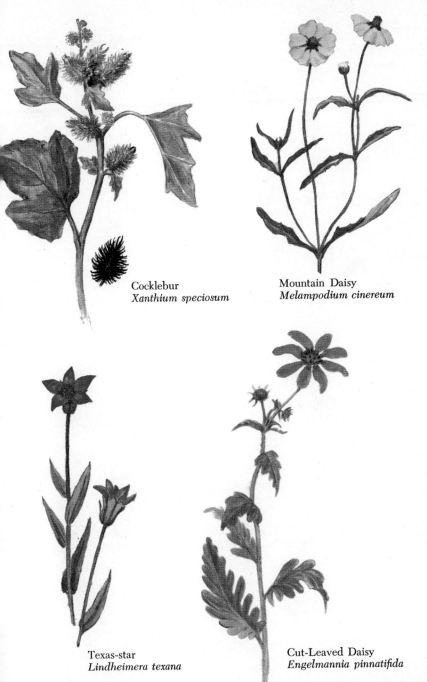

Cocklebur
Xanthium speciosum

Mountain Daisy
Melampodium cinereum

Texas-star
Lindheimera texana

Cut-Leaved Daisy
Engelmannia pinnatifida

57

Mexican-hat
Ratibida columnaris

Black-eyed–susan
Rudbeckia serotina

Cone-flower
Rudbeckia amplexicaulis

Purple Cone-flower
Echinacea angustifolia

Sunflower
Helianthus annuus

58

Sunflower
Helianthus maximiliani

Golden-wave
Coreopsis grandiflora

Thelesperma
Thelesperma filifolium

Thelesperma
Thelesperma simplicifolium

59

Rayless Thelesperma
Thelesperma megapotamicum

Old-plainsman
Hymenopappus artemisiaefolius

Yellow Daisy
Tetraneuris scaposa

Poison Bitterweed
Hymenoxys odorata

Bitterweed
Helenium amarum

Sneezeweed
Helenium latifolium

Fire-wheel
Gaillardia pulchella

Pincushion Daisy
Gaillardia suavis

Paper Daisy
Baileya multiradiata

Milfoil
Achillea millefolium

Ragwort
Senecio plattensis

Threadleaf Groundsel
Senecio longilobus

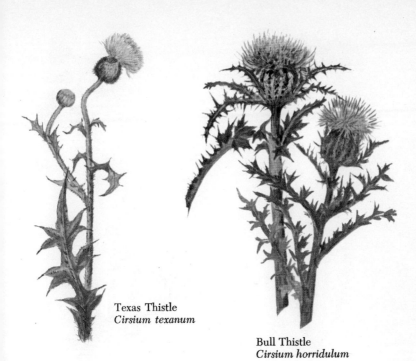

Texas Thistle
Cirsium texanum

Bull Thistle
Cirsium horridulum

Star-thistle
Centaurea americana

Perezia
Perezia wrightii

63

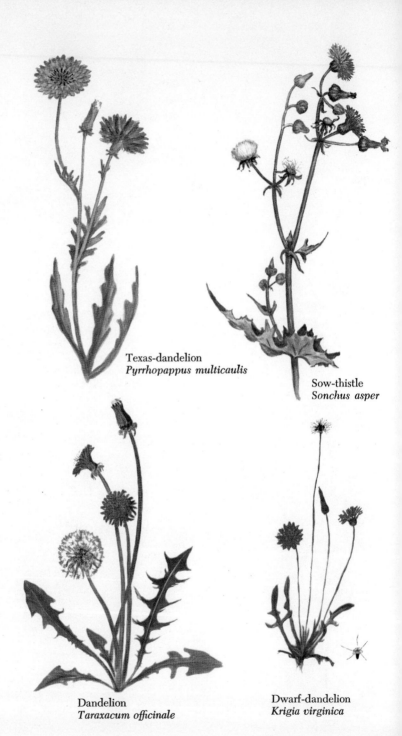

Texas-dandelion
Pyrrhopappus multicaulis

Sow-thistle
Sonchus asper

Dandelion
Taraxacum officinale

Dwarf-dandelion
Krigia virginica

64

A Note to the Amateur Botanist

THE INTELLIGENT LAY BOTANIST who is interested in enlarging his knowledge of the flora around him, and thus his pleasure in it, needs two tools: (1) a set of keys for identifying a species strange to him, and (2) a glossary for the verbal definition of the terms necessary for talk about flowers, supplemented by a set of diagrams for graphic definition of these terms naming the parts of a flower.

Use of the keys. Each key consists of a series of groups of statements, most frequently two statements, but sometimes three, or even more, in each group. All statements within a group are numbered alike, and in accordance with the serial position of the group within the key. To identify a plant the botanical explorer should begin with the first key (A) and, in each successive group of statements, make a choice of the one statement which is true of his specimen. At the end of that statement, next the margin, he will find either a number directing him to a following pertinent group of statements in that same key or a letter directing him to a following key. With each succeeding group of statements or key the same procedure of choice should be followed, resulting finally in the name of the specimen to be identified. Some plants, obviously, will be identified more quickly and with greater ease than others. Discussion and illustration of the plant thus identified can be located through the Index.

Glossaries. Both the graphic and the verbal glossaries are located immediately after the text. References to them will make clear the relationships and functions of the various parts of a flower and will define terms new to the amateur botanist.

(65)

KEY A

1. Plants with flowers in dense heads subtended by 2 or more whorls of bracts (Daisy Family) . . . . KEY B
1. Plants with flowers either not in heads or if in heads then each head with not more than a single whorl of subtending bracts . . 2
2. Plants with flower parts in 3's or 6's; leaves with parallel veins (Cat-tails, Dayflowers, Lilies, Yuccas, Orchids, and their relatives) . . . . KEY C
2. Flower parts in 2's, 4's, 5's or higher numbers (rarely in 3's); leaves net-veined (few exceptions) 3
3. Shrubs, trees, woody vines, and succulent plants with persistent aerial parts . . . . KEY D
3. Herbaceous plants either without persistent aerial parts or dying back most of the way at the end of the growing season . . 4
4. Leaf blades and flowers floating on water; remainder of plant submerged, rooted at bottom . . WATER-LILY—*Nymphaea elegans*
4. Leaf blades (when present) extended in air; plant rooted in dry or wet soil, rarely submerged 5
5. Plants with prickles or spines on leaves and/or stems and/or other parts . . . . KEY E
5. Plants unarmed 6
6. Plants vine, usually climbing but sometimes trailing (the stems mostly 2 ft. long or more) . . . . KEY F
6. Plants not vine, but sometimes prostrate and then the stems mostly less than 2 ft. long 7
7. Leaves compound . . . . KEY G
7. Leaves simple 8
8. Leaves opposite on the stem 9
8. Leaves alternate on the stem or all basal 10
9. Leaf margins entire . . . . KEY H
9. Leaf margins lobed and/or toothed . . . . KEY I
10. Leaf margins entire . . . . KEY J
10. Leaf margins lobed and/or toothed . . . . KEY K

KEY B: Plants with flowers in dense heads subtended by 2 or more whorls of (involucral) bracts (Daisy Family)

1. Leaves opposite 2
1. Leaves alternate (upper ones sometimes opposite in *Lindheimera texana*) 7
2. Rays absent; disc yellowish brown 3
2. Rays present; disc yellow to reddish brown 4

(66)

3. Uppermost leaves entire and filiform; achene *ca.* ¼ in. long, with 2 bristles at one end; plant of West Texas . . . . . .
. . . . . RAYLESS THELESPERMA—*Thelesperma megapotamicum*

3. Uppermost leaves lobed, or if entire not filiform; achene ½ in. long or more, with 3 or 4 hooked projections at one end; plant of East Texas . . . . BEGGAR-TICK—*Bidens bipinnata*

4. Rays white . . . . . MOUNTAIN DAISY—*Melampodium cinereum*

4. Rays yellow or cream-colored 5

5. Inner phyllaries united at least halfway up from the base to form a cup 6

5. Inner phyllaries free nearly to the base . . . .
. . . . GOLDEN-WAVE—*Coreopsis grandiflora*

6. All leaves much divided into several or many filiform segments; disc reddish brown . . . . THELESPERMA—*Thelesperma filifolium*

6. Upper leaves undivided or with only a few filiform segments; disc yellow or yellowish brown . . . .
. . . . THELESPERMA—*Thelesperma simplicifolium*

7. Plants with milky juice; all florets bearing strap-shaped rays . . 8

7. Plants without milky juice; some (not all) or none of the florets bearing strap-shaped rays 11

8. All leaves in a rosette at the base; plants stemless 9

8. Leaves, at least some of them, borne on the stem 10

9. Phyllaries all more or less equal in length; heads mostly less than ⅔ in. across . . . . DWARF-DANDELION—*Krigia virginica*

9. Phyllaries in 2 sets, the inner much longer; heads mostly more than ⅔ in. across . . . . . . DANDELION—*Taraxacum officinale*

10. Achenes flattened; tall coarse herbs seldom branched at the base, the leaves bearing weak marginal spines . . . .
. . . . SOW-THISTLE—*Sonchus asper*

10. Achenes columnar, not flattened; low herbs with ascending branches from the base; leaves without spines . . . . . .
. . . . TEXAS-DANDELION—*Pyrrhopappus multicaulis*

11. Rays absent 12

11. Rays present in 1 or more series around the edge or base of the head 24

12. Leaves with spine-tipped teeth or lobes 13

12. Leaves without spines 15

13. Involucre subtended by a whorl of intensely spiny bracts . . .
. . . . BULL THISTLE—*Cirsium horridulum*

13. Involucre not subtended by bracts 14

14. Leaves densely whitish-pubescent beneath, less so above; heads lavender or rosy lavender; involucre *ca.* ⅔ in. in diameter . .
. . . . TEXAS THISTLE—*Cirsium texanum*

(67)

14. Leaves mostly glabrous; heads pink; involucre *ca.* ¼ in. in diameter . . . . PEREZIA—*Perezia wrightii*
15. Florets rose, purple, lilac, pink, or reddish brown 16
15. Florets some other color 22
16. Heads spherical, deep red-orange to reddish brown, emitting a gardenialike odor; leaves basal . . . .
. . . . PINCUSHION DAISY—*Gaillardia suavis*
16. Heads hemispherical, more or less flat-topped, odorless or only weakly scented; leaves, at least some, borne on a distinct stem . 17
17. Heads 1 in. or more in diameter, rose pink or lilac around the edge, lighter or white in the center . . . .
. . . . STAR-THISTLE—*Centaurea americana*
17. Heads less than 1 in. in diameter; not so colored 18
18. Heads rosy purple, in spikes, spikelike racemes, or narrow panicles 19
18. Heads violet or lilac, in spreading corymbose or cymose clusters . 20
19. Basal leaves 5 to 9 in. long; phyllaries mostly longer than ⅔ in.
. . . . GAY-FEATHER—*Liatris squarrosa*
19. Basal leaves 1½ to 5 in. long; phyllaries mostly less than ⅔ in. long . . . . GAY-FEATHER—*Liatris punctata*
20. Lowest leaves much longer than stem leaves; heads lilac . . .
. . . . ELEPHANT-FOOT—*Elephantopus carolinianus*
20. Lowest leaves only slightly longer than upper ones; heads purple 21
21. Leaves with whitish-felty pubescence beneath; phyllaries with appressed hairs . . . . . . IRON-WEED—*Vernonia lindheimeri*
21. Leaves pubescent but not whitish felty; phyllaries without conspicuous hairiness . . . . . . IRON-WEED—*Vernonia texana*
22. Heads yellowish or greenish, unisexual; leaf blades 5 to 10 in. long and about as broad . . . COCKLEBUR—*Xanthium speciosum*
22. Heads white or sometimes pinkish, bisexual; leaf blades (except the basal ones, if present) mostly less than 5 in. long, always longer than broad 23
23. Inner phyllaries as long as or longer than the disc florets, resembling small rays; lower leaves much cut . . . .
. . . . . . OLD-PLAINSMAN—*Hymenopappus artemisiaefolius*
23. Phyllaries all shorter than the disc florets; leaves all entire . . .
. . . . CUDWEED—*Gnaphalium wrightii*
24. Disc higher than broad, domelike or fingerlike 25
24. Disc (when in flower) broader than high, flat or somewhat rounded 28
25. Rays rosy lavender . PURPLE CONE-FLOWER—*Echinacea angustifolia*
25. Rays at least partly yellow 26
26. Rays entirely yellow . . . BLACK-EYED–SUSAN—*Rudbeckia serotina*

(68)

KEY C: Plants with Flower Parts in 3's or 6's; leaves with parallel veins (Cat-tails, Dayflowers, Lilies, Yuccas, Orchids, and their relatives)

2. Plants with long pendulous branches; flowers yellowish . . .
. . . . SPANISH-MOSS–*Tillandsia usneoides*

3. Flowers (the lower ones) brown . . . CAT-TAIL–*Typha latifolia*

3. Flowers rose-red to salmon-pink . RED YUCCA–*Hesperaloe parviflora*

3. Flowers pink 4

3. Flowers greenish yellow 5

3. Flowers yellow or yellow-orange 6

3. Flowers blue to violet 7

3. Flowers white or cream-colored 11

4. Leaves tubular, all basal . . . WILD ONION–*Allium drummondii*

4. Leaves flat, bladelike, some borne on stem . . . . . .
. . . . SPIDERWORT–*Tradescantia* spp.

5. Flower stalk 1 to 2½ ft. tall . . . .
. . . . GREEN-LILY–*Schoenocaulon drummondii*

5. Flower stalk 6 to 20 ft. tall . . CENTURY-PLANT–*Agave americana*

6. Flowers solitary, *ca.* 2 in. across . . . .
. . . . ATAMASCO-LILY–*Zephyranthes texana*

6. Flowers 2 to 6 together, ½ to 1 in. across . . . .
. . . . YELLOW STAR-GRASS–*Hypoxis hirsuta*

7. Showy petals 2 . . . . DAYFLOWER–*Commelina* spp.

7. Showy petals 3 (or sometimes apparently 6 because of 3 similarly colored sepals) 8

8. Petals (3) showy and sepals (3) inconspicuous . . . . . .
. . . . SPIDERWORT–*Tradescantia* spp.

8. Petals (3) and sepals (3) showy 9

9. Petals erect; sepals reflexed . . . . . WILD IRIS–*Iris hexagona*

9. Petals and sepals all alike 10

10. Flowers less than ¾ in. across . . . .
. . . . BLUE-EYED–GRASS–*Sisyrinchium* spp.

10. Flowers 1 in. across or more . CELESTIAL–*Nemastylis geminiflora*

11. Plants of ponds, swamps, or wet places 12

11. Plants of dry land 13

12. Plants usually growing in water, rooted at the bottom; leaves
arrow-head–shaped . . EASTERN ARROW-HEAD–*Sagittaria latifolia*

12. Plants usually growing in wet soil out of water; leaves broadly
strap-shaped . . . . . . SPIDER-LILY–*Hymenocallis liriosme*

13. Flower stalks 3 ft. tall or taller 14

13. Flower stalks less than 3 ft. tall 16

14. Leaves armed with marginal recurved hooks . . . . . .
. . . . SOTOL–*Dasylirion texanum*

14. Leaves unarmed except for terminal spine 15

(71)

15. Leaf margins bearing threadlike filaments . . . . Yucca—*Yucca arkansana*
15. Leaf margins without filaments . . . Yucca—*Yucca treculeana*
16. Flowers in clusters 17
16. Flowers solitary 18
17. Flowers numerous, arranged in spikes . . . . Ladies'-tresses—*Spiranthes cernua*
17. Flowers few to several, arranged in umbels . . . . Crow-poison—*Nothoscordium bivalve*
18. Petals and sepals ⅓ to ¾ in. long . . . . Rain-lily—*Cooperia pedunculata*
18. Petals and sepals 1 to 1¼ in. long . . . . Rain-lily—*Cooperia drummondii*

KEY D: Shrubs, trees, woody vines, and succulent plants with persistent aerial parts

1. Plants parasitic, attached to branches of trees or shrubs . . . . Texas Mistletoe—*Phoradendron serotinum*
1. Plants not parasitic, rooted in ground 2
2. Plants succulent, without leaves, the stems covered with patches of spines 3
2. Plants not succulent, true leaves present, at least in growing periods; spines, if present, not occurring in patches 6
3. Flowers pink, red, or purplish 4
3. Flowers yellow or orange 5
4. Plants 3 to 12 ft. tall; spines needlelike, straight . . . . Cholla—*Opuntia arborescens*
4. Plants 4 to 8 in. tall; spines flat, recurved . . . . Devil's-head—*Echinocactus texensis*
5. Stems flat, padlike . . Texas Prickly-pear—*Opuntia lindheimeri*
5. Stems cylindrical . . . . . . Tasajillo—*Opuntia leptocaulis*
6. Plants climbing or trailing, without self-supporting erect stems . 7
6. Plants with erect self-supporting stems 17
7. Stems armed with prickles 8
7. Stems unarmed 10
8. Flowers pink . . . . Wild Pink Rose—*Rosa setigera*
8. Flowers white 9
9. Flowers 1½ in. or more across . Wild White Rose—*Rosa bracteata*
9. Flowers 1 in. or less across . . Wild Blackberry—*Rubus trivialis*
10. Leaves simple 11
10. Leaves compound 13

11. Flowers red outside, orange inside . . . .
. . . . CORAL HONEYSUCKLE—*Lonicera sempervirens*
11. Flowers white or cream-colored, at least when young 12
12. Flowers *ca.* ½ in. long; uppermost leaves united around the
stem . . . . WHITE HONEYSUCKLE—*Lonicera albiflora*
12. Flowers *ca.* 1 in. long; leaves all free . . . .
. . . . JAPANESE HONEYSUCKLE—*Lonicera japonica*
13. Leaves alternate; leaflets 3; flowers greenish yellow; fruit berrylike, grayish white . POISON-IVY (POISON-OAK)—*Rhus toxicodendron*
13. Leaves opposite; leaflets 2 to several; flowers and fruit not as
above 14
14. Flowers red or orange outside, yellow or yellow-orange inside;
fruit a pod 15
14. Flowers white or rose-violet; fruit a plumed achene 16
15. Leaflets 7 to 13 . . . . . TRUMPET-CREEPER—*Campsis radicans*
15. Leaflets 2 or 3 . . . . . . CROSS-VINE—*Anisostichus capreolatus*
16. Sepals (petal-like) spreading, white . . . .
. . . . OLD-MAN'S—BEARD—*Clematis drummondii*
16. Sepals (petal-like) erect, urnlike, rose-violet . . . .
. . . . LEATHER-FLOWER—*Clematis reticulata*
17. Leaves simple 18
17. Leaves compound 26
18. Flowers white or cream-colored 19
18. Flowers white and purple or lavender 21
18. Flowers yellow . . . . . . MUSTARD-TREE—*Nicotiana glauca*
18. Flowers pink, red, or purplish 22
19. Conspicuous portion of flower consisting of 4 distinct bracts
notched at apex; the true flowers small and numerous, arranged
in a central head . . . . . EASTERN DOGWOOD—*Cornus florida*
19. Conspicuous portion of flower consisting of several petals
united below, the lobes spreading 20
20. Petals ½ to ⅔ in. long; flowers few to several, arranged in
terminal clusters . . . WHITE HONEYSUCKLE—*Lonicera albiflora*
20. Petals *ca.* ⅓ in. long; flowers in dense globular terminal
heads . . . . . . BUTTON-BUSH—*Cephalanthus occidentalis*
21. Leaves lanceolate, entire . . DESERT-WILLOW—*Chilopsis linearis*
21. Leaves ovate, toothed . . . . . LANTANA—*Lantana camara*
22. Stems armed with stout spines . OCOTILLO—*Fouquieria splendens*
22. Stems not armed 23
23. Flowers reddish purple or pinkish purple 24
23. Flowers scarlet or red 25
24. Flowers appearing with the leaves; leaves glabrous . . . . .
. . . . REDBUD—*Cercis canadensis*

(73)

24. Flowers appearing after the leaves; leaves gray-pubescent . .
. . . . CENIZO—*Leucophyllum frutescens*
25. Leaves alternate . . . . . TURK'S-CAP—*Malvaviscus drummondii*
25. Leaves opposite . . . . . . SHRUBBY RED SAGE—*Salvia greggii*
25. Leaves in whorls of 3 . . . . TROMPETILLA—*Bouvardia ternifolia*
26. Flowers red or red-orange or orange . RED BUCKEYE—*Aesculus pavia*
26. Flowers violet or red-violet . . SHRUBBY DALEA—*Dalea frutescens*
26. Flowers yellow or greenish yellow 27
26. Flowers white or cream-colored 33
27. Stamens red, long and protruding . . . .
. . . . BIRD-OF-PARADISE—*Caesalpinia gilliesii*
27. Stamens some other color 28
28. Stems spiny 29
28. Stems unarmed 30
29. Flowers ⅔ in. or more across, arranged in racemes . . . . .
. . . . PALOVERDE—*Parkinsonia aculeata*
29. Flowers minute, arranged in short dense spikes . . . . . .
. . . . HUISACHE—*Acacia farnesiana*
30. Leaflets 2, resinous; plant emitting a strong odor . . . . . .
. . . . CREOSOTE-BUSH—*Larrea tridentata*
30. Leaflets 3 or more, not resinous; plant with little or no odor . . 31
31. Leaflets 3, firm, spiny-toothed . . . . AGARITA—*Berberis trifoliata*
31. Leaflets 7 to 19, membranous, teeth not spine-tipped 32
32. Flowers bright yellow, *ca.* 1½ in. long, arranged in terminal
racemes . . . . YELLOW-ELDER—*Tecoma stans*
32. Flowers greenish yellow, *ca.* ¼ in. long, in dense terminal
panicles . . . . SHINING SUMAC—*Rhus copallina*
33. Flowers less than ½ in. across 34
33. Flowers ¾ in. or more across 35
34. Flowers arranged in fingerlike spikes; fruit a pod . . . . .
. . . . MESQUITE—*Prosopis juliflora*
34. Flowers arranged in flat-topped clusters; fruit a berry . . . .
. . . . ELDERBERRY—*Sambucus canadensis*
35. Stems armed with prickles . . . WILD BLACKBERRY—*Rubus trivialis*
35. Stems unarmed . . . . . . APACHE-PLUME—*Fallugia paradoxa*

KEY E: Herbaceous plants with prickles or spines on leaves
and/or stems, and/or other parts

1. Flowers pink . . . . . . SENSITIVE-BRIAR—*Schrankia uncinata*
1. Flowers yellow . . . . . . BUFFALO-BUR—*Solanum rostratum*
1. Flowers white 2

1. Flowers lavender to purple 3
2. Leaves palmately 3- to 5-lobed; showy parts of flower (sepals) united below to form a tube; plant with milky juice . . . . .
. . . . BULL-NETTLE—*Cnidoscolus texanus*
2. Leaves not palmately lobed; showy parts of flower (petals) free to the base; plant with orange-colored juice . . . . . .
. . . . PRICKLY-POPPY—*Argemone albiflora*
3. Flowers in heads; leaves spiny margined . . . .
. . . . ERYNGO—*Eryngium leavenworthii*
3. Flowers in loose lateral clusters; leaves prickly on veins only . .
. . . . HORSE-NETTLE—*Solanum dimidiatum*

KEY F: Herbaceous vines, usually climbing but sometimes trailing (the stems mostly 2 ft. long or more)

1. Flowers entirely yellow or orange 2
1. Flowers entirely white 3
1. Flowers red or purple and some other color 4
2. Leaves rough-pubescent, with a strong unpleasant odor; flowers 4 or more in. across . . WILD GOURD—*Cucurbita foetidissima*
2. Leaves warted but otherwise smooth, without noticeable odor; flowers ½ in. across or less . BALSAM GOURD—*Ibervillea lindheimeri*
3. Leaves absent; stem yellow to rusty orange . DODDER—*Cuscuta* spp.
3. Leaves present; stem green . . . .
. . . . WHITE NIGHTSHADE—*Solanum triquetrum*
4. Plants climbing by means of tendrils . MAY-POP—*Passiflora incarnata*
4. Plants climbing by means of twining stems or merely trailing . . 5
5. Flowers 2-lipped, purple and white, open all day . . . . .
. . . . CLIMBING SNAPDRAGON—*Maurandia antirrhiniflora*
5. Flowers bell- or funnel-shaped, colored otherwise, closing in the afternoon 6
6. Leaves gray-green; flowers white or pale pink with a red throat, less than 1 in. across . TEXAS BINDWEED—*Convolvulus hermannioides*
6. Leaves green; flowers pink or lavender and purple, 2 or more in. across 7
7. Leaves longer than broad, the lobes sharp-tipped; plant of inland areas . . . . WILD MORNING-GLORY—*Ipomoea trichocarpa*
7. Leaves broader than long, the lobes rounded; plant of beach dunes . . . . GOAT-FOOT—CREEPER—*Ipomoea pes-caprae*

KEY G: Herbaceous plants with compound leaves

1. Leaves divided into threadlike segments or into indefinite more-or-less-bladelike terminations 2
1. Leaves divided into definite bladelike leaflets 4
2. Flowers red, yellow-spotted within . . . .
. . . . STANDING-CYPRESS—*Ipomopsis rubra*
2. Flowers bluish violet . . . . BLUE GILIA—*Gilia rigidula*
3. Flowers 1½ to 2 in. long . . . . . WHITE GILIA—*Gilia longiflora*
3. Flowers not more than ¼ in. long. . WILD CARROT—*Daucus pusillus*
4. Leaflets 2 . . . . . . TWO-LEAVED SENNA—*Cassia roemeriana*
4. Leaflets 3 5
4. Leaflets 4 or more 12
5. Leaflets toothed 6
5. Leaflets entire or merely wavy-margined 7
6. Flowers white . . . . . WHITE SWEET-CLOVER—*Melilotus albus*
6. Flowers yellow . . . YELLOW SWEET-CLOVER—*Melilotus officinalis*
6. Flowers violet to bluish violet . . . . ALFALFA—*Medicago sativa*
7. Flowers papilionaceous (sweet-pea–like) 8
7. Flowers not papilionaceous 9
8. Flowers cream-colored . . . . WILD-INDIGO—*Baptisia leucophaea*
8. Flowers yellow . . . . BUSH-PEA—*Baptisia sphaerocarpa*
8. Flowers red . . . . CORAL-BEAN—*Erythrina herbacea*
8. Flowers violet . . . . . BUSH-CLOVER—*Lespedeza virginica*
9. Plants sticky; flowers with petals all swept upward; stamens protruding 10
9. Plants not sticky; flowers rotate (petals all arranged in a circle); stamens not protruding 11
10. Petals *ca.* ⅜ in. long . . . .
. . . . . CLAMMY-WEED—*Polanisia dodecandra* var. *trachysperma*
10. Petals ½ in. long or longer . . . .
. . . . CLAMMY-WEED—*Polanisia dodecandra* var. *uniglandulosa*
11. Leaves all basal; flowers lavender-pink to purple . . . . .
. . . . PURPLE WOOD-SORREL—*Oxalis purpurea*
11. Leaves borne on stem; flowers yellow . . . .
. . . . YELLOW WOOD-SORREL—*Oxalis dillenii*
12. Leaflets arising from a common point at the end of the main leafstalk (i.e., leaves palmately compound) 13
12. Leaflets arranged in a row on either side of the main leafstalk (i.e., leaves pinnately compound) 14
13. Leaflets pubescent on both sides . . BLUEBONNET—*Lupinus texensis*
13. Leaflets more or less glabrous above . . . .
. . . . BLUEBONNET—*Lupinus subcarnosus*

(76)

14. Main leafstalks (petioles) opposite on the stem; plant creeping . 15
14. Main leafstalks alternate on the stem; plant usually erect . . . 16
15. Flowers ⅔ in. across or less; fruit spiny . . . .
 . . . . Goat-head—*Tribulus terrestrius*
15. Flowers 1½ in. or more across; fruit not spiny . . . . . .
 . . . . Desert-poppy—*Kallstroemia grandiflora*
16. Leaflets an even number (i.e., terminal leaflet absent) 17
16. Leaflets an odd number (i.e., terminal leaflet present) 18
17. Flowers in short lateral clusters just above the leaf axils; 4 (of
 the 5) petals red-spotted at base . . . .
 . . . . Partridge-pea—*Cassia fasciculata*
17. Flowers in large terminal panicles; petals without spots . . . .
 . . . . Lindheimer's Senna—*Cassia lindheimeri*
18. Flowers yellowish to white . . . . Catgut—*Tephrosia virginiana*
18. Flowers pink or pinkish purple . Goat's-rue—*Tephrosia lindheimeri*
18. Flowers blue to purple or lavender 19
19. Flowers papilionaceous (sweet-pea–like) 20
19. Flowers regular (petals all alike in shape and size) 21
20. Leaflets mostly 5 . . . . . . Scurvy-pea—*Psoralea cuspidata*
20. Leaflets 21 to 31 . . . . . Woolly Loco—*Astragalus mollissimus*
21. Flowers ⅓ in. or less across. . . . Blue-curls—*Phacelia congesta*
21. Flowers ⅔ in. or more across . . . .
 . . . . Baby-blue-eyes—*Nemophila phacelioides*

KEY H: Herbaceous plants with simple, opposite, entire
leaves

1. Flowers yellow . . . . Menodora—*Menodora longiflora*
1. Flowers white or whitish 2
1. Flowers red or rose 7
1. Flowers blue, violet, lavender, or pink 9
2. Petals or petal-like sepals united below to form a tube 3
2. Petals or petal-like sepals all free to the base 6
3. Flower tube 2 to 6 in. long . . . .
 . . . . Angel's-trumpet—*Acleisanthes longiflora*
3. Flower tube less than 2 in. long 4
4. Flowers fragrant, in dense clusters subtended by numerous
 bracts . . . . Sand-verbena—*Abronia fragrans*
4. Flowers without noticeable odor, in diffuse clusters, bracts
 none or minute 5
5. Petals 4; leaf blades ⅓ to 1½ in. long . . . .
 . . . . Star-violet—*Hedyotis nigricans*

(77)

5. Petals 5; leaf blades 1½ to 3 in. long . . . .
. . . . LAMB'S-LETTUCE—*Valerianella amarella*
6. Plants erect, 2 to 6 ft. tall . . SNAKE-COTTON—*Froelichia floridana*
6. Plants spreading, 4 to 12 in. tall . . . CHICKWEED—*Stellaria media*
7. Flowers in heads; stamens protruding . . . .
. . . . DEVIL'S-BOUQUET—*Nyctaginea capitata*
7. Flowers in racemes or cymes; stamens not protruding 8
8. Plants 1½ to 2½ ft. tall, woody below; flowers 2-lipped . . .
. . . . SHRUBBY RED SAGE—*Salvia greggii*
8. Plants less than 1½ ft. tall, herbaceous throughout; flowers
regular . . . . ANNUAL PHLOX—*Phlox drummondii*
9. Flowers regular or nearly so 10
9. Flowers distinctly 2-lipped 18
10. Petals 4 11
10. Petals 5 12
11. Stamens 4 . . . . STAR-VIOLET—*Hedyotis nigricans*
11. Stamens 5 . . . . MEADOW-PINK—*Sabbatia campestris*
12. Flowers fragrant, in dense clusters subtended by numerous
bracts . . . . SAND-VERBENA—*Abronia fragrans*
12. Flowers without noticeable odor, in loose clusters, bracts none
or minute 13
13. Flowers 1¼ in. long or longer 14
13. Flowers less than 1 in. long 16
14. Leaf blades sessile . . . . . . BLUE-BELL—*Eustoma grandiflora*
14. Leaf blades with distinct petioles 15
15. Flowers ¾ to 1¼ in. across . . WILD-PETUNIA—*Ruellia caroliniensis*
15. Flowers 1⅓ to 1½ in. across . . WILD-PETUNIA—*Ruellia occidentalis*
16. Perennial herb from a woody base or branching root 17
16. Annual herb from a slender taproot . . ANNUAL PHLOX—*Phlox* spp.
17. Flowers bright pink; plant of mountains of West Texas . . .
. . . . DWARF PHLOX—*Phlox nana*
17. Flowers pale rose to bluish lavender; plant of fields and prairies
east of the Pecos River . . . . . PRAIRIE PHLOX—*Phlox pilosa*
18. Flowers in spikelike racemes without bracts; calyx bluish gray
. . . . BLUE SAGE—*Salvia farinacea*
18. Flowers in bracted inflorescences or solitary in the leaf axils;
calyx green 19
19. Flowers pinkish purple to rosy lavender 20
19. Flowers blue to bluish purple 21
20. Flowers ⅝ to ¾ in. long; leaves with petioles . . . . . .
. . . . FALSE-MINT—*Dicliptera brachiata*

(78)

20. Flowers ⅓ to ½ in. long; leaves sessile . . . .
. . . . LION-HEART—*Physostegia intermedia*
21. Fruit a many-seeded capsule ⅜ to ½ in. long . . . .
. . . . SNAKE-HERB—*Dyschoriste linearis*
21. Fruit consisting of 4 minute nutlets enclosed by the
persistent calyx 22
22. Plants 1½ to 2 ft. tall; upper leaves linear . . . .
. . . . SKULL-CAP—*Scutellaria integrifolia*
22. Plants 3 to 15 in. tall; upper leaves lanceolate or broader . . . 23
23. Leaves ⅓ to ¾ in. long; flowers solitary in axils of leaflike
bracts . . . . SKULL-CAP—*Scutellaria drummondii*
23. Leaves 1½ to 2½ in. long; flowers arranged in successive whorls
in bracted racemes . . . . TEXAS SAGE—*Salvia texana*

KEY I: Herbaceous plants with simple, opposite, lobed or
toothed leaves

1. Flowers yellow 2
1. Flowers white 3
1. Flowers red 5
1. Flowers pink, lavender, purple, or blue 6
2. Leaves 3- to 7-cleft or 3- to 7-parted; flowers entirely yellow
(buds reddish) . . . . REDBUD—*Menodora heterophylla*
2. Leaves remotely and shallowly toothed; flowers yellow with
reddish-brown dots . . . YELLOW HORSE-MINT—*Monarda punctata*
3. Plants creeping and rooting at intervals . . FROG-FRUIT—*Phyla incisa*
3. Plants erect, 1 to 4 ft. tall 4
4. Leaves with wavy or shallowly round-toothed margins;
individual flowers *ca.* ¼₆ in. long . . SPIDERLING—*Boerhavia erecta*
4. Leaves with shallowly sharp-toothed margins . . . . . .
. . . . LEMON HORSE-MINT—*Monarda citriodora*
5. Flowers subtended by a pale green bell-shaped involucre;
leaves irregularly and unevenly toothed . . . .
. . . . UMBRELLAWORT—*Mirabilis nyctagineus*
5. Flowers not subtended by an involucre; leaves regularly and
evenly toothed . . . . . . SCARLET SAGE—*Salvia coccinea*
6. Leaves with indentations more than halfway to the middle . . 7
6. Leaves with indentations less than halfway to the middle . . . 9
7. Petals all free; leaves palmately lobed . . . .
. . . . STORKSBILL—*Erodium texanum*
7. Petals united at the base to form a tube; leaves pinnately lobed . 8
8. Flowers bluish to reddish purple; plant perennial . . . . .
. . . . PRAIRIE VERBENA—*Verbena bipinnatifida*

8. Flowers rosy purple; plant annual . Low Verbena—*Verbena pumila*
9. Flowers more than 1 in. long 10
9. Flowers less than 1 in. long 14
10. Flowers distinctly 2-lipped, in dense headlike clusters 11
10. Flowers not distinctly 2-lipped, in loose clusters 12
11. Petioles ¼ to ⅓ as long as blades; flowers with purplish spots
within . . . . . . Lemon Horse-mint—*Monarda citriodora*
11. Petioles ⅕ to ¼ as long as blades; flowers not spotted . . . .
. . . . Pink Horse-mint—*Monarda fistulosa*
12. Flowers with purplish markings within . . . .
. . . . Wild-foxglove—*Penstemon cobaea*
12. Flowers without markings within 13
13. Flowers ¾ to 1¼ in. across . . Wild-petunia—*Ruellia caroliniensis*
13. Flowers 1⅓ to 1½ in. across . . Wild-petunia—*Ruellia occidentalis*
14. Fruit of 4 minute nutlets enclosed by the persistent calyx . . . 15
14. Fruit capsular or otherwise 22
15. Stamens 2 16
15. Stamens 4 17
16. Calyx bluish gray; leaves petioled . . . Blue Sage—*Salvia farinacea*
16. Calyx green; leaves sessile or nearly so . . Texas Sage—*Salvia texana*
17. Flowers solitary in axils of leaves or bracts 18
17. Flowers in dense whorls 21
18. Upper lip of calyx with a bump or fold, covering the opening
of the calyx after flowering 19
18. Upper lip of calyx with straight or spreading teeth 20
19. Plants 1 to 3 ft. tall . . . . . Skull-cap—*Scutellaria integrifolia*
19. Plants 3 to 12 in. tall . . . . Skull-cap—*Scutellaria drummondii*
20. Calyx deeply 2-lipped, the teeth very unequal . . . . .
. . . . Brazos-mint—*Brazoria scutellarioides*
20. Calyx with 5 slightly unequal teeth . . . .
. . . . Lion-heart—*Physostegia intermedia*
21. Bracts of the spike abruptly differing from the foliage leaves
below, closely overlapping; flowers bluish violet . . . . . .
. . . . Heal-all—*Prunella vulgaris*
21. Bracts resembling the leaves, the pairs rather distant, not overlapping; flowers rosy purple . . . Henbit—*Lamium amplexicaule*
22. Flowers *ca.* ¹⁄₁₆ in. long; leaves finely black-dotted
beneath . . . . Spiderling—*Boerhavia erecta*
22. Flowers at least ½ in. long or broad; leaves not dotted 23
23. Petals 4, all free; stamens 8 . . Meadow-beauty—*Rhexia virginica*
23. Petals 5, united below to form a tube, the flare 2-lipped;
stamens 2 . . . . False-mint—*Dicliptera brachiata*

KEY J: Herbaceous plants with simple, alternate or basal, entire leaves

1. Flowers or conspicuous parts of inflorescence reddish purple, red, or orange 2
1. Flowers pink 6
1. Flowers or conspicuous parts of inflorescence white or greenish white 8
1. Flowers yellow 23
1. Flowers blue, violet, or lavender 27
2. Conspicuous parts of inflorescence red-, orange-, or purplish-tipped leaflike bracts 3
2. Conspicuous parts of inflorescence flowers 5
3. Bracts usually with a pair of fingerlike lateral lobes . . . .
. . . . PURPLE PAINTBRUSH—*Castilleja purpurea*
3. Bracts entire or with a few terminal teeth 4
4. Bracts ⅗ in. broad or broader; plant of West Texas . . . . .
. . . . WESTERN PAINTBRUSH—*Castilleja latebracteata*
4. Bracts less than ⅗ in. broad; plant of Central and East Texas . .
. . . . SCARLET PAINTBRUSH—*Castilleja indivisa*
5. Leaves fleshy . . . . FLAME-FLOWER—*Talinum lineare*
5. Leaves membranaceous . . . BUTTERFLY-WEED—*Asclepias tuberosa*
6. Plants 3 to 8 ft. tall . . GREAT POKEWEED—*Phytolacca americana*
6. Plants less than 1 ft. tall 7
7. Leaves membranaceous; flowers in erect terminal racemes . .
. . . . PINK MILKWORT—*Polygala polygama*
7. Leaves fleshy; flowers in small terminal clusters . . . . .
. . . . FLAME-FLOWER—*Talinum lineare*
8. Leaves all basal 9
8. Leaves borne on stem 11
9. Spike less than 2 in. long; leaves less than 1 in. broad . . . .
. . . . RIBBON-GRASS—*Plantago lanceolata*
9. Spike 3 in. long or longer; leaves broader than 1 in. . . . .
. . . . HELLER'S PLANTAIN—*Plantago helleri*
10. Plants with milky juice 11
10. Plants with watery juice 13
11. Plants 1 to 1½ ft. tall; leaves ovate; flowers in umbels . . . .
. . . . GREEN MILKWEED—*Asclepias oenotheroides*
11. Plants usually 2 ft. tall or more; leaves mostly lanceolate or linear; flowers not in umbels 12
12. Conspicuous portion of inflorescence the white-margined bracts . . . . SNOW-ON-THE-MOUNTAIN—*Euphorbia bicolor*
12. Conspicuous portion of inflorescence the petal-like cyathium appendages . . . . . FLOWERING SPURGE—*Euphorbia corollata*

(81)

27. Plants with milky juice . . . .
. . . . Purple Milkweed—*Asclepias brachystephana*
27. Plants with watery juice 28
28. Petals (or petal-like sepals) all free to the base 29
28. Petals united, at least below 32
29. Flowers irregular, the petals and petal-like sepals of different
sizes and shapes . . . . . . Blue Milkwort—*Polygala longa*
29. Flowers regular, the petals or petal-like sepals all alike . . . 30
30. Flowers ⅛ to ⅙ in. across . . . Small Pokeweed—*Rivina humilis*
30. Flowers ½ to 1 in. across 31
31. Plants erect; leaves membranous; flowers in racemes . . . .
. . . . Blue Flax—*Linum pratense*
31. Plants prostrate or ascending; leaves fleshy; flowers in small
terminal clusters . . . . Moss-rose—*Portulaca pilosa*
32. Stems silky, much branched, ascending or spreading . . . .
. . . . Shaggy Evolvulus—*Evolvulus nuttallianus*
32. Stems not silky, simple or branched above, mostly erect . . . 33
33. Flowers regular, pale violet; stamens bright yellow . . . .
. . . . Trompillo—*Solanum eleagnifolium*
33. Flowers 2-lipped, light blue to lavender; stamens
whitish . . . . Toad-flax—*Linaria texana*

KEY K: Herbaceous plants with simple, alternate or basal,
lobed and/or toothed leaves

1. Leaves with 3 or more lobes palmately arranged, the indentations extending more than halfway to the middle 2
1. Leaves pinnately toothed or lobed, or palmately toothed or
lobed, in the latter instance the indentations extending not
more than halfway to the middle 7
2. Flowers yellow . . . .
. . . . . Large-flowered Buttercup—*Ranunculus macranthus*
2. Flowers white, pink, lavender, violet, or in various
combinations 3
3. Flowers irregular, the petals or petal-like sepals of different
sizes and shapes 4
3. Flowers regular, the petals all alike 5
4. Leaves all basal; flowers violet and white . . . .
. . . . Bird's-foot Violet—*Viola pedata*
4. Leaves borne on stem; flowers white or pale lavender with
bluish spots . . . . . Prairie Larkspur—*Delphinium virescens*
5. Leaves all basal . . . . Anemone—*Anemone decapetala*
5. Leaves borne on stem 6

(83)

6. Flowers violet to magenta, ⅔ to 1¼ in. across . . . . . .
. . . . Wine-cup—*Callirhoe digitata*
6. Flowers salmon-pink to lavender-pink, *ca.* ½ in. across . . .
. . . . Copper-mallow—*Sphaeralcea angustifolia*
7. Flowers white or greenish white 8
7. Flowers red 12
7. Flowers yellow or orange 13
7. Flowers pink, lavender, reddish violet, or purple 23
8. Flowers funnel-shaped, 2 to 4 in. long . . . .
. . . . Smooth Jimson-weed—*Datura stramonium*
8. Flowers not funnel-shaped, less than 1 in. long (but up to
1¾ in. across in one case) 9
9. Buds drooping; flowers 1 to 1¾ in. across . . . .
. . . . Pink Evening-primrose—*Oenothera speciosa*
9. Buds erect or ascending; flowers ¼ in. across or less 10
10. Fruit an elliptic-cylindrical pod . Whitlow-grass—*Draba platycarpa*
10. Fruit a flattened nearly circular pod 11
11. Plants annual; stem simple below, often much branched
above . . . . Pepper-grass—*Lepidium virginicum*
11. Plants perennial; stems numerous from a woody root . . . .
. . . . Pepper-grass—*Lepidium allysoides*
12. Flowers irregular, in terminal racemes . . . .
. . . . Cardinal-flower—*Lobelia cardinalis*
12. Flowers regular, solitary in the leaf axils . . . .
. . . . Turk's-cap—*Malvaviscus drummondii*
13. Petals purplish at the base 14
13. Petals entirely yellow 15
14. Leaf margins sharply toothed; flowers ¼ to ½ in. across;
plants annual . . . . . . Ground-cherry—*Physalis angulata*
14. Leaf margins bluntly toothed; flowers ½ to ⅔ in. across;
plants perennial . . . . . . Ground-cherry—*Physalis viscosa*
15. Petals 4 16
15. Petals 5 or more 20
16. Leaves and flowers all basal . . . Buttercup—*Oenothera triloba*
16. Leaves and flowers borne on stem 17
17. Sepals longer than petals, rust-red to pinkish . . . . . .
. . . . . . Cut-leaved Evening-primrose—*Oenothera laciniata*
17. Sepals shorter than petals, mostly green or greenish 18
18. Flowers ¾ to 1¼ in. across . . Day-primrose—*Oenothera serrulata*
18. Flowers less than ⅔ in. across 19
19. Stem glabrous; petals yellow . . . Wild Mustard—*Brassica juncea*
19. Stem pubescent; flowers yellow-orange . . . .
. . . . Bladderpod—*Lesquerella gracilis*

(84)

20. Leaves rough-pubescent, sandpapery to the touch 21
20. Leaves soft-pubescent 22
21. Petals 5, ¼ to ⅓ in. long . . . Stick-leaf—*Mentzelia oligosperma*
21. Petals 10, ⅓ to ⅔ in. long . . . . . Stick-leaf—*Mentzelia nuda*
22. Flowers less than ¾ in. across . Indian Mallow—*Abutilon incanum*
22. Flowers 1½ to 2 in. across . . Velvet-leaf—*Wissadula holosericea*
23. Leaves with bases clasping the stem . . . .
. . . . Venus' Looking-glass—*Triodanis perfoliata*
23. Leaves sessile or with petioles, the bases not clasping the stem . 24
24. Conspicuous parts of inflorescence the purplish-red—tipped
leaflike bracts . . . . Purple Paintbrush—*Castilleja purpurea*
24. Conspicuous parts of inflorescence the true flowers 25
25. Flowers irregular, the petals of different sizes and shapes . . . 26
25. Flowers regular, the petals all alike 28
26. Flowers in racemes . . . . Blue Lobelia—*Lobelia appendiculata*
26. Flowers solitary 27
27. Leaves all basal . . . . . Missouri Violet—*Viola missouriensis*
27. Leaves borne on stem . . . . Wild Pansy—*Viola bicolor*
28. Flowers rosy pink; petals 4, free to the base . . . . . .
. . . . Pink Evening-primrose—*Oenothera speciosa*
28. Flowers bluish purple; petals 5, united 29
29. Leaves 1½ to 3 in. long; flowers in axillary pairs . . . . .
. . . . Purple Ground-cherry—*Quincula lobata*
29. Leaves 2½ to 6 in. long; flowers 3 or more in lateral
clusters . . . . Horse-nettle—*Solanum dimidiatum*

The Counties of Texas

County	Code	County	Code	County	Code	County	Code
Anderson	H1	Donley	A19	Kaufman	D22	Real	I9
Andrews	B24	Duval	K7	Kendall	I6	Red River	D4
Angelina	H6	Eastland	C25	Kenedy	K15	Reeves	E4
Aransas	J26	Ector	F3	Kent	B17	Refugio	J25
Archer	C7	Edwards	I4	Kerr	I5	Roberts	A9
Armstrong	A18	Ellis	D28	Kimble	I1	Robertson	G21
Atascosa	I19	El Paso	E1	King	B12	Rockwall	D15
Austin	J16	Erath	G2	Kinney	I11	Runnels	F8
Bailey	B1	Falls	G16	Kleberg	K11	Rusk	D26
Bandera	I10	Fannin	D2	Knox	C5	Sabine	H8
Bastrop	J3	Fayette	J9	Lamar	D3	San Augustine	H7
Baylor	C6	Fisher	B23	Lamb	B2	San Jacinto	H14
Bee	K5	Floyd	B4	Lampasas	G10	San Patricio	K9
Bell	G15	Foard	C4	La Salle	K2	San Saba	F19
Bexar	I14	Fort Bend	J23	Lavaca	J14	Schleicher	F21
Blanco	I3	Franklin	D10	Lee	J4	Scurry	B22
Borden	B21	Freestone	G18	Leon	G22	Shackelford	C18
Bosque	G8	Frio	I18	Liberty	H15	Shelby	H4
Bowie	D5	Gaines	B19	Limestone	G17	Sherman	A2
Brazoria	J29	Galveston	H30	Lipscomb	A5	Smith	D24
Brazos	J6	Garza	B16	Live Oak	K4	Somervell	G4
Brewster	E8	Gillespie	I2	Llano	F24	Starr	K16
Briscoe	A24	Glasscock	F5	Loving	F1	Stephens	C19
Brooks	K14	Goliad	J19	Lubbock	B9	Sterling	F6
Brown	F10	Gonzales	J8	Lynn	B15	Stonewall	B18
Burleson	J5	Gray	A14	Madison	J7	Sutton	F25
Burnet	G14	Grayson	D1	Marion	D20	Swisher	A23
Caldwell	J2	Gregg	D25	Martin	B25	Tarrant	C22
Calhoun	J27	Grimes	J11	Mason	F23	Taylor	C23
Callahan	C24	Guadalupe	I15	Matagorda	J28	Terrell	E9
Cameron	K19	Hale	B3	Maverick	I16	Terry	B14
Camp	D18	Hall	A25	McCulloch	F18	Throckmorton	C12
Carson	A13	Hamilton	G7	McLennan	G12	Titus	D11
Cass	D13	Hansford	A3	McMullen	K3	Tom Green	F16
Castro	A22	Hardeman	C1	Medina	I13	Travis	J1
Chambers	H18	Hardin	H16	Menard	F22	Trinity	H9
Cherokee	H2	Harris	J24	Midland	F4	Tyler	H11
Childress	A26	Harrison	D21	Milam	G20	Upshur	D19
Clay	C8	Hartley	A6	Mills	G6	Upton	F13
Cochran	B7	Haskell	C11	Mitchell	B27	Uvalde	I12
Coke	F7	Hays	I8	Montague	C9	Val Verde	E10
Coleman	F9	Hemphill	A10	Montgomery	J18	Van Zandt	D23
Collin	D6	Henderson	D29	Moore	A7	Victoria	J20
Collingsworth	A20	Hidalgo	K17	Morris	D12	Walker	J12
Colorado	J15	Hill	G9	Motley	B5	Waller	J17
Comal	I7	Hockley	B8	Nacogdoches	H3	Ward	F11
Comanche	G1	Hood	G3	Navarro	G13	Washington	J10
Concho	F17	Hopkins	D9	Newton	H13	Webb	K6
Cooke	C10	Houston	H5	Nolan	B28	Wharton	J22
Coryell	G11	Howard	B26	Nueces	K10	Wheeler	A15
Cottle	B6	Hudspeth	E2	Ochiltree	A4	Wichita	C3
Crane	F12	Hunt	D7	Oldham	A11	Wilbarger	C2
Crockett	F20	Hutchinson	A8	Orange	H17	Willacy	K18
Crosby	B10	Irion	F15	Palo Pinto	C20	Williamson	G19
Culberson	E3	Jack	C14	Panola	D27	Wilson	I20
Dallam	A1	Jackson	J21	Parker	C21	Winkler	F2
Dallas	D14	Jasper	H12	Parmer	A21	Wise	C15
Dawson	B20	Jeff Davis	E5	Pecos	E6	Wood	D17
Deaf Smith	A16	Jefferson	H19	Polk	H10	Yoakum	B13
Delta	D8	Jim Hogg	K13	Potter	A12	Young	C13
Denton	C16	Jim Wells	K8	Presidio	E7	Zapata	K12
De Witt	J13	Johnson	G5	Rains	D16	Zavala	I17
Dickens	B11	Jones	C17	Randall	A17		
Dimmit	K1	Karnes	I21	Reagan	F14		

*Marginal numbers in the text refer
to the plate on which the flower is
illustrated.*

CAT-TAIL FAMILY   Typhaceae

CAT-TAIL   *Typha latifolia* L.   (PL. 1)   **1**

Monoecious marsh or aquatic herb, perennial by creeping rhizomes, with fibrous roots and erect terete stems 3 to 10 ft. tall. Leaves alternate, linear, or strap-shaped ¼ to ¾ in. broad, sheathing at the base, flat, more or less convex on the back, parallel-veined. Flowers densely crowded in compact cylindric spikelike racemes to 1 ft. long, the upper staminate and lower pistillate portions contiguous; staminate flowers falling, the axis persistent. Distribution: marshes and wet places throughout most of North America, Europe, and Asia.

The genus of Cat-tails, *Typha*, is of nearly world-wide distribution in open riparian and estuarine marshes. The stem is divided into two parts: a starchy rhizome which is rooted in the mud and grows horizontally, the tips of its branches turning upward; the leafy aerial stem arising from these rhizome branches and terminated by the familiar cylindrical flower masses. By means of the creeping rhizomes it is not uncommon for enormous stands covering acres to become established. Indeed it is uncommon to see a solitary Cat-tail without an accompanying multitude. The flowers are produced in the summer, the upper male flowers colored pale yellow, the lower female, brown. The tiny brown fruits are covered with minute hairs, facilitating eventual wind transport of the seeds. Another species, *T. domingensis* Pers., is similar but for narrower leaves and a short length of naked stalk separating the male from the female flowers. Both are found in Texas abundantly in coastal marshes and inland, locally, in ditches, along lake borders, and in or near other permanently wet places.

ARROW-HEAD FAMILY   Alismaceae

EASTERN ARROW-HEAD   *Sagittaria latifolia* Willd.   (PL. 1)

Stemless perennial herb of marshes, swamps, or other wet places, emersed or partly submerged, 1 to 3 ft. tall. Rootstock irregularly thickened or tuberous. Leaves erect or ascending, the blades often broader than long, 6 to 15 in. long, usually hairless, the two basal lobes ovate or narrower; leafstalk commonly longer than the blade. Scapes usually exceeding the leaves. Flowers unisexual, but with male and female on the same scape, staminate above, pistillate below; staminate flowers with numerous stamens; pistillate flowers with many distinct carpels. Sepals 3, obtuse. Petals 3, obovate. Fruiting head ½ to 1 in. in diameter; achenes about ⅛ in. long, gradually narrowed to the prominent beak. Distribution: swamps and shallow water in eastern two thirds of U. S., northwest to British Columbia and Washington.

Choosing borders of ponds and swamps and the muddy shallows of quiet streams, Arrow-heads often grow in extensive stands or files, coming to flower in summer and early fall. Of the 35 species of *Sagittaria* known, about a dozen occur in Texas. The Eastern Arrow-head extends into the eastern quarter of the state; it usually has a greater number of flower whorls than shown in the painting. Generally smaller and with narrower leaves is *S. longiloba* Engelm., common southward from Bastrop County, and also occurring in the Panhandle. *S. calycina* Engelm. is a stouter species, chiefly of southeastern Texas, with erect sepals more or less enveloping the achene heads. Most of the other Arrow-heads in Texas have spear-shaped leaves lacking the lower lobes or tails. *S. platyphylla* (Engelm.) J. G. Smith, with reflexed fruiting pedicels, is common east of the Edwards Plateau. Often difficult to distinguish from the preceding, the similarly distributed *S. graminea* (Engelm.) J. G. Smith usually holds its fruiting pedicels upward. In *S. papillosa* Buch. the bracts beneath each whorl of flowers are roughened on the upper surface. Nearly all the Arrow-heads have enlarged tuberous roots, which the Indians gathered, cooked, and ate. Hence another common name, water potato. Many water birds feed on the achenes.

PINEAPPLE FAMILY   Bromeliaceae

Spanish-moss   *Tillandsia usneoides* L. [=*Dendropogon usneoides*
(L.) Raf.]   (PL. 1)

Epiphyte, pendant with festooned stringlike spiral-zigzag stems from branches of trees. Leaves scattered, silvery-scurfy with scales, linear-filiform, 1 to 3 in. long, the base slightly dilated. Flowers perfect, axillary, usually solitary, fragrant, the peduncles shorter than the leaves. Sepals 3, green, ca. ¼ in. long. Petals 3, twice as long as sepals, yellow, tipped with yellow-green, narrowly spoon-shaped. Stamens usually 6. Stigma 3-lobed. Capsule linear, 1 in. or more long, eventually splitting by three valves. Distribution: near the coast, from Virginia to Central America.

BALL-MOSS   *Tillandsia recurvata* L.   (PL. 1)

Rigid epiphyte with slender but firm stems, erect or ascending, 2 to 6 in. long. Leaves softly scurfy, mainly basal, commonly crowded, dilated or saccate at base, tapering to tip. Flowers usually in pairs, perfect, with pedicels equalling or exceeding the leaves. Sepals 3, ⅓ to ½ in. long. Petals 3, violet-blue, ½ in. or more long, each with a slender stalk and somewhat broader blade. Stamens 6. Style thread-like, tipped with 3 spreading stigmas. Capsule (in painting) more or less cylindric, about 1 in. long, eventually splitting by 3 valves. Distribution: coastal regions, especially in swamps, from Florida to Mexico and tropical America.

"Spanish-moss" is a very misleading common name, for the plant concerned is neither Spanish nor moss. Nor is it parasitic, as is commonly believed, but rather relies on the branches of trees, especially of oaks, for support. At the base, each of the slender stems is tangled or wound around its support, and as the tip grows downward the older parts die, leaving only a fine fibrous thread, the "horsehair." Leaves and young stems are coated with gray scales, which help in absorbing moisture. The inconspicuous flowers are neither common nor noteworthy; they appear in early summer. Ball-moss, often found with its more graceful cousin, grows contentedly also on telephone wires and wire fences. Ball-moss, or Bunch-moss, as it is sometimes called, has true roots, but these do not penetrate the living tissues of the supporting host. Instead they trap bits of debris, which in time form a little clump of humus from which nutrient material is absorbed during wet weather. Wind and nest-building birds probably account for the spread of these plants from tree to tree. *T. baileyi* Rose, a much larger, coarser plant with bright rose-pink flowers on scapes up to 1 ft. long, occurs south of Live Oak County, especially along the lower Rio Grande. These three species are the most northerly distributed members of the enormous genus *Tillandsia*, which embraces some 400 species of tropical America.

DAYFLOWER FAMILY   Commelinaceae

SPIDERWORT   *Tradescantia* spp.   (PL. 2)   **2**

Perennial herbs, often of erect habit, sometimes with mucilaginous sap. Leaves alternate, the blades often long and narrow. Flowers perfect, in terminal umbel-like clusters subtended but not enclosed by an involucre of 2 (1-3) leaflike bracts. Sepals 3, distinct, nearly equal. Petals 3, equal. Stamens 6, all fertile, those opposite the petals some-

(91)

times shorter than the others. Capsule 3-celled, exposed. Distribution: tropics; in North America northward to Canada.

2
(Cont.) The Spiderworts are generally more striking plants than Dayflowers, often forming clumps, having morning flowers with three similar petals, ranging in color from light blue to rose-violet. White flowers also occur in some species. Here too, distinctions among the dozen or so Texas species are fine, and the situation is further complicated by considerable hybridization which is known to occur among some kinds. Spiderworts prefer sunny positions in open woods and on prairies. As a group they respond very well to cultivation, requiring little care, and as perennials can be counted on to flower for several years, usually between March and June.

Another member of the Dayflower Family, *Commelinantia anomala* (Torr.) Tharp [= *Tinantia anomala* (Torr.) C. B. Clarke = *Commelina anomala* (Torr.) Woodson], known by some as the Texas Dayflower, is a branched annual to 2 ft. or more found in the Edwards Plateau region. It has lavender flowers rather similar in form to those of the true Dayflowers, but they are subtended by an open bract, which is a little shorter than the stem leaves, a condition suggestive of the Spiderworts.

DAYFLOWER   *Commelina* spp.   (PL. 2)

Annual and perennial herbs, commonly with spreading, node-rooting stems. Leaves alternate, the blades entire, often uprolled (especially in dry weather), sheathing at the base. Flowers irregular, usually a few together, but appearing one at a time, basally enclosed by a folded leaflike involucre. Sepals 3, unequal, the larger two often partly united. Petals 3, two much larger than the third, usually blue. Stamens 3, two much larger than the occasionally absent third. Staminodes 2 or 3, smaller than the fertile stamens. Capsule 2- or 3-celled, hidden in involucre. Distribution: tropics and in North America northward to Texas, Illinois, and New York.

Named for their flowers, which remain open for a single morning, the Dayflowers or Widow's Tears are at once garden favorites and troublesome weeds, depending on their degree of spontaneity. The blue or purplish flowers appear to be 2-petalled, but close examination reveals a third whitish inconspicuous one. The buds and fruit are hidden from view unless one parts the folded bract that encloses them. Since trained botanists have trouble distinguishing at least some of the nine species known to occur in Texas, it seems useless to enumerate them here. Dayflowers are found throughout the state, but are especially abundant in damp shady places.

LILY FAMILY   Liliaceae

GREEN-LILY   *Schoenocaulon drummondii* Gray   (PL. 2)

Scapose herb from fibrous-coated bulb. Leaves basal, channeled, linear, 6 to 15 in. long, curved, the margins inrolled. Scapes erect, unbranched, 1 to 2½ ft. tall. Flowers in slender spikelike racemes, inconspicuous. Sepals and petals alike, yellow-green, narrowly linear, ⅟₁₆ in. long. Stamens 6, yellow. Capsules conical to ovoid, 3-celled, separating into three 1-seeded sections. Distribution: Texas and adjacent Mexico.

Abundant along highways and on hillsides in South Central and Trans-Pecos Texas but hardly commanding of attention is the Green-lily. From among the bases of the slender fleshy leaves there arises the scape, its upper quarter or third bristling with tiny yellow-green flowers. The flowering period extends from April to July, or later with sufficient moisture. The White-lily or Death Camas, *Zigadenus nuttallii* Gray [= *Toxicoscordion nuttallii* (Gray) Rydb.] has numerous slender leaves and one or a few flower stalks sometimes nearly a yard high. These bear crowded creamy white flowers nearly ½ in. across. The White-lily is rather common from April to May, occurring in open woods and hillsides, especially in low places, from northeastern Texas west to the Edwards Plateau.

WILD ONION   *Allium drummondii* Regel [= *A. helleri* Small] (PL. 2)

Odorous, stemless herb from an ovoid, fibrous-coated bulb. Leaves all basal, the blades linear, tubular, 4 to 9 in. long. Flowers perfect, few to many, in umbels subtended by 2 or 3 sheathing papery bracts; scapes simple, usually erect, hollow, terete, as long as the leaves, or longer; pedicels slender, ¼ to ⅗ in. long, erect or ascending; perianth members 6, petal-like, white to rose-pink; stamens 6, their filaments slightly swollen above the base; pistil 1, 3-chambered. Fruit an ovoid capsule 3 to 6 mm. long. Distribution: Nebraska to Colorado, south to Texas and Arizona.

Showing a rather consistent preference for unshaded, frequently barren locations is Wild Onion, Prairie Onion, or Cebollita. The flowers are usually pale pink at first but fade to an ashy white with age. They appear in April and May and sometimes again in the fall when there is unusually heavy rainfall and cool weather. The bulbs are commonly in pairs and are coated with delicately interwoven fibers. Very diminutive when compared with the cultivated Onion, *A. cepa* L., and the Leek, *A. porrum* L., the Wild Onion seldoms exceeds 6 in.

in height and, when the papery capsules are ripe, dies back to the bulb. It is found almost throughout Texas except in the extreme east and west portions. Numerous other species, all with the same general habit, are found in the state.

3   CROW-POISON   *Nothoscordium bivalve* (L.) Britt.   (PL. 3)

Odorless, stemless herb from a membranous-coated bulb ⅓ to ¾ in. long. Leaves all basal, the blades narrowly linear, 4 to 15 in. long. Flowers perfect, few to many in narrow-bracted umbels atop erect scapes 8 to 18 in. tall; pedicels slender, ¾ to 2 in. long; perianth members 6, white, petal-like, oblong-lanceolate to narrowly oblong, acute at the apex, ¼ to ½ in. long; stamens 6, the filaments shorter than the perianth members; pistil 1, 3-chambered. Fruit an obovoid capsule *ca.* ¼ in. long. Distribution: Virginia to Nebraska, south to Florida, Texas, and adjacent Mexico.

Crow-poison looks very much like wild onion but lacks the characteristic odor. From the small rather deep bulb grows a tuft of narrowly linear leaves and a foot-high scape bearing a loose umbel of white flowers. The flowering period is from March to May, but in damp situations a second round of flowering takes place in fall. Crow-poison, sometimes known as False-garlic or Odorless-onion, ranges over most of East, Central, and South Texas, west to Childress, Tom Green, and Val Verde counties, and more sparingly in the Trans-Pecos and Panhandle. Despite its commonness and rather forbidding name, Crow-poison, when massed in an open position, makes an attractive early spring addition to any garden.

YUCCA   *Yucca arkansana* Trel.   (PL. 3)

Short-stemmed plant from a stout root, with 1 to few densely leafy crowns. Leaves simple, alternate, so crowded as to obscure the stem, linear, 12 to 20 in. long, ⅓ to ¾ in. wide, firm, straight, entire, margins shredding into conspicuous white threads. Flowers perfect, drooping, arranged in a narrow raceme or panicle; peduncle shorter than or equalling the leaves with broad-based upwardly reduced bracts; perianth members 6, greenish white, obtuse-ended; stamens 6, the filaments enlarged above; pistil 1, 3-chambered. Fruit an erect capsule *ca.* 2 in. long, containing numerous dull seeds ⅓ to ⅖ in. long. Distribution: Kansas south to East Texas.

YUCCA   *Yucca treculeana* Carr.   (PL. 3)

Plant developing a stem 5 to 10 (exceptionally to 18) ft. tall, usually obscured by the persistent dead leaves or leaf bases. Leaves simple, alternate, crowded, linear, 1½ to 3 ft. long, rigid, straight, entire. Flowers perfect, drooping, arranged in a dense, thick-stalked panicle 3 to

5 ft. high, the lowest flowers well down in the foliage crown; perianth members 6, ovate to broadly lanceolate, creamy-white, 1½ to 2½ in. long; stamens 6, the filaments enlarged above; pistil 1, 3-chambered. Fruit a drooping berrylike capsule, opening very tardily or not at all, 2½ to 4 in. long, terminating with a short blunt beak. Distribution: South Texas and adjacent Mexico.

There are three features of considerable interest in the structure of a Yucca flower: the pollen is sticky; the pollen-receptive stigmas lie inside a cavity; the pollen-bearing anthers are remote from the stigmas. These three characteristics eliminate the likelihood of self-pollination and make necessary the carriage of pollen by some outside agent. The agent most important in this activity is the Yucca Moth, whose life history is so intimately entwined with that of the Yucca that neither can carry on without the other. The moth enters newly opened flowers, one after another, collecting pollen from the anthers, tucking it in a depression behind her head. After she has filled this receptacle, she thrusts her ovipositor into the flower ovary, lays an egg, and then take some of her pollen load and spreads it over the stigmatic surface. This she continues to do, going from flower to flower, plant to plant. The insect egg hatches out in the developing fruit and the larva voraciously eats many of the food-rich seeds, eventually making its way to the capsule wall, where it chews a hole large enough for escape and drops to the ground on a thread. Immediately burrowing into the soil a few inches below the surface, the larva continues its development at a much slower pace, and emerges as a moth when the Yuccas bloom the following year.

   Y. *arkansana* is common in the Blackland Prairie and ranges from Grayson, Travis, and Kenedy counties east to Grimes County. It flowers in April and May. Y. *rupicola* Scheele is the commonest species of the Edwards Plateau and extends from Dallas and Comanche counties southeastward to Kerr and Medina counties. Similar to Y. *arkansana* but larger in most respects is Y. *glauca* Nutt., flowering from April to June and occurring from Kerr, McCulloch, and Midland counties west to the Trans-Pecos. Y. *treculeana*, a clump-forming species of South Texas commonly cultivated in much of the state, bears its showy white flowers in April and May. The Joshua-tree, Y. *brevifolia* Engelm., becomes a many-branched open tree up to 35 ft. tall in its native Arizona and California. There are several additional species in Texas, most of them in the western portion.

RED YUCCA   *Hesperaloe parviflora* (Torr.) Coult.   (PL. 3)

   Yuccalike plant with a sessile or short-trunked densely leafy crown of foliage and a slender, sparingly branched, short-bracted peduncle. Leaves simple, alternate, and crowded, obscuring the stem, linear,

(95)

1 to 2 ft. long, stiff, sharp-pointed, entire, with numerous white or grayish marginal filaments. Flowers perfect, arranged in narrow panicles, the common peduncle 3 to 8 ft. tall; perianth members 6, collectively cylindric with a gentle flare, rose-red; stamens 6; pistil 1, 3-chambered. Fruit an ovate, pointed capsule *ca.* 1 in. long. Distribution: West Texas.

One of Texas' most attractive desert plants, the Red Yucca has long been cultivated outside its native range, thriving especially well on limestone soils. The slender, wandlike flower stalks bear the narrow rosy flowers from May to July, or even later in damp situations. The Ixtli, *H. funifera* (Koch) Trel., is a much larger plant of Mexico with leaves up to 5 ft. long, with purplish-tinged greenish flowers, and capsules about 2 in. long. The long, strong leaf fiber is exported as Tampico fiber.

4 SOTOL *Dasylirion texanum* Scheele (PL. 4)

Coarse plant with little or no visible stem, the numerous leaves forming a large bushy crown. Leaves simple, alternate, crowded, and obscuring the stem, linear, 2 to 4 ft. long, rigid, sharp-pointed, the margins armed with hooked spines and finely toothed between. Flowers unisexual, the staminate and pistillate flowers on different plants, both types small and arranged in close, narrow panicles, the common peduncle 4 to 15 ft. tall; perianth members 6, white or cream, persistent, *ca.* $\frac{1}{12}$ in. long; stamens 6, reduced and functionless in pistillate flowers; pistil 1, 1-chambered. Fruit capsulelike, oval or elliptic, *ca.* $\frac{1}{3}$ in. long, 3-winged, not opening, shallowly notched at the apex, containing a single seed. Distribution: Central and West Texas and adjacent Mexico.

Sotol or Desert-candle grows mostly in dry rocky mesas and hillsides, often in large numbers, conspicuously punctuating the otherwise often unbroken landscape. Frequently seen cultivated elsewhere in Texas, this species is found in the wild state from Gillespie and Bandera counties west to Brewster County. It flowers in May and June. *D. leiophyllum* Engelm. is the common species of the Trans-Pecos, with a short trunk bearing smooth, rather lustrous leaves about 3 ft. long, the marginal spines directed backward, and narrow, more deeply notched fruit. It is found from Pecos and Jeff Davis counties south to the Rio Grande. *D. graminifolium* Zucc., also of the Trans-Pecos, has its smooth leaves abruptly narrowed above the base, spine-margined and widened to no more than ½ in. beyond. Several additional species known from adjacent Mexico may extend into southwestern Texas. In times of drought the leaf crowns, when chopped open, are a valuable food source for stock animals. The leaves have been used in basketry, mats, and thatch, and the alcoholic drink "sotol" is prepared from roasted, fermented stems. The

(96)

closely related Ribbon-grass, *Nolina* spp., of which there are many species, differs by having narrower, rough-margined, or minutely toothed leaves and papery 3-seeded capsules.

AMARYLLIS FAMILY   Amaryllidaceae

YELLOW STAR-GRASS   *Hypoxis hirsuta* (L.) Cov.   (PL. 4)

Stemless perennial herb with a small corm. Leaves basal, with elongate to nearly filiform grasslike blades, to 1 ft. in length, about ⅓ in. in diameter, hairy, with a tubular sheath below. Scape slender but rather rigid, 3 to 8 in. high, 2- to 6-flowered. Bracts small, narrow, pointed. Petals and sepals 3 each and alike, yellow, rarely white, greenish and hairy below, elliptic to narrowly ovate, ¼ to ⅔ in. long. Capsule ovoid or spherical, about ⅛ in. long, finely hairy. Distribution: Maine to Ontario, Florida, and Texas.

Yellow Star-grass, or Yellow-eyed–grass, as it is often called, occurs abundantly in sandy fields and open woods and along highways in the eastern ⅓ of the state, westward to Bell and Hays counties. It can scarcely be found except when in flower, so closely do its leaves suggest those of true grasses. They spring from a corm 5 or 6 in. below the surface. The yellow flowers arranged in umbels appear from March until May. *H. rigida* Chapm. [= *H. humilis* Tharp], with flower stalks less than half as long as the leaves, grows in the southeastern corner of the state. *H. juncea* Smith, of the pine belt of extreme East Texas, has narrow stringlike leaves with well-developed tubular sheaths.

ATAMASCO-LILY   *Zephyranthes texana* Hook.   (PL. 4)

Stemless herb with coated subglobose bulb *ca.* ¾ in. in diameter, the neck 1 to 1½ in. long. Leaves basal, the blades narrowly linear, 2½ to 6 in. long, usually only 3 or 4. Scape very slender, 4 to 8 in. tall, terete, 1-flowered, with a spathe about 1 in. long. Sepals and petals 3 each and alike, coppery yellow, striped with deep red-orange or purple outside, about 1 in. long and ¼ in. wide. Stamen filaments joined to the throat of the floral tube. Ovary 3-celled, borne above the spathe. Capsule 3-celled, somewhat 3-lobed, *ca.* ⅓ in. in diameter. Distribution: prairies in South Central Texas.

The Atamasco-lily resembles the Rain-lilies but for the color of the flowers and their frequently nodding posture. Less common, it is found in sandy soil from Anderson, Montgomery, and San Patricio counties west to McLennan and Bexar counties. The solitary blossoms are produced in late summer as the leaves wither. *Z. longifolia* (Hemsl.) Cockerell occurs in the Trans-Pecos, and a third species, *Z. pulchella* J. G. Smith, grows in the lower Rio Grande Valley, northward to Kleberg County. Bulbs of nearly all the Rain-lilies and Atamascos are marketed by seedsmen under such names as Star-lilies, Zephyr-lilies, Fairy-lilies, and Copper-lilies.

RAIN-LILY   *Cooperia pedunculata* Herb. [= *Zephyranthes drummondii* D. Don]   (PL. 4)

> Stemless herb with a coated subglobose bulb *ca.* 1 in. in diameter, the neck 2 to 3 in. long. Leaves basal, the blades narrowly linear, 6 to 12 in. long, *ca.* ¼ in. wide. Scape erect, unbranched, 4 to 9 in. high, the solitary flower subtended by a bractlike spathe. Petals and sepals 3 each and alike, white, salverform, the tube slender, 1 to 2 in. long, slightly dilated above. Capsule *ca.* ½ in. in diameter. Distribution: prairies in Central Texas.

Two kinds of Rain-lily grow in Texas. The Giant Rain-lily or Prairie-lily is found in fields and open woods over much of the central region, especially in the triangle formed by Travis, Bexar, and Washington counties. It has fleshy strap-shaped leaves growing from a bulb the size of a small onion, which is often a foot below the surface. The flowers appear irregularly from late spring to early fall, most commonly a few days after heavy rains. They open slowly around dusk or earlier on cloudy days, the lobes gradually spreading during the night, and appearing fully expanded the next morning. Ordinarily each flower lasts only one day, turning pale pink before withering, but in dull weather withering may not occur until the second day. The other species, *C. drummondii* Herb. [= *Zephyranthes brazosensis* Traub.] (PL. 4), is smaller in almost every respect with the exception of the longer floral tube. More widespread, it occurs in open woods and fields from the Red River south to the Rio Grande, westward to the mountain valleys in the Trans-Pecos.

5   SPIDER-LILY   *Hymenocallis liriosme* (Raf.) Shinners [= *H. galvestonensis* (Herb.) Baker]   (PL. 5)

> Fleshy stemless herb from a large coated bulb. Leaves basal, the blades linear, 6 to 30 in. long, *ca.* 1 in. wide. Scape 1 to 3 ft. high, terminating with an umbel of 4 to 6 flowers, subtended by a membranous bract. Sepals and petals 3 each and alike, white, from a tube 2 to 4 in. long, narrow, spreading, the tips often recurved. Stamens 6, united by a thin saucer-shaped corona. Ovary 3-celled, with a long usually curved style tipped by a globose or slightly flattened stigma. Distribution: low places in East Texas.

(98)

Scenting still air in the spring with its abundant perfume, the Spider-lily is found, often in large numbers, in roadside ditches, shaded pond borders, and swamps, most commonly near the coast southward to Corpus Christi. The handsome glossy foliage and large but delicate flowers have brought the plant considerable popularity in the garden, its main requirement being an unfailing and generous supply of water. Another less common species, *H. occidentalis* Kunth, known from extreme East Texas (Nacogdoches and Gregg counties east-ward) blooms in summer and early fall, often after the leaves have dried up. It is further distinguished by its leaves measuring more than an inch in width and covered with a whitish waxy bloom.

CENTURY-PLANT   *Agave americana* L.   (PL. 5)

> Large fleshy or somewhat woody plants developing a more or less elongate caudex. Leaves crowded on caudex, persisting for several years, the blades very thick, gray-green, spine-tipped, with conical somewhat recurved marginal spines decurrent for not more than their length, 3 to 7 ft. long, 6 to 9 in. wide. Inflorescence a panicle to 20 ft. high, the lateral branches horizontal. Sepals and petals 3 each and alike, yellow-green, persistent. Stamens 6. Ovary 3-celled. Capsule 3-celled, thick-walled, with numerous flattened black seeds. Dis-tribution: dry soil, from Florida to South and West Texas; naturalized from Mexico and Central America.

There are few rosette-plants known which can match the Century-plant for sheer size and bulk of structure. Reduce it to one twentieth or even one tenth its actual size and we would hardly give a second glance. From among the thick, waxy, blue-green leaves there arises after ten to twenty (not 100!) years an immense asparaguslike shoot which soon expands and branches to display the greenish flowers. The flowering period extends for many weeks; thereafter the dried floral parts persist indefinitely. With the maturing of the flow-ering edifice the leaves usually shrivel and die. Suckers sometimes grow up from the roots at this time. The Century-plant is extensively cultivated for ornament in South Texas, but in Mexico and the Cen-tral American countries, where it is known as Maguey, the sap (aqua mil) from the young decapitated inflorescence stalk is fermented and distilled to make the well-known tequila. Closely related is the smaller *A. havardiana* Trel. of the Big Bend region. Its flower stalk seldom exceeds 12 ft. in height and its spine-tipped leaves have rigid recurved hooks along the upturned margins. Still smaller is the Lechuguilla, *A. lechuguilla* Torr., which bears thinner heavily armed green to bluish leaves to 2 ft. long and 1½ in. wide, often with a pale longitudinal stripe on the upper surface, and flowers in a spikelike cluster.

IRIS FAMILY   Iridaceae

CELESTIAL   *Nemastylis geminiflora* Nutt. [= *N. acuta* (Bart.)
Herb.]   (PL. 5)

> Perennial herb from coated bulb. Stem terete, 6 to 15 in. tall, with
> few or no branches. Leaves bright green, alternate, the blades linear,
> 4 to 12 in. long, most of them exceeding the flower cluster. Flowers
> 2 or 3 from a 2-parted spathe. Sepals and petals 3 each and nearly
> alike, light blue-violet, whitened at the base, ½ to ¾ in. long. Stamens
> 3. Ovary 3-celled, the 3 styles alternating with the stamens and each
> parted into 2 slender filamentous segments. Capsule more or less ovate
> or turbinate, *ca.* ½ in. long, splitting into 3 valves to release the
> numerous seeds. Distribution: Tennessee to Kansas, Louisiana, and
> Texas.

But for the fact that the flowers are open only a few hours, Celestials
might be well-known wildflowers. Hardly suggesting their affinity to
the true iris, they open out flat or saucer-shaped in the late morning,
each petal and sepal slightly cupped. At first the orange anthers
stand erect, but in an hour or two they turn downward. And then,
usually before 3:00 P.M., the perianth parts curl up. Because of their
flat grasslike foliage, the plants are hard to find when out of flower.
Celestials are found blooming in April in sandy fields, open woods,
and on the Blackland Prairie in East Texas, west to Clay, Coleman,
and Kendall counties. The taller, purple-flowered *N. purpurea* Herb.
occurs in the pine belt in extreme East Texas and blooms in May
and June.

5, 6   BLUE-EYED–GRASS   *Sisyrinchium* spp.   (PLS. 5, 6)

> Annual and perennial, usually tufted grasslike herbs with more or
> less well-developed rootstocks bearing fibrous roots. Leaves relatively
> few, sometimes only basal, the blades linear. Flowering stalks flat,
> when branched each node bearing a leaflike bract. Flowers solitary
> or in terminal clusters, arising from two-bracted spathes. Sepals and
> petals 3 each and alike, commonly blue or blue-violet, also white or
> yellow, spreading. Stamens 3, their stalks united nearly to the top.
> Ovary 3-celled, each cavity with few to many ovules. Capsule oval,
> spherical, or depressed, borne on threadlike stalks, opening near
> apex to release the numerous smooth or pitted seeds. Distribution:
> North and South America.

Plants belonging to this large and difficult genus are collectively distinctive, having narrow grasslike leaves and wide open often yellow-
centered flowers which close in the afternoon. Characters separating

the species are very fine and, in some cases, there are intergrading forms from one species to another. While Blue-eyed–grass is found in nearly all parts of the state, the sandy woods and plains near the Gulf Coast show the greatest diversity. Among the commoner and more distinctive species, *S. minus* Engelm. & Gray, an annual with erect or prostrate stems bearing rosy purple flowers up to ½ in. across in March and April, occurs in damp depressions along roadsides and in fields from Liberty County to Bee County, sparingly northward. Another annual, *S. micranthum* Cav., with yellow flowers on much-branched slender stems, is common in Southeast Texas; it is an introduction from South America. *S. albidum* Raf. has white flowers and occurs in the eastern and north-central portions. The commonest species on the Edwards Plateau is *S. ensigerum* Bicknell. *S. pruinosum* Bicknell is its counterpart on most of the Blackland Prairie. Both have flowers in various shades of blue, the sepals and petals being noticeably paler on the underside. *S. varians* Bicknell is the prevailing species in the lower Rio Grande Valley. Among the fewer West Texas species, *S. longipedunculatum* Bicknell of mountain slopes is perhaps the most common. The remaining 12 or 15 species are chiefly blue-flowered, most of them growing in the eastern half of the state. When transplanted to gardens or grown from seed, many species will bloom considerably beyond their normal seasonal limits, especially if the soil is kept damp. As with their iris cousins, the perennial Blue-eyed–grasses form clumps, the consequent massing of the flowers adding to their conspicuity.

WILD IRIS   *Iris hexagona* Walt. [= *I. flexicaulis* Small]   (PL. 6)   **6**

> Perennial herb with long rootstocks bearing thick fibrous roots. Stem 1 to 3 ft. tall. Leaves mostly basal, firm, 1 to 2 ft. long, *ca.* 1 in. wide, the stem leaves smaller. Sepals 3, petal-like, spreading and reflexed, blue-violet with deep violet veins and a yellow spot. Petals 3, smaller, erect or ascending, pale violet. Stamens 3, hidden by the 3 broad petal-like style branches. Capsule 1 to 1½ in. long, 6-angled, the seeds in two rows in each of the 3 cavities. Distribution: South Carolina to Missouri, Florida, and Texas.

Many species of *Iris* grow wild in the eastern half of the country, some of them extending into East Texas, where they occur in low ground and swampy places, even in shallow water. The Wild Iris or Blue Flag pictured occurs southward and eastward from Polk County. *I. virginica* L., var. *shrevei* (Small) E. Anderson, is very similar but has a 3-angled capsule. It occurs as far west as Gonzales, Robertson, and Smith counties. Copper Iris, *I. fulva* Ker., has reddish-brown flowers, is known from western Louisiana and may occur in extreme East Texas. *I. brevicaulis* Raf., also of Louisiana, seldom exceeds 1 ft. in height. It is known from damp woods along the Red River in Bowie and Red River counties. Some of the numerous cultivated types escape and then perpetuate themselves, most notably the White Flag, *I. germanica* L.

ORCHID FAMILY   Orchidaceae

LADIES' TRESSES   *Spiranthes cernua* (L.) L. C. Rich. [= *Gyrostachys cernua* (L.) Kuntze]   (PL. 6)

> Perennial herb with thickened fleshy tuberlike roots. Stem unbranched, 8 to 30 in. tall. Basal and lower-stem leaves with narrow blades, 3 to 10 in. long, often withering at flowering time; upper-stem leaves mere sheathing scales. Flowers in a slender bracted spike, arranged in 1 to 3 gently spiraling rows. Sepals 3, petal-like, white or pale greenish white. Petals 3, unequal, the longest ⅓ to ½ in. long, white. Distribution: meadows and swamps, Nova Scotia to Minnesota, Florida, and Texas.

Of the half dozen genera of orchids occurring in Texas, only *Spiranthes* approaches the classification of a roadside wildflower. The others are for the most part rare items of bogs and deep woods, becoming increasingly uncommon as the thoughtless and ignorant decimate some areas for the pleasure of a few days' beauty in a vase. Because of their unpretentious appearance and the fact that few people suspect their true orchid affinities, Ladies' Tresses are usually left untouched. *S. cernua* may be seen from June to September in open woods and on prairies in East Texas west to Parker and Llano counties. *S. vernalis* Engelm. & Gray, with flowers in one strongly spiraled row from April to June, is common in the southeastern corner of the state, northward to Dallas County. *S. grayi* Ames, with smaller flowers, about ¼ in. long arranged in one spiral row, grows in dry sandy woods west to Houston and Lamar counties. *S. gracilis* (Bigelow) Hook. is occasionally encountered, ranging west to Grayson and Bastrop counties. Both bloom in the summer months. *S. odorata* (Nutt.) Ktze., a species in coastal swamps, occurs eastward from Corpus Christi. It closely resembles the figured species. Most spectacular is the red-flowered Flame Orchid, *S. cinnabarinas* (Llava & Lex.) Hemsl., found at high elevations in Brewster County.

BUCKWHEAT FAMILY   Polygonaceae

WILD BUCKWHEAT   *Eriogonum annuum* Nutt.   (PL. 6)

Annual herb 1 to 3 ft. tall, the stem unbranched to the inflorescence. Leaves and stem covered with soft silky matted grayish hairs. Leaf blades 1 to 3 in. long, flat or slightly undulate, narrowed at the base to a short leafstalk. Inflorescence usually flat-topped; involucres turban- or bell-shaped, *ca.* ⅛ in. high, very short-stalked, densely white-hairy, 5-lobed; sepals 6, in two series, the inner narrower, white or on occasion pink, less than ⅛ in. long, hairless; petals absent; stamens 9; ovary 1-celled, topped with 3 styles. Achenes 3-angled, *ca.* ¹⁄₁₆ in. long, with a globular base and a beak of equal length. Distribution: dry places from Nebraska to Texas, New Mexico, and Chihuahua.

The Buckwheats are a large genus of nearly 200 species of herbs and shrubs, mostly of dry regions of western North America. The Wild Buckwheat figured, one of 20 species in Texas, is an upright plant with one to several stems bearing narrowly oblong, whitish leaves with down-rolled margins and flower clusters in summer and early fall. The pink-flowered form is occasionally seen mixed in populations of the usual white-flowered plants. Although most Buckwheats occur isolated among plants of other kinds, *E. annuum* commonly grows in pure stands in neglected fields rather generally over the entire state. *E. wrightii* Torr., a much-branched shrub or sub-shrub to 2 ft., common in the Trans-Pecos, bears its flowers in summer scattered on the branches or, less commonly, crowded near the ends. Often abundant, it is reputedly a browse plant of considerable importance.

CANAIGRE   *Rumex hymenosepalus* Torr.   (PL. 7)   **7**

Perennial herb from a cluster of swollen roots. Stem erect, 1 to 3 ft. tall, usually unbranched below, often red or red-brown, somewhat fleshy, with a papery collar (the ocrea) at each node. Leaves alternate, the blades entire, plane, rather fleshy, lanceolate to ovate-lanceolate, 4 to 15 in. long, apex acuminate to acute, margin commonly wavy, somewhat crisped, the lower blades narrowing to thick stalks, the upper blades sessile. Inflorescence a somewhat leafy-bracted panicle, dense in fruit, the branches erect, 2 to 8 in. long. Sepals 6, in two series, the inner developing ovate-cordate wings *ca.* ⅓ in. long. Stamens 6. Ovary topped with 3 styles. Fruit a 3-angled achene, invested by the much-enlarged winglike calyx, ovoid, *ca.* ¼ in. long.

The Docks are a group of about 100 species of weedy herbs of north-temperate regions. The Canaigre, of West Texas, is a smooth perennial commonly seen in stream beds and gulches, but readily invading disturbed ground. The plant grows from tannin-rich tuberous roots and bears leaves often exceeding a foot in length. The inconspicuous flowers, borne in large terminal panicles in April, are soon followed by masses of fruit, each achene enclosed in an enlarged rosy or purplish-brown calyx. The plants wither at the onset of hot dry weather. Curly-leaved Dock, *R. crispus* L., is an erect perennial to 3 ft. or more, easily distinguished from the preceding by the very finely wavy margins of its long rather narrow leaves. It occurs more or less generally throughout the state, but is commonest in sandy fields and waste places in East Texas. Similarly distributed is the annual *R. hastatulus* Baldwin, a close relative of the Sheep-sorrel, *R. acetosella* L., a troublesome perennial weed of northern states. Our plant, erect and sometimes reaching 18 in., is easily identified by the basal pair of narrow tail-like lobes on each leaf. It is found in open woods and neglected fields, chiefly on sandy soils in East Texas. In all, there are about 12 species of Dock in the state.

AMARANTH FAMILY   Amaranthaceae

SNAKE-COTTON   *Froelichia floridana* (Nutt.) Moq.   (PL. 7)

> Rather slender annual herb with erect or ascending wandlike puberulent stems 2 to 6 ft. tall. Leaves simple, opposite, the pairs remote, sessile or nearly so; blades lanceolate to linear, reduced upward, 1¼ to 4 in. long, acute at the apex, pubescent with appressed hairs. Flowers perfect, in bracted wooly spikes at the ends of long peduncles; bracts yellowish, shorter than the flowers; sepals 5, united to form a tube, densely wooly outside; petals absent; stamens 5; pistil 1, 1-chambered. Fruit a 1-seeded unopening utricle enclosed by the united filaments and the persistent calyx. Distribution: Georgia west to Texas.

Among the more than 750 species of herbs and shrubs in the Amaranth Family, most are rather weedy plants, a few, such as the Careless-weed, *Amaranthus* spp., having ill repute as stock poisons. Snake-cotton or Cotton-weed, a plant of the eastern half of Texas, is sometimes rather conspicuous by numbers, for it often grows in dense masses along highway shoulders and in abandoned cultivations. The flowers are borne from June to October. Cultivated plants of the Amaranth Family include: Prince's-feather, *Amaranthus hybridus* L. and *Amaranthus hypochondriacus* L.; Cock's-comb, *Celosia argentea* L., var. *cristata* (L.) Ktze.; Globe-amaranth, *Gomphrena globosa* L. Other well-known wild plants of the family are the

Tumbleweed, *Amaranthus albus* L., of West Texas, Chaff-flower, *Alternanthera repens* (L.) Ktze., Green Pigweed, *Amaranthus viridis* L., and Water-hemp, *A. tamariscinus* Nutt.

FOUR-O'CLOCK FAMILY   Nyctaginaceae

UMBRELLAWORT   *Mirabilis nyctagineus* (Michx.)   MacMillan [= *Oxybaphus nyctagineus* (Michx.) Sweet = *Allionia nyctaginea* Michx.]   (PL. 7)

Perennial herb with forking stems 1 to 3 ft. tall, the nodes more or less swollen. Leaves opposite, rather fleshy; blades triangular-ovate, 1 to 4 in. long, the apex acute or acuminate, the margin ragged or irregularly uneven, the base obtuse or cordate; petioles ½ to 1 in. long. Inflorescence a cluster of 3 to 5 flowers within a pale green broadly bell-shaped involucre *ca.* ⅝ in. across; calyx red, hairy outside, soon falling; petals absent; stamens 3 to 5, unequal in length, protruding. Fruit an achene whose wall is in part composed of the persisting base of the calyx tube, ⅛ in. long, pubescent, shallowly ridged, the faces minutely lumpy. Distribution: Montana and Wisconsin south to Louisiana, Texas, and New Mexico.

As with other members of the Four-o'clock Family, the flowers of the Umbrellawort have no true petals, the enlarged bell-shaped calyx taking their place. In the Garden Four-o'clock, *M. jalapa* L., the calyx is brightly colored, but in this species it is pale greenish and commonly escapes notice. If cross-pollination does not occur when the stamens and style are fully extended, self-pollination is certain to take place later when these structures roll up together. After the flowering period of April and May, most of the calyx soon falls away, its narrow base persisting as a jacket over the ovary. The subtending involucre enlarges and persists as the small hairy club-shaped 1-seeded fruits mature. In the same family are the spectacular South American Bougainvillaeas, which owe their attractiveness not to the flowers but to the richly colored leaflike involucres.

SPIDERLING   *Boerhavia erecta* L.   (PL. 7)

Slender annual herb with forking, erect, or sometimes more or less spreading stems 1 to 4 ft. long. Leaves opposite, occasionally alternate; blades unequal, ovate or triangular-ovate, sometimes asymmetric, 1 to 3½ in. long, apex acute to obtuse, margin wavy or very shallowly round-toothed, base wedge-shaped to cordate, the pale undersurface finely black-dotted; petioles at least half as long as the blades. Inflorescence a panicle of many small 2- to 6-flowered clusters on slender stalks; calyx white to purple, commonly pink, *ca.* $\frac{1}{16}$ in. long; petals absent; stamens 1 to 5, protruding. Fruit an achene *ca.* $\frac{1}{8}$ in. long, 5-angled, the grooves transversely wrinkled, the top flat. Distribution: South Carolina to Florida, Texas, Mexico, and tropical America.

Of the dozen species of *Boerhavia* in Texas this is the most extensively distributed. A common weed in waste places and disturbed ground, the Spiderling, which flowers from June to September, grows in East Texas, west to Taylor and Bexar counties, south to the Mexican border. It also occurs (in the var. *intermedia*) in the Trans-Pecos. The purplish-margined black-dotted leaves are paired on divergent branches which end in loose delicate clusters of small white-to-pink flowers. The Wine-flower, *B. coccinea* Mill. (PL. 7), is rather more attractive, with numerous spreading branches arising from a perennial root and producing on long sticky stalks tight clusters of deep red flowers. These are followed by viscid fruits. The leaves have a purplish cast above. A native of South and West Texas, this species is gradually spreading eastward along roadsides and railways.

8   SAND-VERBENA   *Abronia fragrans* Nutt.   (PL. 8)

Viscid-hairy annual with much-branched stems spreading to 2½ or 3 ft. Leaves opposite; blades often of unequal size, thick, entire, 2 to 4 in. long, rounded at both ends; petiole usually somewhat shorter than the blade. Flowers fragrant, numerous in a whitish many-bracted involucre; calyx petal-like, opening in late afternoon, ½ to 1¼ in. long, the white tube gradually expanded upward to the white or pale lavender limb; petals absent; stamens 3 to 5, included within calyx tube, the very slender filaments of varying lengths; style long and slender. Fruit an achene *ca.* ⅓ in. long, minutely hairy, 5-winged, wrinkled. Distribution: Montana southward to Texas and Mexico.

One of the most beautiful Texas plants in the Four-o'clock Family is the Sand-verbena, conspicuous on sandy plains from April to June with its heads of white or pale lavender flowers. Also known as Heart's-delight, this species has been introduced as a garden plant, especially in South Texas, where it has acquired yet another common name, Lasater's-pride. Its natural range is in the Panhandle, south to Ward County and east to Wichita County. Desert Ground-cover, also cultivated in the sandy soils of South Texas, is *A. villosa* Wats., a species of dry areas in Arizona and California. Its long bristly hairs distinguish it from the Pink Sand-verbena, *A. angustifolia* Greene, of the far Trans-Pecos, the latter having short hairs usually with a sticky secretion. *A. ameliae* Lundell, native of sandy prairies from Live Oak County southward, closely resembles *A. fragrans*.

DEVIL'S-BOUQUET   *Nyctaginea capitata* Choisy   (PL. 8)

Perennial herb with viscid-hairy foliage, the stem erect or spreading, 1 to 1½ ft. long. Leaves opposite; blades thick, ovate to triangular, apex usually acuminate, margin undulate, base rounded or sub-cordate; petiole at least half as long as the blade. Flowers 8 to 15 in an involucrate head; involucral bracts 8 to 12, linear-lanceolate, ½ to 1 in. long, sharp-pointed; calyx red to salmon-rose, villous with glandular hairs on the outside, tube constricted above the ovary, ¾ to 1¼ in. long; petals absent; stamens 5, long-exserted, the slender filaments of varying lengths; style very slender, with a capitate stigma. Fruit a turbinate achene *ca.* ¼ in. long, many-ribbed. Distribution: West Texas and southern New Mexico.

Flowering from April until fall, especially after wet periods, the Devil's-bouquet or Musk-flower is an arresting plant. The bright red or pink flowers are arranged in bracted clusters about 3 in. in diameter, arising from straggling knobby stems. As with most members of this family, the blooms open in late afternoon, closing early the next day or persisting longer in cloudy weather. Widespread but seemingly nowhere abundant, Devil's-bouquet ranges eastward from the Trans-Pecos to Burnet, Karnes, and Hidalgo counties.

ANGEL'S-TRUMPET   *Acleisanthes longiflora* Gray   (PL. 8)

Smooth or finely pubescent perennial herb with brittle creeping much-branched stems, at length forming a mat 3 or 4 ft. across. Leaves opposite; blades thick, unequal, entire, lanceolate to rhombic-lanceolate, ½ to 1¼ in. long, apex acute to acuminate, base acute to rounded; petiole short. Flowers solitary in leaf axils, subtended by tiny bracts; calyx white, the tube pronouncedly elongate, constricted above the ovary, 4½ to 6 in. long, the 5-lobed limb salverlike; stamens 2 to 5, the exserted anthers on very slender filaments of unequal lengths; style elongate, exserted, tipped with a capitate stigma. Fruit a 5-ribbed achene, constricted beneath apex, *ca.* ⅓ in. long. Distribution: Texas and adjacent Mexico.

Possessed of one of the longest flowers of all Texas plants, Angel's-trumpet appears in April and May but may sporadically bloom through the summer until mid-autumn, especially after rains. It is commonest on sandy roadsides in South Texas and the Trans-Pecos, ranging locally northward to Motley County. True to the character of the Four-o'clock Family, Angel's-trumpet is nocturnal, opening at dusk and closing the following morning. *A. obtusa* (Choisy) Standl., with blunt-ended leaves and much shorter calyx tubes, grows in South Texas from Maverick, Bexar, and Goliad counties southward. Several other species, all with flowers less than 3 in. long, occur in the Rio Grande Valley and the Trans-Pecos.

POKEWEED FAMILY   Phytolaccaceae

SMALL POKEWEED   *Rivina humilis* L.   (PL. 8)

Perennial herb with erect or ascending stems 1 to 3 ft. high, the stems and leaves smooth or somewhat hairy. Leaves alternate; blades ovate to oblong or lanceolate, 1 to 5 in. long, ½ to 2½ in. broad, membranous, margin entire or undulate, apex acuminate or acute, base wedge-shaped to subtruncate; petiole ½ to 3 in. long. Flowers in slender several- to many-flowered racemes 1½ to 8 in. long; pedicels slender, ⅛ to ¼ in. long; sepals 4, green to pinkish purple, *ca.* ¹⁄₁₆ in. long; petals absent; stamens 4, shorter than the sepals, filaments about ¹⁄₃₂ in. long, the anthers shorter; ovary 1-celled with 1 ovule, the style short, bearing a capitate stigma. Fruit a drupe, about ⅛ in. in diameter, yellow to red. Distribution: Arkansas to Florida, Texas, Mexico, and the tropics.

9   GREAT POKEWEED   *Phytolacca americana* L. [= *P. decandra* L.] (PL. 9)

Glabrous, succulent, often malodorous perennial herb to 8 ft. from a large parsniplike poisonous root. Leaves alternate; blades entire, oblong-lanceolate to ovate, 4 to 12 in. long, 1 to 5 in. broad, acute or acuminate at both ends; petioles slender, ½ to 2½ in. long, grooved above. Inflorescence a raceme, erect in bud, ascending in flower, nodding in fruit, 3 to 12 in. long; pedicels smooth or finely hairy, often reflexed, ⅛ to ¼ in. long, each with a narrow bract at its base and two smaller ones closer to the supported flower; sepals 5 (rarely 6), greenish white to pale pink, ovoid, about ⅛ in. long; petals absent; stamens 9 to 12 (usually 10), shorter than the sepals; ovary 10-celled, bearing recurved styles. Fruit a depressed berry about ⅓ in. in diameter (shorter than the pedicels), deep violet. Seed orbicular, ⅛ in. long, black, shining. Distribution: Maine to Minnesota, south to Florida and Texas.

Pokeweeds are probably better known for their attractive fruit clusters than for their modest pale flowers. Members of a predominantly tropical family, the Texas representatives have plus and minus merits. The red or violet fruits attract many birds and the often handsome foliage suits the plants for cultivation as seasonal hedges or screens—but beware of the poisonous root! The Pigeonberry or Small Pokeweed is found rather commonly, in places abundantly, in woods in the rolling hills of Central Texas, south to the Rio Grande, west to the Trans-Pecos. It is distinguished from the Scoke, or Great Pokeweed, by wavy-margined leaves, pale pink flowers, and red fruit. The Scoke on the other hand is an inhabitant of low moist woods, principally in East Texas, and has flat leaves, white flowers,

(108)

and purple berries. Both species flower from May or June to early fall. The early spring shoots of the Great Pokeweed are sometimes eaten as greens but this is utility fraught with danger; the entire plant, especially the root, carries a poisonous substance, hence the water in which the greens are boiled should be discarded. *Phytolacca rigida* Small differs from the Great Pokeweed by distinct fruiting characters: berries globose, longer than their supporting pedicels, disposed in erect racemes. It occurs in extreme southeastern Texas.

PORTULACA FAMILY   Portulacaceae

MOSS-ROSE   *Portulaca pilosa* L.   (PL. 9)

> Succulent prostrate or ascending annual herb, the stems up to 8 in. long, usually with tufts of hairs in the leaf axils. Leaves alternate; blade fleshy, thick, narrowly oblong, ¼ to ⅝ in. long, *ca.* ¹⁄₁₆ in. broad, apex acute, margin entire, base narrowed to a short petiole. Flowers perfect, terminal, subtended by a whorl of 6 to 10 leaves interposed with long grayish or pale brown hairs; sepals 2, ovate or somewhat triangular, *ca.* ⅛ in. long; petals usually 5, rose-pink or pinkish purple, ⅕ to ⅓ in. long, obovate, the apex often notched; stamens 15 to 30, the filaments crimson; style lobes 4 or 6. Fruit a 1-chambered capsule *ca.* ⅛ in. in diameter, opening by a hoodlike membranous cap which falls away to liberate the numerous black seeds. Distribution: Missouri southward to Florida, Texas, California, and tropical America.

In Central, South, and West Texas the Moss-rose grows here and there along roadsides and in sandy fields, producing its pinkish-purple flowers during the brightest hours. In some places it becomes so abundant as to carpet the ground, blanketing barren waysides with a rosy mantle. The familiar Garden Portulaca or Sun-plant, *P. grandiflora* Hook., a native of Argentina, is very similar but for its generally larger size. The abundantly produced metallic gray seeds sometimes escape gardens in sandy regions, establishing plants in nearby fields and roadsides. Pusley, *P. oleracea* L. (PL. 9), is a persistent weed of European origin which forms mats of thick flat leaves among which may be seen little yellow flowers. Young leafy shoots are sometimes included in salads or boiled as greens, and the seeds are sometimes substituted for poppy seed in baked goods. Also with flattened leaf blades is *P. lanceolata* Engelm. of South Texas. It bears yellowish-pink petals, which, unlike those of Pusley, are rounded, not notched, at the apex. A few additional species are known from West Texas.

FLAME-FLOWER   *Talinum lineare* H. B. K. [= *T. aurantiacum* Engelm.]   (PL. 9)

Fleshy-rooted perennial herb with slender, erect, or ascending simple or branched stems 4 to 15 in. tall. Leaves alternate; blades linear, fleshy, rather flat, 1 to 2½ in. long, apex acute, margin entire, sessile at the narrowed base. Flowers borne on short peduncles in the axils of the leaves; sepals 2, soon falling; petals 5, ¾ to 1¼ in. long, yellow to red-orange, withering in late afternoon; stamens *ca.* 20, the filaments red; styles 3, somewhat united, orange. Fruit a subglobose capsule *ca.* ¼ in. long, splitting three ways to discharge the numerous shiny black seeds, borne on a strongly recurved stalk. Distribution: western half of Texas, southern New Mexico, and adjacent Mexico.

The Flame-flower grows from an edible root and bears its solitary vividly colored blooms on brittle stems from March to September. Soon after the petals fall, the flower stalk turns downward while the capsule matures. Commonest in the western and southern portions of the state, the Flame-flower is known locally as far east as Stephens and Travis counties. *T. parviflorum* Nutt. is a low plant having leaves margined with a colorless membranous band and small pink flowers borne in terminal clusters. It grows in East Texas, west to Llano County, and also in the Trans-Pecos. Rather similar is *T. calycinum* Engelm. of the Panhandle and locally eastward to Cooke County. It differs by having larger flowers, the petals measuring ⅜ in. or longer, and 25 or more stamens. *T. paniculatum* Willd. is a taller plant, sometimes reaching 5 ft., bearing leaves nearly ovate in outline, and large loose panicles of small rose-pink–to–yellow flowers. Its range is from southeastern Texas west to Bexar County and also in the Trans-Pecos.

PINK FAMILY   Caryophyllaceae

10   CHICKWEED   *Stellaria media* (L.) Villars [= *Alsine media* L.] (PL. 10)

Annual herb with branched spreading or weakly ascending stems, 4 to 12 in. long, finely hairy in alternating lines. Leaves opposite; blades ovate, ¼ to ¾ in. long, apex acute, margin entire, more or less tapering at base; petioles of lower leaves often about as long as blades, but shorter in later growth. Flowers in cymes, the peduncles at first short, but lengthening in age; sepals 5, sometimes 4, oblong-lanceolate, *ca.* ⅛ in. long; petals as many as sepals, white, 2-cleft or 2-parted nearly to the base (superficially appearing as 10 or 8), slightly shorter than the sepals; stamens as many as the sepals, the spreading filaments slender; ovary 1-celled, the styles 3. Fruit an elliptic or ovoid capsule about as long as the sepals, opening by 6 short teeth. Distribution: Europe and western Asia; introduced and generally distributed in temperate North America.

Chickweed, one of the numerous weedy members of the Pink Family, is a diffusely branched, usually matted winter annual with small white flowers appearing from late January or February until mid-spring, or later in damp shady places. The abundantly produced pendant fruits shed multitudes of seeds, which germinate in damp periods in late fall or early winter, the young plants often carpeting the ground in lawns, gardens, and waste places. In Texas Chickweed is commonest in the eastern third of the state and in the Panhandle. Starwort, *S. nuttallii* Torr. & Gray [= *Arenaria drummondii* Shinners], is a more attractive species, more or less erect to 1 ft., found in moist low ground in prairies and open woods in northeastern Texas, and rather conspicuous in April and May with white flowers about 1 in. across. Other members of the Pink Family include the native Sleepy Catchfly, *Silene antirrhina* L., and several popular garden subjects (all natives of Europe), Baby's-breath, *Gypsophila elegans* L., Sweet-william, *Dianthus barbatus* L., and Carnation, *D. caryophyllus* L.

BUTTERCUP FAMILY   Ranunculaceae

PRAIRIE LARKSPUR   *Delphinium virescens* Nutt.   (PL. 10)

Woody-rooted perennial herb with erect stems 1 to 3½ ft. tall, often somewhat branched. Leaves basal and alternate on lower portion of stem; blades finely hairy, somewhat viscid, 2 to 5 in. broad, repeatedly palmately divided into linear segments or teeth, those of the lowest leaves sometimes oblong. Flowers in simple racemes 6 to 20 in. long; pedicels ⅓ to ¾ in. long, erect, bearing bractlets ⅛ in. long *ca.* ¼ in. below the sepals; sepals 5, white or pale lavender, each with a bluish-purple spot, the uppermost sepal prolonged into a spur; petals 4, the two lateral ones bearded, 2-cleft; stamens many; pistils few, each containing many ovules. Fruit a cylindric follicle ⅝ to ⅞ in. long, opening by little pores to discharge the many sharply angled brown seeds. Distribution: Wisconsin and Illinois, south to Texas and New Mexico.

Prairie Larkspur, or Rabbit-face, is a slender perennial seen most commonly on flat grassy prairies and plains but occurring throughout most of the state. The white-to-pale-lavender flowers, appearing in April and May, are borne on the upper half or third of slender graceful stems which in some localities become waist-high. The peculiar

(111)

flowers consist of 5 colored sepals, the uppermost of which is drawn backward into a spur, then 4 petals, the upper 2 with long nectar-bearing spurs extending into the sepal spur, the lower 2 arching over the upper ones, shielding the numerous stamens and 3 pistils. On opening, a flower shows the stamens in front of the nectar-bearing spurs; with age, after the pollen is dispersed, the stamens relax and the pistils assume an exposed position. Thus bees, moving upward through a raceme, as is their custom, seeking nectar in any open flowers, carry pollen from the younger upper flowers of one raceme and place it quite accidentally on the pistils of the older lower flowers of the next. In this way cross-pollination is effected. When the sepals and petals fall, the enlarging pistils turn upward and at maturity open by means of terminal pores, enabling the wind to shake out the seeds. In sandy woods and open places in the eastern half of the state is the Carolina Larkspur, *D. carolinianum* Walt., easily told by its deep blue or blue-violet flowers. This is not to be confused with the cultivated but often escaped Annual Larkspur, *D. ajacis* L., a native of Europe, with very narrow threadlike leaf segments and blue, violet, white, or pink flowers crowded in racemes.

ANEMONE   *Anemone decapetala* Ard.   (PL. 10)

> Perennial herb from a small corm. Leaves basal, few, finely hairy; blades 3-divided, the segments ovate or ovate-oblong, bluntly toothed, ½ to 1½ in. long; petioles slender, 2 to 8 in. long. Flowers solitary, on erect scapes 4 to 20 in. tall bearing three lobed bracts usually above the middle but well below the flower; bracts nearly sessile, once or twice palmately cleft, the segments linear; sepals petal-like, 10 to 20, greenish white to purplish blue or occasionally pink; petals absent; stamens many, shorter than the sepals; pistils numerous, spirally arranged on an elongating column. Fruit mass cylindric, ¾ to 1½ in. long, consisting of many tiny 1-seeded achenes obscured by copious wool. Distribution: Dakotas and Illinois, south to Florida and Texas; through Mexico to Central America and the mountains of South America.

The commonest of five or six species known to occur in Texas, this Anemone has a basal rosette of 3-parted leaves, often purple beneath, each part being more or less 3-lobed and coarsely toothed. Each stem has a whorl of 3 bracts, very unlike the leaves, and bears a solitary flower. The flowers have a single series of colored parts, usually regarded as sepals, which vary from white through shades of violet and lavender on the underside and are paler above. One of our first wildflowers, the Anemone blooms from February (even January) to March or April, brightening fields and open woods throughout most of the state but thriving especially well in the Blackland Prairie and in the Limestone Hill Country. Very similar but more restricted to the sandy soils of East Texas is the Carolina Anemone, *A. caroliniana* Walt. It is distinguished by the bracts, their position being on the lower half of the stem, and by the rhizomatous, not cormous, underground parts. The basal leaves are usually finely divided, frequently resembling the bracts, and the sepals, while often white or lavender, commonly take on shades of pink.

OLD-MAN'S–BEARD   *Clematis drummondii* Torr. & Gray
(PL. 10)

Woody-stemmed vine climbing or straggling by means of tendrils produced on some leafstalks. Leaves opposite, with 5 to 7 leaflets pinnately arranged; leaflets ½ to 1¼ in. long, coarsely cleft or parted, the segments acute or acuminate, sometimes toothed. Flowers unisexual, the male and female flowers on separate plants, usually arranged in broad much-branched clusters; male flowers: sepals ½ in. or less in length, white, spreading, slightly broadened near apex, petals absent; stamens many, spreading; female flowers: sepal and petal characters the same; bearing numerous long-styled pistils. Fruiting heads conspicuous, each consisting of many achenes *ca.* ⅛ in. long, tailed with the slender, silky-plumose styles 2 to 4 in. long. Distribution: Texas to Arizona, southward into Mexico.

LEATHER-FLOWER   *Clematis reticulata* Walt. [= *Viorna reticulata*   **11**
(Walt.) Small]   (PL. 11)

Much-branched vine 6 to 12 ft. tall or more, climbing by means of twisting or coiling petioles. Leaves opposite, pinnately compound; leaflets usually several, lanceolate to oval or oblong, firm, usually glabrous, conspicuously veiny, entire or the lowest ones lobed or again divided, ¾ to 1½ in. long. Flowers unisexual, the staminate and pistillate ones on different plants, terminal or solitary in the axils, borne on long stalks; sepals 5, petal-like, *ca.* ¾ in. long, pale rose-violet or lavender at the base, nearly white at the apex, whitish-margined; petals absent; stamens numerous (absent in pistillate flowers); pistils numerous (absent in staminate flowers). Fruit a 1-seeded elliptic achene *ca.* ⅕ in. long, topped with a silky-pubescent style 1½ to 2 in. long. Distribution: South Carolina to Florida and Texas.

Most species of *Clematis* are climbing shrubs with opposite compound leaves whose petioles or modified tendril-like terminal leaflets are sensitive to contact, bending once around the support, thickening, and turning woody. Old-man's-beard, or Texas Virgin's-bower, is a common climber of fences or component of thickets in Central, South, and West Texas. The rather inconspicuous white flowers are borne from May to early fall, but the plant gains in conspicuity as the clusters of achenes mature, making such dense masses as to obscure the foliage in grayish-white fluff. In the species of *Clematis* known as Leather-flower, it is the flowers which are worthy of note. The nodding blooms have no petals, but the sepals are joined to form a colored urn-shaped calyx. Commonest among them is the Purple Leather-flower, *C. pitcheri* Torr. & Gray, a denizen of damp shaded stream banks, producing brownish-purple flowers from April to July. Its range is about the same as that of Old-man's-beard. Less widely distributed are the Marsh Leather-flower, *C. crispa* L., of southeastern Texas, with pale ruffled tips on the lavender or bluish-purple calyx lobes; the Scarlet Leather-flower, *C. texensis* Buckl., of the Edwards Plateau, with a bright red calyx; and the Pine-woods Leather-flower, *C. reticulata,* of the pine forests of extreme East Texas, with characters much like those of the Purple Leather-flower. The Leather-flowers are placed in the genus *Viorna* by some botanists.

LARGE-FLOWERED BUTTERCUP   *Ranunculus macranthus* Scheele
   (PL. 11)

> Perennial herb with numerous erect or ascending stems 4 to 24 in. tall, simple or sparingly branched. Leaves mainly basal; blades long-stalked, divided into more or less wedge-shaped smooth or toothed segments. Flowers solitary; sepals 3 to 5, green, reflexed; petals 8 to 18, yellow, ⅓ to ¾ in. long; stamens many, yellow to yellow-green, in a broad band beneath the many spirally arranged green pistils. Fruit mass consisting of numerous achenes, each ⅛ to 3/16 in. long, borne on the elongate receptacle. Distribution: western half of Texas to southern Arizona, southward into Mexico.

Of the dozen or more native Buttercup species, the Large-flowered Buttercup is certainly the most striking. The waxy yellow flowers, up to 2 in. across, are produced in profusion in March and April. The handsome 5- or 7-lobed leaves are supported on long stalks with clasping bases. In upward progression on a stem, the leaves are seen to become smaller and to have fewer lobes. The Large-flowered Buttercup is found in damp ground in Central Texas and in scattered localities in the Trans-Pecos and along the Rio Grande. The Pine Buttercup, *R. fascicularis* Muhl., so common in sandy woods in the eastern third of the state, is smaller in all respects. Its flowers, appearing in February and March, have 5 to 9 petals, and the large basal leaves three lobes. The Low Buttercup or Spearwort, *R. pusillus* Poir., is a curious little plant, usually less than a foot high, bearing uncut hairless spoon-shaped leaves and small yellowish or whitish flowers. It grows in ditches, pond borders, stream bottoms, and other wet places in the eastern half of the state.

(114)

WATER-LILY FAMILY   Nymphaeceae

WATER-LILY   *Nymphaea elegans* Hook. [= *Castalia elegans* (Hook.) Greene]   (PL. 11)

Perennial herb from short branching horizontal rhizomes. Leaves alternate from the rhizome; blades floating or slightly elevated, peltate, cleft at base, nearly circular in outline, 6 to 10 in. long, about 1 in. less in width, coarsely net-veined beneath; petioles slender, circular in cross section, spongy. Flowers solitary, floating or elevated; sepals 4, purplish green on outer surface, often purple-veined; petals many, cream-colored, often bluish near the apex, grading into the numerous yellow stamens; pistils many, their stigmas joined to form a disc with many radiating lines. Fruit a berry, maturing beneath surface. Distribution: South Texas and adjacent Mexico.

The Water-lilies are herbaceous aquatic perennials with thickened horizontal stems called rhizomes, which are rooted in the mud. From these grow true roots into the sunken rotting vegetation and large leaves and solitary flowers to or above the surface. As a group, the Water-lilies show preference for quiet fresh water, as in oxbows, ponds, and lake coves. In cultivation are many hybrids whose identities are difficult to determine. The species illustrated grows in shallow water where there is at least several hours' exposure to the sun. The flowers, diurnal and often elevated several inches above the surface, vary from white to shades of bluish lavender. They appear from May to October, each one lasting but a single day. This Water-lily ranges along the Gulf Coast, from Jefferson to Cameron counties, northward in the eastern third of the state, becoming quite local and, in the upper counties, perhaps entirely introduced. *N. odorata* Ait. [= *Castalia odorata* (Ait.) Woodville & Wood], a species of Louisiana and extreme East Texas but commonly cultivated elsewhere, has cleft leaves circular in outline and flowers varying from white to pink. The Banana Water-lily, *N. mexicana* Zucc., has yellow flowers and occurs in scattered localities in the eastern half of Texas. Closely related is the Spatterdock, *Nuphar advena* (Ait.) Ait., with nearly circular cleft leaves held a little above the water and small cuplike flowers with 5 incurved sepals, yellow-green on the outside, waxy yellow within. The curious berrylike fruit breaks up into 1-seeded sections which float until they decompose, dropping the seeds to the bottom. The American Lotus, *Nelumbo lutea* (Willd.) Pers., found in East and South Texas, cousin to the Sacred Lotus of the eastern tropics, has large circular uncleft elevated leaves usually depressed in the center and with slightly drooping margins. The flowers have many pale-yellow-to-nearly-white petals which, on dropping, expose the thickened flat-topped receptacle in which are buried numerous 1-seeded pistils. At maturity the dried receptacle breaks off, floats about in the water, and as it decays the heavy seeds are set free to settle to the bottom. The Royal Water-lily, *Victoria regia* Lindl., of the Amazon and Guiana regions in northern South America, is the giant of the family, having leaves to 6 ft. across with upturned margins and a spiny undersurface. The creamy white nocturnal flowers take on a beautiful pink tone the second night, and often measure 14 in. in diameter. Requisite of a constant water temperature of 70° F. and much room, this truly regal plant is very seldom attempted in cultivation.

BARBERRY FAMILY   Berberidaceae

AGARITA   *Berberis trifoliata* Moric. [= *Mahonia trifoliata* (Moric.) Fedde]   (PL. 11)

> Evergreen shrub 3 to 6 ft. high with yellow wood, often forming thickets. Leaves alternate, trifoliolate; leaflets firm, leathery, gray-green or blue-green above, greener beneath, narrowly lanceolate to ovate, margins with 1 to 4 pairs of spine-tipped teeth. Flowers in compact umbel-like clusters; sepals 6, petal-like, pale yellow, each with two glandular spots at the base; petals 6, yellow, cupped; stamens 6, pistil 1. Fruit a pea-sized red berry, acid to the taste. Distribution: Central, West, and South Texas, and adjacent Mexico.

The Agarita is usually a low shrub occurring abundantly in the limestone hills of Central Texas, but extending west to the Trans-Pecos and along the Rio Grande to Webb and Jim Hogg counties. The small yellow flowers appear from January to March and, in common with other members of *Berberis*, show a curious pollination mechanism. Inside the sepals and petals there are 6 stamens, each with a touch-sensitive base. When contacted by a nectar-seeking insect, the stamens flail the insect's head, covering it with pollen, which may be placed on the pistils of the next flower visited. The red berries, sometimes called "currants," ripen in May and are used in making preserves. Early settlers valued the yellow wood as a dye source. *B. swaseyi* Buckl. of Central Texas from Travis and Hays to Real counties, has 5 to 9 pinnately arranged leaflets, each with 3 to 8 pairs of spine-tipped teeth, and whitish or pinkish translucent berries. *B. haematocarpa* Woot. has red berries, but the leaflets, generally smaller than those of Agarita, number 5 or 7, the lowest pair occurring very near the petiole base. It grows in the mountains of the Trans-Pecos. Oregon-grape or Holly-grape, *B. aquifolium* Pursh, a native of western Washington and Oregon commonly cultivated in Texas, has 5 to 11 dark green glossy leaflets, yellow flowers in racemes, and deep blue berries. Japanese Barberry, *B. thunbergii* DC., is a much-branched shrub with small simple untoothed deciduous leaves borne on grooved spiny stems. It is often cultivated as a hedge plant. The introduced English or European Barberry, *B. vulgaris* L., with simple toothed leaves that are also deciduous, is a noxious plant in wheat-growing regions owing to its role as obligate host to one phase of wheat rust.

POPPY FAMILY   Papaveraceae

TEXAS PRICKLY-POPPY   *Argemone albiflora* Hornem., var. *texana*   **12**
(G. Ownb.) Shinners   (PL. 12)

> Annual or biennial herb with branched prickly stems 1½ to 4 ft. high. Leaves alternate, gray-green; blades lanceolate to ovate, 2 to 10 in. long, those of the lower leaves lobed almost to the midrib, the smaller upper blades more shallowly so, upper surface smooth or with a few weak prickles along the midrib, lower surface spiny along midrib and main veins, apex with prominent spine, base (especially of upper blades) clasping stem. Flowers solitary or in loose cymes; sepals 3, soon falling, each ending with a stout spine or horn less than ¼ in. long; petals 6, white, ovate to nearly circular, outer margin irregularly ragged; stamens numerous, yellow or reddish; ovary 1-chambered, containing many ovules, topped with a 3- to 5-lobed purple stigma. Fruit a spiny capsule opening by terminal splits. Seeds black-brown. Distribution: East Texas, north to Arkansas and Missouri.

Native to North and South America, the Prickly-poppies, or Mexican-poppies, are striking components of our spring roadside flora. But to those who attempt to gather the flowers the spiny stems, buds, and leaves are discouraging. It is just as well, for when picked the flowers quickly wilt beyond any use. It seems that only the insects that visit to partake of the abundant pollen—and incidentally effect pollination—are rewarded. Of the 20 or more species growing in North America, 8 occur in Texas. *A. polyanthemos* (Fedde) G. Ownb. is similar to the Texas Prickly-poppy but its sepal horns range in length from ¼ to ⅝ in. Found in the Panhandle and in North Central Texas, it is spreading eastward. The Texas Prickly-poppy has a similar distribution, but extends south to Brazoria and Karnes counties. Also with white flowers are two other species, their leaves very prickly on both surfaces. *A. aurantiaca* G. Ownb., of the limestone hills and adjacent Blackland Prairie in Central Texas, has red-orange juice and long-branched spines ¾ to 1½ in. long on the capsules. *A. squarrosa* Greene, var. *glabrata* (G. Ownb.) Shinners has yellowish juice and capsular spines ⅜ to ⅝ in. long, usually unbranched. It is found in dry hills and valleys west of the Pecos River. Of the 2 yellow-flowered Prickly-poppies, *A. aenea* G. Ownb. (PL. 12) has larger flowers, usually 3 to 4½ in. across, and 150 to 250 stamens. It occurs mainly along the Rio Grande, but ranges northward to San Patricio, Uvalde, and Reeves counties. The other, with flowers only 1¼ to 2½ in. across bearing less than 75 stamens, is *A. mexicana* L., native in the triangle formed by Webb, Val Verde, and Travis counties, but is widely cultivated and perhaps escaped elsewhere. The two remaining Prickly-poppies have rosy-lavender flowers, although they are known to vary to white and may therefore be difficult to identify. Common on roadsides and in other disturbed areas of Bexar County is *A. sanguinea* Greene (PL. 12). *A. chisosensis* G. Ownb. of the Trans-Pecos is similar at lower elevations, but in the Chisos Mountains it is distinct with copiously bristly or prickly stems and buds.

MUSTARD FAMILY   Cruciferae

VIRGINIA PEPPERGRASS   *Lepidium virginicum* L.   (PL. 12)

Annual herb, more or less finely hairy. Stem simple below, commonly much-branched above, 8 to 24 in. tall. Leaves alternate; blades of the lower leaves more or less spoon-shaped in outline, irregularly toothed and lobed, soon withering; blades of upper leaves lanceolate, erect or ascending, sharply toothed or incised, the uppermost usually entire or nearly so. Flowers in racemes; pedicels spreading, *ca.* ⅛ in. long; sepals 4, equal in size, *ca.* 1/16 in. long, blunt-tipped; petals 4, white or pale green, only slightly longer than the sepals; stamens 6 or fewer; pistil 1. Fruit a nearly circular flattened silicle, ⅛ to 3/16 in. broad, notched at apex. Distribution: Quebec to Minnesota, south to Florida, Texas, and Mexico; naturalized in Europe.

The Peppergrasses, named for their pungent seeds and narrow grass-like leaves, are usually weedy plants, frequently abounding in disturbed places such as vacant lots, roadside embankments, fallow fields, and neglected lawns. The species are in some cases rather difficult to determine because of much variability according to conditions and the ability of some to hybridize. Virginia Peppergrass grows in East Texas, extending westward to Eastland, Llano, and Webb counties, and flowers from March to June. *L. austrinum* Small is very similar, differing chiefly by having long soft hairs at right angles to the stem. It is found from East Central Texas, where it ap-

(118)

parently hybridizes with the preceding species, west to the Trans-Pecos. *L. oblongum* Small has stem leaves rather uniform in size, all of them deeply lobed and toothed. It ranges from the Panhandle to the Trans-Pecos, eastward to Wichita and Comanche counties. *L. alyssoides* Gray (PL. 13) of plains, hillsides, and valleys in West Texas is a perennial with numerous stems from a woody root, reaching 10 in. or more in height. The flowers are more conspicuous because of the larger petals, which measure about ⅛ in. long.

13

WHITLOW-GRASS   *Draba platycarpa* Torr. & Gray [= *D. cuneifolia* Nutt., var. *platycarpa* (Torr. & Gray) Wats.]   (PL. 13)

Annual herb, finely hairy all over. Stem 2 to 12 in. tall, simple or branched. Leaves alternate, usually fewer than 12, scattered along the stem; blades ½ to 1 in. long, the lower ones wider than the progressively reduced upper ones, all more or less coarsely saw-toothed. Flowers in racemes, the peduncles erect, 2 to 8 in. long; pedicels at length ⅜ to ⅓ in. long, spreading or ascending; sepals 4, oblong, *ca.* ⅟₁₆ in. long; petals 4, white, *ca.* ⅛ in. long, broadly spoon-shaped. Fruit an elliptic pod, *ca.* ¼ in. long, finely hairy. Distribution: Texas to Arizona.

From a short stem with relatively few leaves there rises in February or March a slender stalk which bears little white flowers. Were Whitlow-grass a May or June flower it would· be lost in the riotous display of those months. But in late winter, when colors other than the drab are seldom seen, this little plant presents its diminutive blossoms, enticing the season's first bees and flies. Whitlow-grass ranges from Wichita and Grayson counties on the Red River to Calhoun and Nueces counties on the Gulf, westward to the Trans-Pecos. Also common, and very similar except for its leaves all crowded near the base, is *D. cuneifolia* Nutt. Its range is very nearly the same as that of the preceding species, although it is not known along the coast. *D. reptans* (Lam.) Fern., a species of fields and roadsides in Central Texas and northward, is commonly very small and bears leaves lacking teeth. Differing from all the above by having stem leaves more than twice as long as wide is *D. brachycarpa* Nutt., often inconspicuous because of its frequent lack of petals. It is common in central and east-central portions, north to the Red River.

BLADDERPOD   *Lesquerella gracilis* (Hook.) Wats.   (PL. 13)

Annual herb, simple or branched, to 20 in., the young parts gray with appressed branched hairs, older parts green and less pubescent. Leaves alternate; blades entire or toothed or irregularly lobed, lanceolate-oblong to linear, ¾ to 2 in. long, ⅟₁₆ to ⅔ in. wide, sessile or nearly so at base. Flowers in racemes; sepals 4; petals 4, bright yellow, about

(119)

¼ in. long; stamens 6, two of them shorter than the other four; pistil
1. Fruit a globose silicle. Distribution: Nebraska to Texas.

13
(Cont.) Of the 50 species of Bladderpods known in North America, perhaps
15 grow in Texas. All are distinctive with their pea-sized bladderlike
pods which pop when stepped on, hence another common name,
Popweed. The figured species blooms from March to May and is
found in fields and roadsides from Grayson and Lamar counties south
to Nueces County, west to Crockett and Val Verde counties and the
lower Panhandle. *L. auriculata* (Engelm. & Gray) Wats. of northeastern Texas has stem-clasping leaf bases. *L. engelmannii* (Gray)
Wats. is a much-branched perennial with petals about ⅓ in. long and
grayish-white foliage, found in Central Texas from Medina and Caldwell counties north to Wise and Dallas counties. Also with large
flowers but distinct with broad leaves to 1½ in. long is *L. grandiflora*
(Hook.) Wats. It occurs southward from Llano and Waller counties.
L. recurvata (Engelm.) Wats. has pedicels which turn downward
after the petals have fallen. It grows sometimes abundantly on limestone soil from Johnson, Travis, and Bexar counties west to Menard
and Kinney counties.

WILD MUSTARD   *Brassica juncea* (L.) Cosson   (PL. 13)

Annual herb with smooth, often bloomy, stems and leaves. Stems 1
to 4 ft. tall, often little branched. Leaves alternate; blades 2 to 6½
in. long, oblong to oval below, the upper ones lanceolate to linear and
reduced in size, all shallowly and coarsely toothed, the lower more
pronouncedly so, sessile or with a distinct petiole, base never clasping
stem. Flowers in racemes; pedicels ¼ to ⅓ in. long, diverging from
main stem; sepals 4, ⅛ to 3⁄16 in. long; petals 4, bright yellow, fading
with age, about twice as long as the sepals. Fruit a silique, 1 to 2 in.
long, apically narrowed, splitting longitudinally to release the brown
seeds. Distribution: western Asia and eastern Europe; naturalized in
North America from New Hampshire to Michigan, south to Georgia
and Texas.

Mustards belong to the large family of Crucifers, named in allusion
to the opposite pairs of petals forming a cross. Members of the genus
Brassica are natives of the Old World and among them are both
pernicious weeds and long-valued garden vegetables, most of the
latter being modified varieties of *B. oleracea* L.: cabbage, cauli-
flower, broccoli, Brussels sprouts, collards. Wild Mustard, a coarse
weed of fields and roadsides, bears its yellow flowers in April and
May, or for more prolonged periods in moist places. It is common in
East Texas and is spreading as more land is brought under cultivation. Black Mustard, *B. nigra* (L.) Koch, also found in East Texas,
is similar but can be distinguished by its strictly erect siliques less

(120)

than ¾ in. long borne on pedicels closely appressed to the stem. Field Mustard, *B. kaber* (DC.) L. C. Wheeler [= *B. campestris* (L.) Rabenhorst = *Sinapis arvensis* L.], a common weed of waste places, principally in the eastern half of the state, is distinctive with bristly-hairy leaves and stems. Similarly distributed is the Wild Turnip or Birdrape, *B. campestris* L., which, as with the first two species, is quite hairless, but differs from them in that the bases of the upper-most leaves clasp the stem. This plant is considered by many botanical workers to be derived and scarcely distinct from the cultivated Turnip, *B. rapa* L.

CAPER FAMILY Capparidaceae

CLAMMY-WEED *Polanisia dodecandra* (L.) DC., var. *trachy-sperma* (T. & G.) Iltis [= *P. trachysperma* T. & G.] (PL. 13)

Annual clammy-pubescent herb. Stems simple or branched, 1 to 2 ft. high. Leaves alternate, each consisting of three leaflets; leaflets ½ to 1½ in. long, elliptic to narrowly ovate, apex obtuse to broadly acute, margin entire, base similar to apex, sessile. Flowers somewhat irregular, in terminal bracted racemes 2 to 10 in. long; bracts mostly of 1 blade, ovate; sepals 4, lanceolate, ³⁄₁₆ in. long, the margins hairy; petals 4, about ⅜ in. long, the narrowed clawlike base as long as the notched blades or slightly longer; stamens 8 to numerous, long-exserted, purple; pistil 1, the ovary elongate and viscid. Fruit a slender erect capsule 1½ to 2½ in. long, about twice as long as the support-ing pedicel. Seeds about ¹⁄₁₆ in. broad, wrinkled. Distribution: Texas, New Mexico, and Arizona, northward to Iowa and British Columbia.

The Clammy-weeds, glandular annuals of warm dry regions, are members of the predominantly tropical Caper Family. From the flower buds of a Mediterranean species of *Capparis* are prepared the capers of commerce. Better known in this country are the Spider-flowers, members of the genus *Cleome*, several of which are native in the western United States, and a few, notably *C. houtteana* Schlecht. (offered by seedsmen as *C. spinosa*) of South America, are popular in the flower garden, where they are distinctive with 4 white petals which turn pink with age, and 6 long stamens. The flowers of Clammy-weeds are similar to those of *Cleome* but differ by having 8 or more stamens and the ovary not extended on a long stalk or gynophore. The plant illustrated blooms from April to fall and occurs over much of the state in various soils, most frequently along high-ways and in neglected gardens, fallow fields, and waste places. It is common along the coast from Harris to Cameron and Starr counties, and from McLennan, Travis, and Bexar counties northward and westward. In the Trans-Pecos the Large-flowered Clammy-weed, *P. dodecandra* (L.) DC., var. *uniglandulosa* (Cav.) Iltis [= *P. uniglandulosa* (Cav.) DC.] (PL. 13), is found. It has larger petals, measuring ½ in. or more in length, and stamens 1¼ to 2 in. long. Diminutive in every respect is *P. jamesii* (T. & G.) Iltis of the upper Panhandle, with petals about ¼ in. long, stamens no longer, and capsules to 1 in. The linear leaflets measure less than 1 in. long and are ¹⁄₁₆ to ⅛ in. wide.

ROSE FAMILY   Rosaceae

14   WILD WHITE ROSE   *Rosa bracteata* Wendl.   (PL. 14)

Spreading evergreen or semievergreen shrub with trailing or arching stems, forming tangled masses up to 8 ft. high, the branches armed with recurved prickles. Leaves alternate, pinnately odd-compound, 1¼ to 2½ in. long, leaflets 5 to 9, obovate or oval, ⅓ to ⅔ in. long, rounded or shallowly notched at the apex, finely sharp-toothed, lustrous deep green above, finely pubescent or glabrous beneath. Flowers perfect, solitary or a few together; sepals 5, elliptic to triangular-lanceolate, acute or acuminate, reflexed at maturity; petals 5, white, ½ to ⅔ in. long, notched at the apex; stamens numerous; pistils numerous, hidden within the cup-shaped receptacle. Fruit an achene, the numerous ones of each flower enclosed within the swollen, berry-like receptacle (the rose "hip"). Distribution: native to China; naturalized from Virginia to Florida and East Texas.

WILD PINK ROSE   *Rosa setigera* Michx.   (PL. 14)

Climbing or trailing shrub, the stems often arched over nearby vegetation, up to 9 ft. long, the finely striate branches armed with remote recurved prickles. Leaves alternate, pinnately odd-compound; leaflets 3 or sometimes 5, elliptic or oval, ¾ to 2½ in. long, acute at the apex, sharply toothed, glabrous or tomentose. Flowers perfect, usually in small corymbose clusters; sepals 5, lanceolate, reflexed at maturity, arising from the rim of the glandular-pubescent receptacle; petals 5, pink, obovate, indented at apex, ⅜ to ⅞ in. long; stamens numerous; pistils numerous, sessile on inner surface of cuplike receptacle. Fruit an achene, those of a single flower enclosed within the swollen receptacle. Distribution: Ontario to Wisconsin, south to Florida and Texas.

Of the nearly 200 species of *Rosa* which have been described, about a dozen occur as wildflowers in Texas. The flowers are usually showy, with five petals and a central ring of stamens encircling the extended styles of the pistils. After pollination and fertilization the petals and stamens drop, and the receptacle enlarges, enclosing the achenes. When the achenes are mature, the investing receptacle or "hip" usually reddens. They are readily devoured by various birds and mammals who unwittingly distribute the unaffected seeds in their droppings. Wild White Rose, or McCartney Rose, a vigorous introduced species formerly planted as a windbreak and soil-binder, has run wild in southeastern Texas, to the extent of becoming a pest in some areas. Its presently known range is from Calhoun and Kerr counties east to the Louisiana border and north to Harrison and Jack counties. Wild Pink Rose is found in fields and roadsides in northeastern Texas, southwest to Dallas, Henderson, and Nacogdoches counties. Both species bloom in May and June, sporadically later. The White Prairie Rose, *R. foliolosa* Nutt., a small many-stemmed shrub not over 18 in. tall, bears solitary white flowers from May to July on erect stems with a few straight prickles. It is found mainly on limestone soils from Kerr and Travis counties northeastward to the Red River. Most of the remaining wild species are found in the northeastern corner of the state, with a few from scattered localities in the mountains of the Trans-Pecos. The Tea Rose, *R. X dilecta* Rehd., Polyantha Rose, *R. X rehderiana* Blackb., and Multiflora Rose, *R. multiflora* Thunb., are commonly met with in cultivation.

WILD BLACKBERRY   *Rubus trivialis* Michx.   (PL. 14)

> Semievergreen trailing or scrambling shrub, the stems bristly or prickle-armed, 3 to 6 ft. long, the flowering branches commonly erect, 2 to 4 in. high, with recurved prickles. Leaves alternate, palmately compound with 3 or 5 leaflets, on prickly petioles; blades ovate-lanceolate to elliptic, ½ to 2½ in. long, glabrous, sharply and irregularly toothed, rounded or cuneate at the base. Flowers perfect, solitary or a few together; sepals 5, lanceolate to ovate; petals 5, white, or sometimes pinkish in the bud, *ca.* ½ in. long; stamens numerous; pistils numerous on a dome-shaped receptacle, each becoming a 1- or 2-seeded drupelet, purplish black when mature. Distribution: Virginia to Florida and Texas.

Blackberries, Dewberries, Loganberries, Raspberries, Cloudberries, Trimbleberries—these are all common names of plants in the large cosmopolitan genus *Rubus,* one embracing over 250 species. *R. trivialis,* our commonest one, flowers in March and April, and occurs in East Texas west to Jack, San Saba, and Kerr counties, forming thickets and bramble patches in fields, along highways, and in fence-rows. Most of the several remaining species of Texas are found in the eastern half of the state. Of the numerous cultivated species, the following are especially worthy of note: American Highbush

(123)

Blackberry, *R. ostryifolius,* source of many large-fruited varieties; Dewberry, *R. caesius* L., a European blackberry with a pronounced bloom on the drupelets; Loganberry, *R.* sp., a presumed hybrid first noted by Judge Logan on his grounds in Santa Cruz, California, in 1881, prized for its large fruit; American Red Raspberry, *R. strigosus* Michx., source of most of our cultivated raspberries, and not to be confused with its stouter-stemmed European counterpart, *R. idaeus* L.; Cloudberry, *R. chamaemorus* L., a small-fruited European blackberry sometimes grown in the northern states; Trimbleberry or Black-cap, *R. occidentalis* L., a black-fruited raspberry.

APACHE-PLUME   *Fallugia paradoxa* (D. Don) Endl.   (PL. 14)

Shrub or subshrub 2 to 3 ft. tall, usually much-branched, the twigs with persistent whitish bark. Leaves simple, alternate, linear, and entire or more commonly with 3 to 7 linear divisions, the margins downrolled, with fine rusty-red pubescence beneath, ⅓ to ¾ in. long. Flowers perfect, solitary, or in few-flowered terminal clusters; sepals 5, triangular, united at the base; petals 5, white, *ca.* ½ in. long, ovate or elliptic; stamens numerous; pistils numerous. Fruit a narrowly oblong achene *ca.* ⅛ in. long with an elongate plumose style 1 to 2 in. long, the fruits massed on the receptacle. Distribution: Colorado and Nevada south to Texas, Arizona, and adjacent Mexico.

The Apache-plume is an attractive plant that affords fair browse for cattle and sheep and is useful as a soil-binder. Known also as the Ponil, this, the only species of *Fallugia,* found considerable use among Indians in the Southwest and in nearby Mexico: small branches tied together served as brooms, straight older stems were used as arrow shafts, and it was believed that an infusion of the leaves washed into the scalp would promote hair growth. Apache-plume is found in the Trans-Pecos and eastward to Upton, Real, and Zavala counties. It blooms from February to October, but most freely from March to July.

PEA FAMILY   Leguminosae

15   HUISACHE   *Acacia farnesiana* (L.) Willd. [= *Vachellia farnesiana*
     (L.) Wight & Arn.]   (PL. 15)

Shrub or small tree armed with short stout stipular spines. Leaves alternate, pinnately bicompound, the leaf-rachis and its branches finely hairy; leaflets small, numerous, 3/16 to ¼ in. long. Flowers in spikes ⅜ in. or more in diameter, the spikes borne on finely hairy peduncles; sepals *ca.* 1/16 in. long; petals *ca.* ⅛ in. long, yellow; sta-

(124)

mens numerous, yellow, long-exserted. Fruit a stout pod, 1½ to 3¼ in. long, pulpy within, the valves leathery and very tardily dehiscent. Seeds *ca.* ¼ in. long. Distribution: South Texas and Mexico, southward along the Gulf and Caribbean coasts to the Guianas; naturalized in southern Florida.

Along the Gulf Coast Huisache grows as a spreading shrub, but inland, especially in creek bottoms in South Texas and along the Rio Grande, it becomes a small tree to 20 ft. Elsewhere Huisache has probably been introduced, intentionally or by accident. The branches have thorns in pairs and bear among the finely divided leaves fragrant yellow flowers in tight globular heads, usually from January to March or April. Few plants of Texas have as many uses as the Huisache. In South Texas it is a valued honey plant. Elsewhere in Central and northern South America the leaves are used as forage during dry periods. The ground seeds yield a good meal and the fruit pulp is used in preparing a dark dye. Tannin is extracted from the bark. In the Mediterranean region, where Huisache is cultivated under the name of Cassie, the flowers are used in perfume manufacture. *A. berlandieri* Benth. is a similar species with smaller leaflets and globose to somewhat elongate spikes, found in Texas south of Karnes County and westward along the Rio Grande to Brewster County. Catclaw, *A. greggii* Gray, also a shrub or small tree, bears whitish flowers in short spikes. It grows on the Edwards Plateau west to the Trans-Pecos, but is known locally from as far northeastward as Young County. Very similar is *A. wrightii* Benth., which, except for its absence from the Trans-Pecos, has about the same distribution. Its flowers are borne on short stalks, not sessile as in *A. greggii*, and its leaflets are rather less than twice as long as wide (more than twice in *A. greggii*). Fern-acacia or Shame-weed, *A. angustissima* (Mill.) Ktze., a herbaceous perennial, has leaves which fold on being touched, a condition common to numerous species of the Pea Family, and bears creamy white spherical clusters of flowers. It occurs generally except in the most extreme reaches of the state.

SENSITIVE-BRIAR   *Schrankia uncinata* Willd. [= *Leptoglottis nuttallii* DC.]   (PL. 15)

Prostrate or procumbent perennial herb. Stems copiously prickly, 2 to 3 ft. long. Leaves alternate, pinnately bicompound; petiole and its branches prickly; pinnae 4 to 8 pairs; leaflets 8 to 13 pairs, elliptic, glabrous or sparingly hairy along the margins, membranous, ³⁄₁₆ to ³⁄₈ in. long, strongly net-veined, especially beneath; apex pointed. Flowers in spherical heads; peduncles prickly, 1 to 3½ in. long; sepals 4 or 5, united; petals 4 or 5, united, pink; stamens 8 to 10, exserted, pink or rose-purple; pistil 1, its style resembling a stamen. Fruit a curved prickly pod, round in cross section, 2½ to 6 in. long, *ca.* ⅛ in. thick. Distribution: South Dakota southward to South Carolina, Alabama, and Texas.

The Sensitive-briar or Catclaw, a rather shrubby creeper from a thick woody root, trails over low plants and among grasses, flowering from April to June or July. Stems, leafstalks, flower stalks, and pods are beset with slender but rigid prickles, making the plant a formidable one to trip over. When the sun shines the many tiny opposite leaflets spread out, but at dusk or in stormy weather, the members of each pair close upward against each other. When touched or walked on they react quickly. The mechanism of this response is not understood in all respects, but it is known to involve pressure changes in the tiny swollen joint or pulvinule at the base of each leaflet. Slightly larger joints are found at the bases of the secondary axes or pinnae, and a much larger one, the pulvinus, at the base of the main leafstalk where it joins the stem. Pulvini and pulvinules are characteristic of nearly all members of the Pea Family, witness the perpendicular nocturnal position assumed by the leaf blades of the great majority of its species. Relatively few, however, are touch-sensitive. The several species of Sensitive-briar in Texas are very similar in appearance. The illustrated plant prefers sandy soils in the east-central and northern portions of the state as well as the mesquite savannahs of the lower Panhandle. The other species lack the raised prominent veining on the undersides of the leaflets. *S. roemeriana* (Scheele) Blankinship, common in the Blackland Prairie and limestone hills of North and Central Texas, has small prickles on the flattened sides of the pods, larger ones on the margins. *L. latidens* (Small) has pods scarcely flattened at all, the sides armed but the margins with few or no prickles. It grows in South Texas below Bexar and Victoria counties. *S. microphylla* (Dryander) Macbride, a species of open places of the pine forests of extreme Southeast Texas, has pale pink or white flowers. Very similar to *S. roemeriana* is *S. occidentalis* (Woot. & Standl.) Standl., distributed in the lower Panhandle from Crosby and Mitchell counties west to Winkler and Ward counties, and differing mainly by having finely hairy rather than glabrous stems.

MESQUITE   *Prosopis juliflora* (Swartz) DC. [= *P. glandulosa* Torr.]
(PL. 15)

Shrub or small tree to 30 ft., often with a tortuous trunk, the branches commonly bearing stipular spines ½ to 1¼ in. long. Leaves alternate, pinnately bicompound, quite or nearly devoid of pubescence; petioles slender, ½ to 1½ in. long; pinnae 1 pair, rarely 2 pairs; leaflets 6 to

20 pairs, linear to oblong, mostly ½ to 1½ in. long, apex obtuse to acute, distant or approximate, strongly pinnately veined. Flowers in drooping spikelike racemes; peduncles ¼ to ¾ in. long, glabrous or very finely hairy; sepals united, *ca.* 1/16 in. long; petals basally united, whitish or cream, ⅛ to 3/16 in. long; stamens numerous, *ca.* ¼ in. long, white, becoming pale yellow with age; pistil 1, the style exceeding the stamens. Fruit a pod 3 to 9 in. long, ¼ to ⅜ in. wide, slightly compressed, more or less narrowed between the seeds. Distribution: Kansas southward to Texas, California, and Mexico.

The Mesquite, romantically associated with the history of the Southwest, often surprises the visitor with the airy gracefulness of its pale green drooping feathery foliage. How can it thrive with such ease in places where other plants superficially better adapted seem to battle with sun and drought for existence? Excavations in these dry areas have provided one answer: the roots of a Mesquite of moderate size descend to 60 ft.! Once rather limited in distribution, Mesquite seems to have profited by human destruction of natural vegetation; it is now the predominant plant in places where 150 or 200 years ago it was entirely unknown. The small whitish or yellowish sweet-scented flowers borne in catkinlike racemes in April and May (intermittently afterward) are followed by straw-colored pods which when dried were ground by Indians and used in making bread. This practice is still followed, especially in northern Mexico. The bark yields a useful gum and the stems and roots are valued as fuel, particularly in regions where Mesquite is the only woody plant of consequence. In times of drought the foliage and fruit are in some places the sole food for stock animals. The dense, hard wood takes a high polish and has been used to some extent in cabinet work. But its chief virtues are dessication- and rot-resistance; hence its wide use as fence posts. Mesquite grows on calcareous soils from Grayson and Wichita counties, southward along the Blackland Prairie to the sandy soils of the Rio Grande plain, westward to the Trans-Pecos. It also occurs, though rather sparingly, in the lower Panhandle and along the Gulf Coast to Chambers County. The Screwbean, *P. odorata* Torr. & Frem. [= *Strombocarpa odorata* Torr.], is a shrub or small tree found along the Rio Grande in Brewster and Presidio counties, distinct with 5 to 9 pairs of leaflets and a tightly coiled pod.

REDBUD   *Cercis canadensis* L.   (PL. 15)

Shrub or small tree, occasionally exceeding 30 ft. in height. Leaves alternate; blades entire, circular or kidney-shaped, flattened or cordate at the base, short-pointed or obtuse at the apex, 2 to 6 in. across, smooth or rarely sparingly hairy beneath. Flowers several in sessile clusters; pedicels ⅓ to 1 in. long; sepals 5, united; petals 5, irregular, papilionate, the longest *ca.* ⅓ in. long, pinkish purple; stamens 10;

pistil 1. Pod smooth, 2 to 3 in. long, *ca.* ½ in. wide, flat, thin, oblong, several-seeded, indehiscent or opening tardily. Distribution: Ontario to Michigan, south to Florida and Texas.

In our area Redbud, perhaps more than any other kind of familiar plant, signifies the beginning of flowering time in woods and fields. The tightly clustered pink flowers appear in March, a little before the leaves, on twigs of the previous season. The attractive purplish pods finally turn brown at summer's end and often hang on most of the winter. Four kinds of Redbud are known in Texas, 3 of them native and 1 from Asia. In the northeast corner of the state grows the illustrated type, the Eastern Redbud, its leaves typically pointed. In a crescent-shaped area extending from Dennison County southward through Tarrant County to McLennan County, this kind gradually passes into the Texas Redbud, *C. canadensis,* var. *texensis* (Wats.) Hopkins, a rather lower, more intricately branched shrub having round-tipped leaves of a more leathery texture. Texas Redbud extends westward to Taylor and Uvalde counties, reaching its maximum development in limestone soil in valleys of Central Texas. In draws and valleys of Val Verde, Pecos, Terrell, and Brewster counties grows the Mexican Redbud, *C. canadensis,* var. *mexicana* (Rose) Hopkins, with leaves similar to those of the Texas Redbud but for their increased pubescence and diminished size. The Asiatic Redbud, or Judas-tree, *C. siliquastrum* L., is cultivated in some of the larger cities and may be told by the notched apex of its leaves. In all cases white flowers are known to occur as rarities and occasional trees may flower a second time in early fall.

16 Two-leaved Senna   *Cassia roemeriana* Scheele [= *Earleocassia roemeriana* (Scheele) Britt.]   (PL. 16)

Herbaceous perennial from a woody root. Stems 1 to several, erect or ascending, simple or branched, 1 to 2½ ft. high, somewhat angled, very finely downy. Stipules linear, persistent. Leaves alternate, compound with 1 pair of leaflets; leaflets lanceolate, 1 to 2½ in. long, up to ½ in. wide, apex acute or nearly so, more or less appressed-hairy on both sides, gland between leaflets narrow. Flowers in axillary clusters, the inflorescence longer than the leaves, each with 2 to 5 flowers; sepals 5, sparingly hairy, *ca.* ¼ in. long; petals 5, yellow or yellow-orange, about twice as long as the sepals; stamens 10, yellow, 7 of them functional, 3 much reduced; pistil 1, the ovary pubescent. Fruit a narrowly oblong, slightly compressed pod ¾ to 1¼ in. long and *ca.* ¼ in. wide, short-pointed, slightly hairy. Distribution: Oklahoma, Texas, and New Mexico, to Nuevo Leon and Coahuila in Mexico.

Sennas, members of the genus *Cassia,* are a large assemblage of plants of very diverse habit, mainly native in warm regions. Some of the African species are cultivated for their leaves, used in the preparation of the drug senna. Others are highly valued for ornament. Most abundant of the Texas species is the Two-leaved Senna, found principally on limestone soils in the central and western portions of the state. Usually there are several stems radiating from a woody crown. The yellow-orange flowers appear in April and May and often again in the early fall, sometimes intermittently all summer. The cylindrical brown pods open by an apical slit. Two-leaved Senna occurs from Dallas, McLennan, and Gonzales counties, west to the Trans-Pecos. Three other two-leaved kinds are found. One, the Pygmy Senna, *C. pumilio* Gray [= *Tharpia pumilio* (Gray) Britt. & Rose], is a tufted inconspicuous plant less than 6 in. high with very narrow grasslike leaflets and bright yellow flowers. *C. durangensis* Rose and the very similar *C. bauhinoides* Gray reach 2 ft. and bear broad silky-hairy leaflets. All three are found in West Texas, the first venturing as far east as Throckmorton and Mills counties. The other Texas sennas have numerous leaflets. Lindheimer's Senna, *C. lindheimeriana* Scheele [= *Earleocassia lindheimeriana* (Scheele) Britt.] (PL. 16), of Central and West Texas is a tall several-branched perennial, its grayish silvery-hairy foliage surmounted by panicles of clear yellow flowers in late summer. In East Texas three others grow. The Coffee Senna, *C. occidentalis* L., with 4 to 6 pairs of pointed leaflets, and the West Indian Senna, or Stinking-toe, *C. obtusifolia* L. (often listed as *C. tora* L.), with 2 or 3 pairs of round-tipped leaflets, are both malodorous weeds from tropical America. The third, the July-flowering American Senna, *C. marilandica* L., produces a large terminal cluster of yellow flowers and, like several others, is worthy of garden cultivation. Mention should be made of the Candle-tree, *C. alata* L., a large-leaved tender shrub of the tropics, usually cultivated in Texas as a perennial herb, and the Argentine Senna, *C. corymbosa* Lam., a hardy evergreen shrub to 6 or 8 ft. Both are commonly planted, flowering in late summer.

PARTRIDGE-PEA   *Cassia fasciculata* Michx. [= *Chamaecrista fasciculata* (Michx.) Greene]   (PL. 16)

Erect branched annual 1 to 4 ft. high, the stem and branches finely hairy or apparently hairless. Stipules narrowly linear, long-pointed, hairy on their margins, ¼ to ⅓ in. long. Leaves alternate, in two ranks, even-pinnately compound; petiole with a sessile or short-stalked, brown or reddish gland near the base; leaflets 6 to 15 pairs, linear-oblong, finely hairy along the margins, the faces glabrous or barely

(129)

downy, abruptly sharp-pointed, distinctly veined, $\frac{1}{3}$ to $\frac{5}{8}$ in. long, $\frac{1}{16}$ to $\frac{3}{16}$ in. wide. Flowers in small clusters of few to 12 or more in or just above the axils of the leaves; pedicels finely hairy, $\frac{1}{2}$ to $\frac{3}{4}$ in. long; sepals 5, lanceolate, $\frac{1}{3}$ to $\frac{1}{2}$ in. long, pubescent along the mid-vein; petals 5, yellow, 4 red-spotted at the base, $\frac{1}{2}$ to $\frac{3}{4}$ in. long, withering after midday; stamens 10, in two unequal sets, 7 functional and colored deep red-violet or yellow, or occasionally mottled, the other 3 very small and greenish white. Pod linear-oblong, flat, smooth, or finely hairy, $1\frac{1}{2}$ to 3 in. long, $\frac{1}{4}$ to $\frac{1}{3}$ in. wide, opening by elastically twisting valves. Seeds black or dark brown, shining, hard. Distribution: Massachusetts to Minnesota, south to Florida and Texas.

The Partridge-pea and its relatives comprise a section of the very large, predominantly tropical genus *Cassia*. Many are weedy, small-flowered, rather inconspicuous plants, but Texas is graced with several attractive ones. The Partridge-pea is the commonest of them, abounding in fields and along highways, principally in sandy soils in Central and East Texas. It is an erect, usually few-branched annual, most commonly 2 to 3 ft. high. The flowers, favorites with bees as they open at dawn, are produced in profusion from June to September, or later where there is sufficient moisture. The little clusters, each with a few buds, bear the flowers one at a time. The 5 petals are slightly dissimilar, one of them cupped inward and each of the other 4 with a small red spot at the base. The flat brown pods burst open explosively, especially on warm dry days in late summer, showering the ground with shiny black seeds. The slightly touch-sensitive leaves regularly fold outward at dusk, markedly changing the appearance of the plant. Similar, but much-branched and nearly prostrate in habit is the Beach Partridge-pea, *C. fasci-culata*, var. *ferrisiae* (Britt.) Turner, a red-stemmed annual of coast-al dunes from Galveston County southward to Cameron County, and inland as far as Webb, Bastrop, and Robertson counties. The two commonly hybridize where their ranges overlap, hence are often difficult to distinguish. *C. fasciculata*, var. *rostrata* (Woot. & Standl.) Turner, is more or less intermediate in habit, having numerous ascending branches from the base. It grows in dry sandy soil along the Rio Grande in Maverick County, eastward to Frio and Lasalle counties, sparingly northward to Wichita County and the Panhandle. The Eastern Partridge-pea, *C. nictitans* L., of sandy fields and open woods in the eastern third of the state, is a rounded bushy plant with very small yellow flowers in late summer. Three or 4 other kinds are found in South and West Texas. Partridge-peas in general often colonize poor soils and should be encouraged in fallow fields, for the tiny nodules on their roots harbor nitrogen-fixing bacteria whose activities contribute to the nitrogen fertility of the soil.

PALOVERDE   *Parkinsonia aculeata* L.   (PL. 16)

Spiny shrub or tree to 30 ft. Bark green to brown, smooth or shallowly fissured into small plates. Branches slender, spreading or drooping, the young twigs finely hairy. Spines 1¼ in. long or less. Leaves alternate, even-pinnately bicompound, the common petiole very short and spine-tipped; pinnae 1 pair (rarely 2), suggesting paired once-compound leaves, 8 to 15 in. long, with flat narrowly winged axes bearing 10 to 25 pairs of short-stalked, linear to narrowly obovate deciduous leaflets, each ⅛ to ⅓ in. long. Flowers few to several in axillary racemes usually shorter than the leaves; pedicels very slender, ¼ to ⅔ in. long; sepals 5, ¼ to ⅓ in. long; petals 5, yellow, about twice as long as the sepals; stamens 10, about as long as the sepals; pistil 1. Fruit a drooping linear-cylindric pod 2 to 6 in. long, much constricted between the seeds. Seeds about ⅓ in. long. Distribution: Florida to South Texas, south to tropical America.

Of the many attractive shrubs in the Pea Family, the Paloverde must be placed high on the list of ornamentals; it is useful in situations where an open, airy effect is desired. The unusual leaves consist of a very short, usually spine-tipped petiole from which arise 2 more or less parallel stalks. These bear small leaflets which often fall during the summer, leaving the flattened stalks to carry on the food-making processes. Appearing in April and May and then sporadically until fall, the flowers are at first uniformly yellow, but one petal soon shows a red spot at its base. Eventually the entire petal reddens and shrivels. The brown fruit is noticeably constricted between the relatively few seeds. Paloverde is found wild in Central and West Texas, but is commonly cultivated well outside this range.

BIRD-OF-PARADISE   *Caesalpinia gilliesii* Wall. [= *Poinciana gilliesii*   **17** (Wall.) Hook. = *Erythrostemon gilliesii* (Hook.) Link, Klotsch, & Otto]   (PL. 17)

Unarmed shrub or low tree, occasionally reaching 25 ft., glandular throughout. Leaves alternate, even-pinnately bicompound, 4 to 12 in. long; pinnae 7 to 15 pairs; leaflets 7 to 10 pairs per pinna, oblong, ¼ to ⅓ in. long, smooth, with a row of tiny black glands near the margin on the underside. Flowers in terminal racemes 4 to 12 in. long; pedicels ¾ to 1¼ in. long; bracts saw-toothed, soon falling; sepals 5, united, slightly unequal, thin, *ca.* ⅔ in. long; petals 5, yellow, spreading, obovate, 1 to 1½ in. long; stamens 10, several times longer than the petals, the filaments bright red; pistil 1. Fruit a flat pod, dotted with black glands, 2½ to 4 in. long, obliquely oblong-lanceolate. Distribution: native of Argentina; escaping cultivation in Texas, New Mexico, and Arizona.

The striking Bird-of-paradise, a widely cultivated shrub native to southern South America but frequently escaping in South Central and West Texas, has delicate twice-compound leaves and flowers borne in erect terminal clusters from May to October. From near the base of the 5 pale yellow petals spring the 10 blood-red stamens, sometimes 4 in. long, imparting something of a gossamer quality to a distantly viewed specimen. Closely related is the Barbados-pride, *C. pulcherrima* Sw., a large shrub with long racemes of yellow, orange, or red flowers, cultivated under glass, or occasionally out of doors in extreme South Texas. Better known is another close relative, the Royal Poinciana or Flamboyante, *Delonix regia* (Bojer) Raf., a flat-topped tree native to Madagascar, widely planted in tropical and subtropical regions for its large scarlet flowers.

WILD-INDIGO   *Baptisia leucophaea* Nutt.   (PL. 17)

> Bushy perennial herb 1 to 2½ ft. tall from a large tough woody root. Stems stout, divaricately branched, smooth or somewhat pubescent. Leaves alternate, 3-foliolate, stipulate; leaflets entire, oblanceolate or narrowly elliptic, apex acute or rarely retuse, 1½ to 4 in. long, persistent. Flowers in declined, apparently 1-sided, bracteate, axillary racemes 4 to 8 in. long; sepals 5, united; corolla papilionaceous, the 5 petals creamy white. Fruit an ovoid-elliptic pod 1½ to 2 in. long. Distribution: Michigan and Indiana to southwestern Arkansas and Texas.

BUSH-PEA   *Baptisia sphaerocarpa* Nutt.   (PL. 17)

> Erect perennial herb with 1 to several stems 1 to 4 ft. tall. Leaves alternate, 3-foliolate; leaflets firm, elliptic to elliptic-oblanceolate, obtuse or notched at apex. Flowers in erect racemes 4 to 12 in. long; sepals 5, united; corolla papilionaceous, the 5 petals deep yellow. Fruit a broadly oval, short-beaked woody pod ½ to ¾ in. long. Distribution: Arkansas and Texas.

About half of the 25 species of *Baptisia*, all North American, occur in Texas. They are perennial herbs with leaves divided into three leaflets and bear racemes of yellow, cream-colored, white, or blue flowers. Commercial indigo is not prepared from these plants but rather from two species of the related genus *Indigofera*.

The illustrated Wild-indigo has horizontal or somewhat pendulous clusters of flowers in March and April, mostly below the level of the foliage. It is commonly found dotting pastures and hillsides in the eastern third of the state. Bush-pea, or Yellow-wisteria, is of quite erect habit and bears its bright yellow flowers in April and May well above the foliage. It too prefers open woods and fields in sandy soils of East Texas. Perhaps the most handsome is *B. minor* Lehmann, found on the Blackland Prairie from Dallas County to the Red River, with erect terminal racemes of bluish-purple flowers in April.

BLUEBONNET   *Lupinus subcarnosus* Hook.   (PL. 17)

> Winter annual to 15 in. tall. Stems pilose with ascending hairs. Leaves alternate, long-petioled, palmately compound; leaflets 4 to 7, glabrous or nearly so above, apices blunt or rounded or notched. Flowers loosely disposed in erect terminal racemes 3 to 5 in. long; pubescence of raceme axis partly ascending, partly spreading; pubescence of buds yellowish gray, dull, hence inconspicuous from a distance; sepals united, *ca.* ¼ in. long; corolla papilionaceous, the 5 petals deep blue or rarely white; banner petal exceeding wing and keel petals, with white yellow-green dotted spot turning red in age. Fruit a pubescent pod. Distribution: East Texas.

BLUEBONNET   *Lupinus texensis* Hook.   (PL. 18)   **18**

> Similar but commonly larger, sometimes up to 24 in., and differing in the following respects: pubescence of raceme axis nearly all ascending; pubescence of buds silvery or white, hence conspicuous from a distance; leaflets pubescent on both sides, the apices acute to obtuse and short-apiculate; racemes rather densely flowered, 2 to 6 in. long; sepals ¼ in. long or more. Distribution: Central Texas.

The Lupines comprise a group of some 150 species, centered in western North America and the Mediterranean region. The generic name, *Lupinus,* is from the Latin *lupus,* wolf, in popular allusion to the plants' once supposed greed for soil nutrients. But the truly beneficial effect of Lupines on the soil was known even by Pliny, who wrote, "there is nothing more beneficial than to turn up a crop of lupines before they have set pod." The nature of this effect was not understood until the close of the nineteenth century. It was then discovered that the frequently observed swellings on the roots of these and most other members of the Pea Family were both caused and inhabited by certain bacteria that combine nitrogen in the air with plant carbohydrates, forming nitrogen compounds which serve as food for the plant and are ultimately incorporated into its structure. When the plant decays, after being plowed under, the nitrogen compounds are freed to the soil in a form that other kinds of plants can use for making their own nitrogenous constituents.

Of further interest is the pollination mechanism of Lupines. As in most papilionaceous flowers, the two lowest petals are united to form an envelope (the keel) which contains the pollen-bearing stamens and the egg-bearing pistil. While the flower is still in the bud stage, the pollen is shed at the base of this tube and the stalks of the stamens thicken to form, en masse, a sort of piston. The stalks then lengthen as the flower opens, pushing the pollen forward to the outer opening of the keel. The receptive end of the pistil, the stigma, lies in the opening and although it ultimately becomes immersed in pollen, its receptivity depends on its being rubbed, most likely by a hungry bee dusted with pollen from other flowers. Thus the chance for cross-pollination is preserved.

In addition to the two illustrated species, *L. havardii* Wats. should be noted. This is the Big Bend Bluebonnet, reaching 20 in. in height, and bearing in spring racemes of blue flowers, the standard marked with a lemon-yellow blotch. The number of leaflets per leaf is most commonly 7. In the field the two former species seem similar, but with a little care they can be readily distinguished. *L. texensis,* widely distributed on calcareous soils through the central portions of the state, has silvery upswept pubescence on all parts except the petals, and each leaflet ends with a definite point. The silvery hairs impart to a partly expanded cluster the appearance of having a cap, even at a considerable distance. *L. subcarnosus* is more limited in distribution, mostly confined to sandy plains within the quadrant formed by Houston, Hearne, Corpus Christi, and San Antonio, and commonest in the northwestern portion of this range. It does occur locally outside of these limits, chiefly southward. In this species the leaflets, especially of the lower leaves, have round or even indented ends, and the pubescence is yellowish or rusty brown, hence the lack of the cap effect. It seems unfortunate that this, the least attractive of our Bluebonnets, has been designated the state flower.

WHITE SWEET-CLOVER   *Melilotus albus* Desv.   (PL. 18)

Erect annual or biennial herb 2 to 6 ft. tall, copiously and widely branched, with fragrant glabrous foliage. Leaves alternate, compound with 3 leaflets; leaflet blades linear-oblong to elliptic, ⅓ to 1½ in. long, margin sharply toothed, apex obtuse or flattened. Flowers in elongate wandlike racemes; sepals 5, united; corolla papilionaceous, the 5 petals white, the standard exceeding the wings. Fruit a short, thick pod *ca.* ⅛ in. long, wrinkled, glabrous. Distribution: native to Europe and Asia, widely established throughout the United States and southern Canada, especially in disturbed areas.

YELLOW SWEET-CLOVER   *Melilotus officinalis* Lam.   (PL. 18)

Very similar to White Sweet-clover, but petals yellow, the standard about equalling the wings. Distribution: native to Europe and Asia, widely established in North America, especially in disturbed areas.

ALFALFA   *Medicago sativa* L.   (PL. 18)

Glabrous perennial herb with ascending stems to 3 ft. Leaves alternate, compound with 3 leaflets; leaflets cuneate-ovate to oblanceolate, ⅓ to ⅔ in. long, sharply toothed near the apex. Flowers pedicellate in rounded racemes; sepals 5, united; corolla papilionaceous, the blue-violet to violet petals ¼ to ⅓ in. long. Fruit a pod twisted in tight coils *ca.* ⅛ in. broad. Distribution: native to Asia, widely cultivated and locally escaped throughout much of North America.

The Sweet-clovers are tall plants of the Old World with 3-parted leaves and racemes of cloverlike flowers. Flowering from April to June, the two illustrated species occur over much of Texas, although the White Sweet-clover is decidedly commoner on calcareous soils. A third species, Sour-clover, *Melilotus indicus* All., occurs as an escape in the eastern half of the state, especially southward. It is lower in stature and bears yellow flowers in April and May. All three species are valued for hay and forage, as soil renovators, and as early summer honey plants. Alfalfa produces its flowers all summer and occurs as an escape mainly on the sandy soils of East Texas, more commonly northward. The plant hardly needs introduction, although the usefulness of its seeds as wild life food is not so well known as its virtues as forage and in soil improvement.

SHRUBBY DALEA   *Dalea frutescens* Gray   (PL. 18)

Glabrous subshrub with erect widely branched stems 1 to 3 ft. tall. Leaves alternate, odd-pinnately compound; leaflets 13 to 17, blades obovate to cuneate, ½ to 2 in. long, notched at apex, glandular beneath. Flowers rather few, in subglobose to oblong spikes 1 to 3 in. long; bracts ovate, obtuse at apex; sepals 5, united, strongly ribbed, covered with large glands, the tube longer than the lobes; corolla papilionaceous, the 5 petals violet or red-violet; stamens 10, the filaments united to form a collar around the single pistil. Fruit a tiny membranous indehiscent pod enclosed within the calyx. Distribution: Texas to New Mexico, southward into northern Mexico.

Named in honor of Samuel Dale, an English botanist of 200 years ago, the Daleas are shrubs, herbaceous perennials, and annuals which, taken together, show a preference for dry desertous places. The pinnately divided leaves are nearly always glandular-dotted, and the rather small flowers are aggregated in heads or spikes which appear very dense because of the many sheathing bracts. Fine distinctions among many species make identification difficult.

Shrubby Dalea is a rounded bushy plant of dry limestone soils in Central Texas, from Dallas, Bell, and Comal counties west to the Trans-Pecos, flowering from late summer through fall. Purple Prairie-clover, *D. purpurea* Vent., grows to 2 ft. or more in sandy fields and prairies along the Red River. Very similar and extending in limestone soils to the southwestern portion of the state is *D. helleri*

Shinners. *D. lasiathera* Gray has rosy-violet flowers in early summer, and is found from Taylor, Travis, and Live Oak counties southwest to the Rio Grande, and also in the Davis Mountains of Jeff Davis County. Golden Dalea, *D. aurea* Nutt., restricted to West Texas, has scantily clothed stems to 2 ft. terminating in dense spikes of yellow flowers. These species and the numerous others known in the state bloom principally in May and June. The flowers are rather peculiar in that the two lowest petals, collectively the keel, are joined to the stalks or filaments of the stamens.

SCURVY-PEA *Psoralea cuspidata* Pursh [= *Pediomelum cuspidatum* (Pursh) Rydb.] (PL. 18)

> Herbaceous perennial from fusiform or ellipsoid root. Stems usually ascending, ½ to 2 ft. tall, branched, glabrous below or sparingly strigose. Leaves alternate, 5-foliate; stipules lanceolate, ½ to ¾ in. long, glabrous above, strigose beneath; leaflet blades oblanceolate to spatulate, entire, ½ to 1½ in. long. Flowers in short, dense racemes, each flower subtended by a lanceolate bract *ca.* ½ in. long; sepals 5, united, strigose, *ca.* ⅓ in. long; corolla papilionaceous, ½ to ⅔ in. long, the 5 petals blue-violet. Fruit an ovoid pod. Distribution: Minnesota to Montana, south to Arkansas and Texas.

The Scurvy-peas are perennial herbs with enlarged tap roots, and in most Texas species the stems, leaves, and fruit are glandular-dotted. The pods contain a single seed and do not open. The illustrated species has much-branched creeping or ascending branches with the flower clusters directed upward. It is found on clay and limestone soils in North Central Texas and flowers in April and May. Indian Breadroot, *P. esculenta* Pursh, makes up for its rather sparse top by having a large tuberous root, which at one time formed a significant part of the diet of the Plains Indians in the West Central and Panhandle regions. The Wild-alfalfas, *P. simplex* Nutt. and *P. psoralioides* (Walt.) Gory, var. *glandulosa* (Ell.) Freeman, are erect plants to 3 ft. in height with alfalfalike flowers in April and May. They are found chiefly in the pine belt of East Texas. *P. rhombifolia* Torr. & Gray, a prostrate plant with reddish-brown flowers in late spring, is commonly seen in sandy soil from Travis County southward, and rather locally further north. About 15 additional species occur in the state, most with blue or purple flowers in late spring.

19 CATGUT *Tephrosia virginiana* (L.) Pers. [= *Cracca virginiana* L.] (PL. 19)

> Perennial herb from a branched woody caudex with several erect stems 1 to 2 ft. high. Leaves alternate, odd-pinnately compound; leaflets 11 to 27, striate, oblong or elliptic, the upper surface glabrous and

with numerous parallel side veins, the fine veinlets among them forming a network, undersurface silky villous, ¾ to 1½ in. long. Flowers
in short terminal racemes, 1 to 3 flowers at each node; bracts subulate; sepals 5, united, silky villous; corolla papilionaceous, the 5 petals
pale yellow, cream-colored, or white, the wings and keel partly or
wholly pink to red, especially in age. Fruit a flat, straight or slightly
curved, bristly pod 1¼ to 2 in. long. Distribution: eastern Canada
south to Florida, Texas, and Mexico.

GOAT'S-RUE   *Tephrosia lindheimeri* Gray [= *Cracca lindheimeri*
(Gray) Kuntze]   (PL. 19)

Perennial herb from a woody tuberous root, the angled, grayish-hairy,
zigzag, prostrate or ascending stems reaching 2 to 3 ft. in length.
Leaves alternate, odd-pinnately compound; leaflets 7 to 13, velvety-
pubescent beneath. Flowers loosely arranged in racemes 4 to 9 in.
long; sepals 5, united, velvety; corolla papilionaceous, the 5 petals
deep pink or purplish pink. Fruit a pod 1 to 1½ in. long, densely
velvety-pubescent, yellowish brown. Distribution: Texas and northern
Mexico.

The large, predominantly tropical and subtropical genus *Tephrosia*
is represented in Texas by about 8 species of hairy perennial herbs,
usually with numerous stems arising from a deep woody root. Catgut
is an erect herb occurring in sandy open woods and fields in the
eastern half of the state, westward to the lower Panhandle. The
hoary stems bear leaves with numerous narrow leaflets and, in May,
terminal racemes of flowers with the upper petals all yellowish white,
the others with more or less pink or red. Goat's-rue, with wider
whitish-margined leaflets and large rosy red flowers in April and
May, is found in open sandy places from Bexar County southward
and also in the Edwards Plateau between Burnet and Mason counties. *T. onobrychoides* Nutt., of East Texas, especially in the pine
forests, is a spreading plant bearing in early summer loose elongate
racemes of flowers which are initially creamy white, but change
with age to reddish purple.

Tephrosias may have some wildlife value, as seeds have been
found in the stomachs of several kinds of wild birds, and it is also
worthy of note that Indians crushed the plants and used the juice
as fish poison. The roots are particularly potent; hence one of the
common names, alluding to the dyspepsia suffered by close-cropping
goats.

WOOLLY LOCO   *Astragalus mollissimus* Torr.   (PL. 19)

Perennial herb with much-branched decumbent stems usually less
than 1 ft. high, from a woody caudex. Leaves alternate, odd-pinnately

compound, ascending 4 to 8 in. long; leaflets 21 to 31, obovate to oval, obtuse or rounded at apex, ⅓ to 1 in. long, densely silky with long loosely appressed yellowish or brownish hairs. Flowers in racemes 2 to 4 in. long; sepals 5, united, densely silky; corolla papilionaceous, the 5 petals lavender to purple; stamens 10, 9 united around the single pistil, one free. Fruit a glabrous pod, narrowly oblong, ½ in. long or longer, arcuate. Distribution: West Texas.

Of the nearly 1000 species of *Astragalus,* over 200 occur in the United States, about 35 of them in Texas. Those members of the genus that are poisonous to livestock are called Locoweeds, while the harmless ones are known as Milk-vetches. In the former category is the Woolly Loco of the Panhandle and the Trans-Pecos area, a tufted, soft-hairy, deeply rooted perennial with dense racemes of purplish flowers in late spring. Quite innocuous looking to the eye, the Woolly Loco is among the "early risers" in the spring, and so tempts cattle, even though its taste is so disagreeable that they normally avoid it. Later, in periods of drought when grasses succumb, the persistent Woolly Loco remains, seemingly unaffected. Nor are browsing animals the only ones concerned. The nectar contains poisonous substances, sometimes causing decimation of bee populations.

Ground-plum, *A. carnosus* Pursh, a Milk-vetch, is a clump-forming perennial of varying habit but usually with spreading stems, occurring in the Central, Panhandle, and Trans-Pecos regions. It has purplish flowers in March and April, followed by broad fleshy legumes, purple above, green underneath, which rest on the ground. *A. lindheimeri* Gray, a harmless annual with spreading stems, grows in North Central Texas and bears white-spotted purple flowers in March and April. A taller variety with less conspicuous flowers is found between Bexar and Travis counties. The most widely distributed Milk-vetch in Texas is the Turkey-pea, *A. nuttallianus* DC., an abundant weedy vetchlike annual, often lost to view among grasses but for the small lavender-to-purple flowers borne in spring. These are followed by curved pods.

BUSH-CLOVER   *Lespedeza virginica* (L.) Britt.   (PL. 19)

Perennial herb 1½ to 4 ft. high, simple or sparingly branched. Leaves alternate, 3-foliolate; leaflets linear-oblong, ½ to 1½ in. long, the terminal one more than 4 times longer than wide, truncate, obtuse or sometimes acute at the apex, glabrate on both surfaces or finely pubescent beneath. Flowers of two types, the normal ones with petals, the cleistogamous ones apetalous and not opening, arranged together in dense clusters in upper leaf axils; sepals 5, united; corolla papilionaceous, the 5 petals violet-purple, *ca.* ¼ in. long. Fruit an ovate to

(138)

orbicular pod *ca.* ⅕ in. long. Distribution: Massachusetts to Minnesota, south to Florida and East Texas.

The *Lespedezas* are annual or perennial herbs with 3-parted leaves and vary in growth habit from erect to trailing. Bush-clover, common in sandy open woods and fields in East Texas, is an erect slender perennial with narrow leaflets. As in several other members of the Pea Family, two types of flowers are borne: those with the normal pinkish corolla and encouraging of insect visitation for cross-pollination; those without a corolla, opening little or not at all, and in which self-pollination occurs. They are produced together throughout the summer. *L. stuevii* Nutt. is very similar in range and habit, but for its wider leaflets. *L. hirta* (L.) Hornem. of East Texas, west to Denton and Bastrop counties, has much larger leaves and spreading or ascending stems reaching 5 ft. in length, bearing small yellowish flowers in the summer. *L. repens* (L.) Bart. is a smaller freely branched plant, often somewhat creeping, the stems sometimes lengthening to 3 ft. Occurring in northeastern Texas and locally southwestward to Gonzales County, it bears pink flowers throughout the summer. This species and *L. virginica* are the presumed parents of numerous intergrading forms. Two introduced annual species are quite common. Common Lespedeza, *L. striata* (Thunb.) Hook. & Arn., of Japan and Korea was introduced over 100 years ago and is now extensively planted as a cover crop. The very slender stems, much branched near the base, are usually prostrate and matted, and produce purplish-pink–and–white flowers from July to September. This is a common escape. Korean Lespedeza, *L. stipulacea* Maxim., a more recent introduction, is preferred as a cover crop in many places because of its hardiness. The purple-and-white flowers are borne terminally in late summer. This species has not yet commonly escaped cultivation in Texas.

CORAL-BEAN   *Erythrina herbacea* L.   (PL. 20)   **20**

Perennial herb from a woody root. Stems more or less spreading, 1½ to 4 ft. long, sometimes sparingly armed. Leaves alternate, 3-foliolate; stipules glandlike; leaflets deltoid to hastate, 1¼ to 3½ in. long. Flowers in bracted but otherwise leafless racemes 1 to 2 ft. long; sepals 5, united, *ca.* ¼ in. long; corolla papilionaceous, 1½ to 2 in. long, the 5 petals scarlet; stamens 10, 9 united to form a collar around the single pistil, 1 free. Fruit a pod 2½ to 5 in. long, constricted between the seeds. Distribution: North Carolina to Florida, Texas, and Mexico. In eastern and southern Texas in sandy soils.

Worthy of a place in anyone's garden is the Coral-bean, or Cherokee-bean. Although native only along the coast and in extreme East Texas, it is cultivated as far north as Abilene and San Angelo. The

(139)

generic name, *Erythrina,* is from the Greek and signifies the redness which this plant manifests twice each year: first, in the flowers, arranged in spikelike racemes from purplish waist-high leafless stalks in April and May; later in the seeds, which appear when the pods open in the fall. The 3-parted leaves are borne on separate stems. Fireman's-helmet, *E. crista-galli* L., a native of southern South America, with leafy flowering shoots and scarlet flowers from March to June, is commonly cultivated. *E. arboracea* (Chapm.) Small is a shrub or small tree found near the coast in southeastern Texas. Its flower clusters are shorter than those of the Coral-bean, usually less than 1 ft. in length.

GERANIUM FAMILY   Geraniaceae

Storksbill   *Erodium texanum* (L.) L'Her.   (PL. 20)

Annual herb, at first acaulescent, later with definite stems extending to 15 in. or more. Leaves opposite; blades ovate or triangular-ovate, ½ to 2 in. long, round-toothed and 3- to 5-lobed; base cordate; basal and lower-stem leaves long-stalked. Flowers in clusters of 2 to 7; peduncles and pedicels hoary-gray with short hairs; sepals 5, minutely bristle-tipped, canescent; petals 5, purple or rose-violet, much exceeding the sepals (sometimes of lesser size late in the season); fertile stamens 5, alternating with 5 sterile stamens; pistil of 5 united carpels, style column (beak) 1¼ to 2½ in. long; carpel bodies narrow, acute at base. Seeds smooth. Distribution: Texas to California and Baja California.

Storksbill, an often abundant roadside wildflower appearing in March and April, is a member of the Geranium Family, most of whose members are found in Europe and South Africa. The delicate purple flowers seem intolerant of intense sunlight; they open in late afternoon, closing the following morning unless cloudy weather prevails. Of singular interest is the fruit. The 5-seeded ovary divides into as many segments at maturity, each 1-seeded segment being flung off by the elastically coiling beak. This dispersal usually occurs during periods of low humidity. When the humidity rises, the beak straightens, its backward-directed hairs catching on debris and driving the slender, sharp-tipped fruit proper toward the soil. The process may be repeated many times, until at length the fruit is pushed into the soil. After germination in late fall, the seedlings vegetate until early spring, when they begin flowering. Storksbill is found most commonly in Central Texas, but ranges north to Tarrant and Childress counties, west to the Trans-Pecos.

With very similar fruits but much smaller pink flowers and larger finely dissected leaves is Filaree or Pin-clover, *E. cicutarium* (L.) L'Her. (PL. 20). A native of Europe now widely naturalized in North America, this species is welcome on ranges as a forage plant. In Texas it is found from the Blackland Prairie in Travis County west to the Trans-Pecos, north to the lower Panhandle. Cranesbill, *Geranium carolinianum* L., has palmately 5-parted leaves, the divisions again lobed and round-toothed, and clusters of whitish or pale pink flowers in April and May or later. The fruit is a small version of the Storks-bills', but differs by splitting from the base upward. Cranesbill inhab-its open woods, pastures, roadsides, and cultivated ground, mostly in East Texas, westward to the Edwards Plateau. The florists' Gera-niums are hybrids derived from species of the large South African genus *Pelargonium*.

WOOD-SORREL FAMILY   Oxalidaceae

YELLOW WOOD-SORREL   *Oxalis dillenii* Jacq. [referred to in some manuals as *O. stricta* L. or *Xanthoxalis stricta* (L.) Small] (PL. 20)

Perennial herb, to 15 in., flowering the first year, developing a deep taproot. Stems erect or ascending, slender. Leaves alternate, palmately trifoliate; leaflets obovate or obcordate, entire or notched at apex, folding in low light intensities, glabrous to pilose on upper surface, green to yellow-green. Flowers solitary or in few-flowered clusters, borne in leaf axils on slender stalks; sepals 5; petals 5, yellow, ½ to 2 in. long; sometimes with red spots inside at base; stamens 10; pis-tils 5, coalescing to form a narrow erect capsule ⅔ to 1 in. long. Dis-tribution: Central Texas and northward. Var. *radicans* Shinners is of lower more prostrate habit, the stems often rooting where in contact with moist soil, and the petals average slightly smaller. Distribution: East Texas.

PURPLE WOOD-SORREL   *Oxalis violacea* L. [= *Ionoxalis violacea* (L.) Small]   (PL. 21)

21

Perennial herb to 1 ft., from bulblike rootstock. Leaves all basal, fewer or absent in fall; leaflets 3, up to 1½ in. long, shallowly notched at apex, somewhat fleshy, gray-green to bluish gray above, green to reddish purple beneath. Flowers borne on scapes at first shorter than, later exceeding the leaves, 8 to 15 in a cymose cluster; sepals 5; petals 5, lavender-pink to purple, rarely white. Capsule ovoid or globose, *ca.* ¼ in. long. Distribution: eastern North America.

The Wood-sorrels comprise a very large genus of some 800 species, commonest in South Africa and in North and South America, and restricted to mountains in the tropics. Most are perennial herbs with cloverlike leaves that have a slightly sour but nonetheless pleasant taste. The leaves exhibit "sleep movements," that is, they fold, in this case downward, at dusk or in cloudy weather. The flowers, usually borne in small clusters, vary considerably in size and color among the species, although yellow, pink, and white predominate. At the close of the day the individual flower stalks, or pedicels, turn downward and the petals come together. The capsular fruits contain many small seeds, each with a tiny cuplike appendage at its base. When mature, and particularly on being disturbed, the appendages, or arils, quickly turn inside-out, flinging the seeds a considerable distance away.

Yellow Wood-sorrel is found commonly on the Blackland Prairie in North and Central Texas, extending westward to Crockett and Brewster counties. The creeping variety occurs in the sandy soils of East Texas, where it is a persistent weed of lawns and gardens. Purple Wood-sorrel is common in most of East Texas west to the limestone hills of the central portion, locally further westward to Brewster County. Both species, and the variety, flower freely in the spring from March to June and often, though less prolifically, in late summer and early fall. *O. drummondii* Gray is another purple-flowered species, usually larger than the foregoing, widespread over South Texas and extending locally northward across the Edwards Plateau to Somervell County. It flowers in September and October. *O. berlandieri* Torr. [= *Lotoxalis berlandieri* (Torr.) Small] is a taprooted, often much-branched subshrub to 1 ft. or more tall, bearing yellow flowers in spring and summer. It grows in South Texas, northward to Webb County, and along the coast to Nueces County. *O. dichondraefolia* Gray [= *Monoxalis dichondraefolia* (Gray) Small] differs from other Wood-sorrels in that its leaves each have a solitary nearly circular leaflet up to 1½ in. across. This species, a perennial herb with a deep woody taproot, occurs southward from Maverick and Nueces counties, and bears its yellow flowers throughout the summer. A few additional species are known from Texas, chiefly from the mountains of the Trans-Pecos.

FLAX FAMILY   Linaceae

YELLOW FLAX   *Linum rigidum* Pursh [= *Cathartolinum rigidum* (Pursh) Small]   (PL. 21)

Annual herb, with pale green, erect, glabrous stems to 1½ ft., simple or more commonly loosely branched above, the branches erect or ascending and sharply angled or winged. Leaves alternate, estipulate, rather numerous, linear to linear-lanceolate, rather early deciduous, erect or ascending, firm, ⅛ to ¼ in. long, acute or acuminate, usually entire, sessile. Flowers in terminal bracted racemes; bracts subulate, gland-toothed; sepals 5, with gland-tipped teeth; petals 5, yellow, red-brown or coppery at base, *ca.* ½ in. long; stamens 5, staminodes 5 and minute or absent. Pistil 1. Fruit an ovoid capsule, usually 5-celled, with firm cross walls. Seeds 10 or fewer by abortion. Distribution: Ontario and Manitoba to Georgia and Texas.

BLUE FLAX   *Linum pratense* (Norton) Small [= *L. lewisii*, var. *pratense* Norton]   (PL. 21)

Hairless annual or perennial herb to 2 ft., the stems often clustered at the base. Leaves linear-lanceolate, commonly crowded, acute, ⅓ to 1 in. long. Flowers in terminal bracted racemes, the bracts usually leaflike; pedicels reflexing after the petals fall; sepals 5, entire, glandless; petals 5, blue, rarely white, ¼ to ⅝ in. long; other characters as above. Distribution: western North America south to northern Mexico.

The Flaxes of Texas are members of a difficult, predominantly Mediterranean, genus, some species of which have long been important to man. Commercial flax is obtained from the stem fibres of the European *L. usitatissimum* L., and linseed oil is expressed from seeds of the same species. Purging Flax, from which a cathartic and diuretic are prepared, is *L. catharticum* L., another European annual. Several kinds are cultivated in gardens, most notably the red-flowered *L. grandiflorum* Desf.

Of the numerous wild Flaxes occurring in the state, the 2 illustrated species are perhaps most commonly seen. Blue Flax, found most abundantly on calcareous soils, flowers from March to June, and ranges from Grayson and DeWitt counties westward to the Trans-Pecos and Panhandle. Yellow Flax blooms from April to June and is distributed over most of the state west of Fannin, Houston, and Calhoun counties. Very similar to the latter is *L. sulcatum* Riddell, distinguished by its lack of the deeper flower center, and found rather locally in the central and north-central portions of the state. *L. imbricatum* (Raf.) Shinners [= *L. multicaule* Hook.] is a heathlike annual with short, closely appressed leaves and orange, brown-centered flowers borne on numerous stems. It flowers in April and May and ranges from Taylor and Stephens counties south and westward to Kleberg and Harris counties. *L. medium* (Planch.) Britt., var. *texanum* (Planch.) Fern. sometimes reaches 3 ft. and produces its yellow to coppery-orange noctural flowers from April to June. It grows in East Texas west to Dallas, McLennan, and Gonzales counties. Several other species, mostly with yellow, often smaller flowers, are known.

(143)

CALTROP FAMILY   Zygophyllaceae

GOAT-HEAD   *Tribulus terrestris* L.   (PL. 21)

Diffuse, trailing annual herb, the stems hirsute and somewhat swollen at the nodes. Leaves opposite, 1 to 2 in. long, pinnately even-compound; stipules subulate, caducous; leaflets 5 to 7 pairs, somewhat oblique, oblong or elliptic, acute to obtuse at apex, silky hispid beneath, ⅛ to ½ in. long, the terminal pair smaller. Flowers solitary on axillary peduncles; sepals 5, soon falling; petals 5, yellow, rarely white, obovate, ⅕ to ¼ in. long; stamens 10; pistil 1, 5- or, by abortion, 4- or 3-celled, each carpel with 2 stout divergent spines and 2 or more smaller ones. Distribution: South Carolina and Nebraska, south through Texas and Arizona to Brazil; native to Mediterranean region.

22   DESERT-POPPY   *Kallstroemia grandiflora* Torr.   (PL. 22)

Spreading annual herb with few to numerous striate, pubescent stems 2 to 4 ft. long. Leaves opposite, pinnately compound; leaflets 5 to 10 pairs, lanceolate to narrowly ovate, oblique at the base, ⅔ to 1 in. long, copiously silky-pubescent when young, the upper surface becoming glabrate with age. Flowers perfect, solitary in the leaf axils; sepals 5, ⅖ to ⅗ in. long, hirsute; petals 5, yellow-orange to orange, ¾ to 1¼ in. long; stamens 10, pistil 1, 5-chambered. Fruit smooth, breaking into 8 to 12 1-seeded nutlets. Distribution: West Texas to Arizona and adjacent Mexico.

The Caltrop Family is a relatively small group having world-wide distribution in warm regions. Of the three genera represented in our area, *Tribulus* is perhaps best known, owing to two traits of its only species here in Texas: persistent recurrence in waste and cultivated ground; adherence of the spiny fruit to feet and hide of stock animals. Though believed to have been introduced into Texas not more than 100 years ago, Goat-head is now distributed throughout most of the state, its spread no doubt having been effected largely by animal agency. Flowering from May to October, the plants quite commonly form dense and extensive mats. The 7 or 8 members of the related genus *Kallstroemia* are similar in general aspect, but in no case produce spiny fruit. Desert-poppy, with clear yellow-orange flowers up to 2½ in. in diameter, is found in the counties of the Trans-Pecos bordering the Rio Grande. Similarly large-flowered, but the only perennial species occurring in the state, is *K. perennans* Turner, known thus far only from Val Verde County. *K. parviflora* Norton is frequently mistaken for Goat-head, as is the often very hairy *K. hirsutissima* Vail, a species reputedly toxic to sheep and cattle. Both of these plants have about the same distribution in Texas as Goat-head.

CREOSOTE-BUSH   *Larrea tridentata* (DC.) Cov. [= *L. mexicana* Moric.]   (PL. 22)

Diffusely branched shrub 4 to 10 ft. tall, the branches swollen and blackened at the nodes. Leaves opposite, each consisting of two thick, resinous, yellowish-green leaflets ¼ to ½ in. long, sessile on a common petiole ¹⁄₁₂ to ⅛ in. long. Flowers perfect, solitary in the leaf axils; sepals 5, soon falling; petals 5, yellow, the bases narrowed into a stalk; stamens 10, the filaments winged below; pistil 1, 5-chambered. Fruit a densely hairy, short-stalked capsule *ca.* ⅕ in. across, with one seed in each chamber. Distribution: West Texas and Utah, west to southern California, and south to central Mexico.

Common on gravelly mesas and hillsides west of the Pecos River and south along the Rio Grande to Webb County, the Creosote-bush gets its name from the strong-smelling resin copiously deposited on the leaflets. It is one of the most characteristic shrubs of the region, often found in great numbers almost to the exclusion of other woody vegetation. The flowers are borne throughout most of the year, but most abundantly from February to June. In addition to its importance as a soil-binder, Creosote-bush, also known as Greasewood, Gobernadora, or Hediondilla, has been a source of food, fire, and medicine to Indians of the Southwest. A brownish lac, deposited on the stems by a scale insect, has been used by Indians in Mexico as a leather dye and as a cement.

MILKWORT FAMILY   Polygalaceae

WHITE MILKWORT   *Polygala alba* L.   (PL. 22)

Stems numerous, glabrous, from a perennial root, often with a cluster of short leafy branches at the base, erect or ascending, simple or sparsely branched, 8 to 15 in. tall. Leaves alternate except for 1 to 2 whorls at the base, the lower spatulate or narrowly obovate, ⅛ to ½ in. long and *ca.* ¹⁄₁₆ in. wide, the others linear. Flowers in rather dense racemes; racemes cylindric or conic-cylindric, ⅛ to ¼ in. in diameter, 1 to 4 in. long; sepals 5, 2 large and petal-like; petals 3, white, rounded, ⅛ to ⅕ in. long; stamens 8, joined to form a collar around the single pistil. Fruit an elliptic to oblong-elliptic capsule ¹⁄₁₆ to ⅛ in. long. Seed 1, pilose. Distribution: Louisiana and Texas north to the Dakotas and Washington, south to central Mexico.

PINK MILKWORT   *Polygala polygama* Walt.   (PL. 22)

Perennial herb with 1 to several stems to 1½ ft. tall. Leaves alternate, somewhat fleshy, often crowded, elliptic below, narrower and longer above, apex rounded to broadly acute. Flowers in loose racemes up to 5 in. long; sepals 5, 2 larger and petal-like; petals 3, pale to deep pink, oval, ⅛ to ¼ in. long; stamens 8, united to form a collar around the pistil; whitish cleistogamous flowers arise from the rhizome near the ground. Fruit a ridged, oval capsule up to ⅜ in. long. Seed 1, ellipsoid, *ca.* ¼ in. long. Distribution: southeast Canada to Florida, west to Texas.

23

BLUE MILKWORT   *Polygala longa* Blake   (PL. 23)

Several-stemmed perennial herb or subshrub 4 to 14 in. tall, densely fine-hairy. Leaves alternate, the lower oval to oblong and ⅓ to ¾ in. long, the upper narrower and up to 1¼ in. long, apex acute to obtuse. Flowers in loose racemes 1 to 5 in. long; sepals 5, 2 larger and petal-like; petals 3, bluish violet, oval, up to ¼ in. long; stamens 8, joined and forming a collar around the pistil. Fruit an oval hairy capsule ¼ to ⅓ in. long. Seed 1, *ca.* ⅕ in. long. Distribution: West Texas to Arizona and Chihuahua, Mexico.

The name Polygala is from the Greek *polys,* much, and *gala,* milk, for it was once believed, as Pliny wrote, that "taken in drink it increases the milk in nursing women." The Milkworts comprise a genus of some 500 species found throughout the world except in western Pacific islands. The flowers, nearly always arranged in racemes, are so modified in structure as to suggest the Pea Family, but close examination reveals numerous distinctions. Senega or Snakeroot, used as an expectorant and diuretic, is obtained from *P. senega* L. of the eastern states. In Texas, the most widely distributed species is the White Milkwort, which occurs in fields and open woods, chiefly on calcareous soils, from the Blackland Prairie and south-coastal area westward. It flowers from April to July. The rhizomatous Pink Milkwort is found eastward from Anderson, Brazos, and DeWitt counties and bears both its types of flowers from April to June. Blue Milkwort grows west of the Pecos River and blooms in June and July. *P. tweedyi* Britt. is a tufted perennial, chiefly from Erath County westward, with finely pubescent stems, linear-lanceolate leaves, and pink to lavender flowers in early summer. With strongly veined, wider leaves and coarse, diverging stem pubescence, *P. lindheimeri* Gray, an otherwise similar species, grows from Travis County to the Rio Grande and west to the Trans-Pecos. About 12 additional species are known from Texas, mainly in the Trans-Pecos and extreme southeastern portions.

SPURGE FAMILY Euphorbiaceae

BULL-NETTLE *Cnidoscolus texanus* (Muell. Arg.) Small [= *Jatropha texana* Muell. Arg.] (PL. 23)

Erect perennial herb from a long tough root, the stems, petioles, and leaf veins densely clothed with translucent stinging hairs. Leaves alternate; petioles stout, 2 to 4 in. long; blades circular in outline, 5 to 8 in. across, cordate at base, palmately 5-lobed, the lobes coarsely and irregularly toothed or again lobed. Flowers unisexual, *ca.* 1 in. across, arranged in terminal corymbs usually borne among the leaves, but sometimes held above; staminate flowers numerous and borne at ends of inflorescence branches; pistillate flowers fewer and lower; sepals 4 to 5, petal-like, white, united below to form a tube; petals absent; stamens 10 or more; pistil 3-lobed, becoming a bristly capsule *ca.* 1 in. long, each lobe containing an oblong grayish-mottled seed which is flung away when the fruit explodes. Distribution: Texas to Arkansas.

A member of the very large nearly cosmopolitan family, Euphorbiaceae, the Bull-nettle, Malo Mujer, or Tread-softly, as it is variously known, is certainly one of the best-armed plants among Texas wildflowers. It commonly occurs in patches or masses in fields, roadsides, and waste places, even in the midst of heavily grazed pastures. The sweet-scented flowers are produced from March to July, and may recur intermittently until fall. Bull-nettle is most common from Cooke, Mills, and Frio counties eastward, but occurs sparingly further south and west, thriving best on sandy soils. The bad reputation of the stinging hairs is in some degree mitigated by the appeal the tasty seeds have for schoolboys.

SNOW-ON-THE-MOUNTAIN *Euphorbia bicolor* Engelm. & Gray [= *Dichrophyllum bicolor* (Engelm. & Gray) Kl. & Garcke = *Lepadena bicolor* (Engelm. & Gray) Niewland] (PL. 23)

Erect hairy annual herb 1 to 4 ft. tall with few or several branches arising from the simple stem. Leaves alternate, mostly sessile, narrowly ovate or lanceolate, entire, rather thick, the upper ones whitemargined, 2 to 4 in. long, ⅕ to ⅓ as wide. Flowers unisexual, very small, in cuplike structures (cyathia), each bearing one pistillate and several staminate flowers. Fruit a 3-lobed capsule exserted from the cyathium and containing 3 round flackish seeds. Distribution: East Central Texas and adjacent Oklahoma.

This is one of two common plants called Snow-on-the-mountain, the other being the closely related *E. marginata* Pursh, differing chiefly in its wider leaves and reduced pubescence, and ranging mainly from the Edwards Plateau westward and northward in limestone and clay soils. Both are attractive annuals with milky juice, brightening late summer fields and roadsides with their white-bordered upper leaves. Unfortunately the white latex of these and other Euphorbias may cause dermatitis in some people.

One of the largest genera of flowering plants, *Euphorbia* contains over 1600 species and is represented in all tropical and subtropical areas. Many species are found in dry places in Africa where they characteristically show a cactuslike habit. Quite a number of these are prized in cactus gardens in this country. Other well-known cultivars include the Crown-of-thorns, *E. splendens* Boj. and the Poinsettia, *E. pulcherrima* Willd.

FLOWERING SPURGE   *Euphorbia corollata* L. [= *Tithymalopsis corollata* (L.) Small = *Agaloma corollata* (L.) Raf.]   (PL. 23)

> Perennial herb from a stout root, the stem rather slender, lightly pubescent to nearly glabrous, reaching 3 ft. Leaves scattered, sometimes apparently opposite, usually sessile; blades linear to oblong-spatulate, 1 to 2 in. long, entire. Flowers unisexual, in loose open clusters; minute, in cuplike cyathia, the rim of each bearing 5 white petal-like appendages. Fruit a globose capsule ⅛ to ¼ in. in diameter containing 3 smooth seeds. Distribution: Massachusetts to Minnesota, south to Florida and Texas.

Flowering Spurge occurs as a solitary plant with one or a few rather erect stems, and frequents fields and woodland borders from Grayson, Tarrant, and Hays counties eastward. The white petal-like appendages of the cyathium attract flies and short-tongued bees for pollination. Though an attractive plant along summer waysides, Flowering Spurge must be considered poisonous, especially when taken internally. Cattle avoid it in pastures.

Closely related is the Wax-plant, or Candelilla, *E. antisyphilitica* Zucc., of West Texas, a leafless shrub to 5 ft. with thickened roots. The pencil-like stems bear small whitish flowers near their tips in spring. In Mexico the waxy excrescence on the stems is used in polishes, insulation, and candles. The purgative properties of the juice and the fine stem fibres also find considerable use there.

SUMAC FAMILY   Anacardiaceae

24   SHINING SUMAC   *Rhus copallina* L., var. *latifolia* Engl.
[= *Schmaltzia copallina* (L.) Small]   (PL. 24)

> Shrub 6 to 12 ft. tall, the stout twigs downy at first, later becoming

(148)

warted. Leaves alternate, pinnately compound; leaflets 7 to 19, entire or few-toothed, oblong to narrowly ovate, *ca.* 3 times longer than wide, softly pubescent to nearly glabrous. Flowers mostly perfect, small, in dense terminal pyramidal panicles; sepals 5; petals 5, greenish yellow; stamens 5; pistil 1. Fruit a drupe, ⅕ to ¼ in. long, deep red or reddish brown. Distribution: Maine to Ontario, south to Florida and Texas.

In a state where high autumnal coloration of leaves is not commonly seen, the Shining or Flame-leaf Sumac is indeed welcome. Around the time of the first frost in the fall the dark glossy green leaflets turn brilliant scarlet, but unfortunately soon drop to the ground. Perfectly harmless, this species, readily distinguished from others by the winged rhachis, might well be encouraged in cultivation but for its annoying habit of spreading by underground stolons. Occasional in the sandy woods of East Texas, the Shining Sumac usually grows in clumps. The clusters of deep maroon fruit, very suitable for winter bouquets, are eaten by numerous kinds of birds. *R. copallina*, var. *lanceolata* Gray, similar except for narrower leaflets, is common in the limestone hills of Central Texas.

SMOOTH SUMAC   *Rhus glabra* L. [= *Schmaltzia glabra* (L.) Small]
(PL. 24)

Shrub 5 to 8 ft. tall, sometimes treelike to 15 ft. Twigs stout, bloom-covered, violet-brown, becoming warted. Leaves alternate, pinnately compound, the rhachis not winged; leaflets 11 to 33, oblong to narrowly lanceolate, glabrous, sharply toothed. Flowers usually perfect, small, in dense terminal panicles; sepals 5; petals 5, greenish yellow; stamens 5; pistil 1. Fruit a drupe, maturing brown, covered with crimson hairs. Distribution: Nova Scotia to British Columbia, south to Arizona, Texas, and Florida.

Once an important commercial source of tannin, the Smooth Sumac occurs frequently in Indian and pioneer lore. Indians used the dried leaves in kinnikinnick, a tobacco substitute. Early settlers found the stem pith to have purgative properties. All parts are rich in malic acid. As with the Shining Sumac, the leaflets take on hues of crimson with the approach of cool autumn weather, and birds relish the persisting fruit in winter. In Texas, Smooth Sumac grows in woods and fields from Eastland, Williamson, and Washington counties northeastward.

POISON-IVY; POISON-OAK   *Rhus toxicodendron* L.   (PL. 24)

Woody, but varying from a vine, climbing by short aerial roots to 25 ft. or more, to a rounded shrub 3 to 5 ft. high. Leaves alternate,

(149)

compound; leaflets mostly 3, but on vigorous shoots occasionally 5 and then pinnately arranged, ovate to lanceolate, entire or wavy-margined or with a few coarse teeth, usually shining and glabrous above, sometimes pubescent beneath. Flowers polygamous, in small axillary panicles; sepals 5; petals 5, greenish yellow; stamens 5; pistil 1. Fruit a smooth, whitish, berrylike drupe ⅕ to ¼ in. in diameter. Distribution: Nova Scotia to British Columbia, south to Texas and Florida.

One of the best-known and least-liked members of the flora of North America, Poison-ivy or Poison-oak (the names are used interchangeably) occurs in Texas as 3 equally troublesome varieties. Var. *toxicodendron,* with entire or bluntly toothed leaflets, the terminal one with a broad, blunt tip, grows in sandy woods, chiefly in Northeast Texas. Var. *vulgaris* Michx. is commonest in Central Texas, but ranges over most of the state, and is distinguished by pubescent petioles and undersurfaces of blades, and has a narrower, distinctively pointed terminal leaflet. Var. *eximia* (Greene) McNair, with petioles and leaves glabrous but otherwise resembling those of the above variety, tends to grow as a clump-forming shrub, often spreading over a considerable area. It is confined to limestone soils from Grayson County southwestward to Taylor, Menard, and Uvalde counties. All varieties produce their inconspicuous flowers from March to May, after the leaves have appeared.

The poison is a somewhat volatile oil occurring in resin ducts throughout the plant. There is much diversity of opinion regarding aerial carriage of the oil in droplet form or on pollen grains, but it seems fairly well established that, for those who are susceptible, touching of the plant or of the extracted resin is necessary for poisoning to be effected. Many people are quite immune, and others may temporarily become so by washing exposed skin with a 5 per cent solution of ferric chloride in a 50-50 mixture of water and alcohol not long before or just after contact with Poison-ivy.

The bad reputation of Poison-ivy has spread erroneously to numerous quite innocent plants. The closely related red-fruited Sumacs, *R. copallina* and *R. glabra,* are often suspected, as is the shrubby Aromatic Sumac, *R. aromatica* Ait., of northeastern Texas, which, despite its 3 leaflets, may be told by the *terminal* position of the clusters of yellow flowers, these appearing in March *before* the leaves. Perhaps the most common victim of confusion is Virginia-creeper or 5-finger-ivy, *Parthenocissus quinquefolia* (L.) Planch. (PL. 24), a commonly cultivated wall-covering vine of the Grape Family, native in the woods of East Texas, and having small clusters of blue-black grapelike berries among the palmately 5-parted leaves. Poison Sumac, *Rhus vernix* L., a justly named white-fruited shrub or small tree of swamps, is unknown in Texas except for a small area in Shelby County.

HORSE-CHESTNUT FAMILY   Hippocastanaceae

RED BUCKEYE   *Aesculus pavia* L. [= A. *discolor* Pursh, in part]
(PL. 24)

Shrub or small tree 6 to 18 ft. tall, with smooth bark. Leaves opposite, palmately compound, long-petioled; leaflets 5 to 7; blades oblanceolate to elliptic, 2 to 6 in. long, dark green, frequently finely pubescent beneath, acuminate at apex, margins finely serrate, base acute. Inflorescence a terminal panicle; flowers *ca.* 1 in. long; sepals 5, basally united; petals 5, united, minutely glandular, red to yellow-orange, often with orange markings; stamens 5 to 10, exserted; pistil 1, of 3 united carpels each with 2 ovules, only 1 of which matures. Fruit a 3-segmented unarmed leathery capsule 1 to 1¾ in. in diameter. Distribution: Virginia to Missouri, south to Florida and East Texas.

Aesculus is a genus of some 18 species of trees and shrubs of North America and Asia. Red Buckeye, widely cultivated within its natural range and far beyond, is an attractive understory shrub, flowering in April and May. The corolla is most commonly red, but occasional specimens bear yellow-orange blooms, these being highly prized in cultivation. In Texas this species is most frequently met with in sandy woods in the east portion, but it ranges westward into the Edwards Plateau region to Real and Uvalde counties, and along the Red River to Wichita County. White Buckeye, *A. glabra* Willd., var. *arguta* (Buckl.) Robins., also a shrub, is distinguished by its yellowish-white flowers borne in March and April. While its range is much the same as that of Red Buckeye, it shows a preference for limestone soil.

MALLOW FAMILY   Malvaceae

INDIAN MALLOW   *Abutilon incanum* (Link) Sweet   (PL. 25)   **25**

Downy-stemmed perennial herb to 6 ft. from a stout root. Leaves alternate, the blades broadly cordate, ½ to 2½ in. long, finely grayish-tomentose, with crenate or dentate margins. Flowers perfect, arranged in leaf axils and in small terminal panicles; sepals 5, united below; petals 5, distinct, yellow-orange, often violet near base, *ca.* ⅓ in. long; stamens ∞, their filaments united to ensheath the style; pistil of 7 to 30 united carpels. Fruit a fluted capsule ½ in. long, the mature carpels arranged around, and eventually separating from, the central axis, each carpel with 1 to 6 kidney-shaped seeds. Distribution: Arkansas to Arizona, southward to Mexico.

The North American *Abutilons* are rather weedy members of a large

(151)

group distributed the world over in warm regions. Several Asiatic species, especially *A. theophrastii* Medic, are commercially valued for their stem fibres, from which a kind of jute is made. A few South American species, e.g., *A. megapotamicum* St. Hil. & Naud. and *A. vitifolium* Presl., attain treelike proportions and bear drooping cup-shaped flowers up to 2½ in. long. Commonly known as "Flowering-maples" in the horticultural trade, these are sometimes grown under glass. Indian Mallow flowers throughout the summer and is found chiefly in limestone soil from Wise, McLennan, Aransas, and Cameron counties west to El Paso County.

VELVET-LEAF   *Wissadula holosericea* (Scheele) Garcke   (PL. 25)

Erect heavily scented perennial herb, densely velvety tomentose nearly throughout. Stems 3 to 6 ft. tall, usually much branched. Leaves alternate; petioles usually shorter than the blades; blades ovate to suborbicular, broadest below the middle, 5 to 8 in. long, apex acute or acuminate, margin more or less distinctly dentate and often 3-lobed, base cordate. Flowers perfect, solitary in upper leaf axils, 1½ to 2 in. in diameter; sepals 5, partially united; petals 5, yellow-orange; stamens ∞, the filaments enclosing the 5 styles; pistil of 5 pubescent carpels, each *ca.* ¼ in. high. Fruit a capsule splitting 5 ways, each carpel containing 2 seeds. Distribution: Texas and adjacent Mexico.

Velvet-leaf rather closely resembles the Indian Mallow, but may be distinguished by its larger size in nearly all respects and particularly by the 5 (rarely more) carpels, each with a horizontal septum or partition. The plants most usually grow alone or widely spaced in dry soil, and are found in South Texas from Travis, Nueces, and Cameron counties westward to Brewster County. *W. amplisericea* (L.) Fries, of extreme South Texas north to Kenedy County, is similar but more finely pubescent and bears yellow flowers, usually less than 1 in. in diameter. Both species flower in the summer months.

COPPER-MALLOW   *Sphaeralcea angustifolia* (Cav.) G. Don, var. *cuspidata* Gray [= *S. cuspidata* (Gray) Britt.]   (PL. 25)

Perennial herb with numerous erect or spreading stems 1 to 4 ft. tall from a woody root, the stems and leaves ashy-gray with branched pubescence. Leaves alternate, long-petioled; blades 1½ to 3 in. long, palmately 5-parted (on upper stem often 3-parted) with lanceolate or linear-lanceolate lobes, margin irregularly crenulate. Flowers perfect, axillary and in terminal racemes; sepals 5, partially united; petals 5, salmon-pink to lavender-pink, *ca.* ¼ in. long; stamens ∞, the united filaments forming a tube around the styles; pistil of 5 or more carpels, becoming ⅕ to ⅓ in. high in fruit. Distribution: Kansas, Colorado, and southern Nevada, south to West Texas and adjacent Mexico.

(152)

Rather resembling a small hollyhock, the Copper-mallow is an attractive plant flowering from April to October, and growing in dry exposed places from Stephens, Travis, and Webb counties westward through the Trans-Pecos. *S. hastatula* Gray, usually lower and bushier, bears rose or pinkish-orange flowers mainly in late spring, but sometimes through the summer in wet years. It prefers gravelly or sandy soils from the southern Panhandle to the Trans-Pecos, and has spread eastward to Erath County. The Scarlet-mallow, *S. coccinea* (Pursh) Rydb., is still lower, with erect or spreading stems seldom exceeding 1 ft. The leaves are 3- to several-lobed or -divided, and the yellowish-red–to–scarlet flowers are borne in late spring, sometimes on to early fall. This species is common in the Panhandle and Trans-Pecos and, like the former species, is moving eastward, thus far to Jack and Montague counties.

WINE-CUP   *Callirhoe digitata* Nutt.   (PL. 25)

Perennial herb from a thickened root, the stems usually erect, 8 to 20 in. tall, more or less villous below, nearly glabrous above. Leaves alternate; the basal leaves with hirsute petioles about as long as the blades or somewhat longer, blades coarsely crenate to palmately lobed or parted; stem leaves few, the petioles relatively shorter, blades palmately divided with linear or lanceolate and usually entire divisions 1 to 3 in. long. Flowers perfect, axillary or in leafy racemes, slender-stalked; sepals 5, united below, nearly glabrous; petals 5, violet to red-violet, sometimes white, ⅓ to ⅝ in. long, apically fringed; stamens ∞, their united filaments ensheathing the styles; pistil of 10 to 20 carpels, each ⅛ to ⅙ in. high. Fruit a flattened dislike capsule ¼ to ⅜ in. across, breaking into 1-seeded segments at maturity. Distribution: Kansas and Missouri south to Texas.

The Wine-cups or Poppy-mallows are a genus of 10 or 12 species of spring-flowering herbs, most of which occur in Texas. In the flowers the anthers discharge pollen before the style branches emerge from the staminal tube; hence, cross-pollination must be effected. This is accomplished mainly by bees which get pollen on their backs while extracting nectar from newly opened flowers and transfer it when pushing past the widely spread styles of older flowers. *C. digitata* blooms in April and May and often colonizes extensive areas along highways and in fields in Central Texas, from Grayson, McLennan, and Bexar counties west to Taylor and Edwards counties.

C. alceoides (Michx.) Gray bears white (infrequently pink) flowers ¾ to 1¼ in. across, closely arranged in terminal clusters, with the petals unevenly dentate at their tips. This rather local species prefers limestone soils, and ranges from Lamar and Kaufman counties southwestward to Eastland County. The most widespread Texas Wine-cup

(153)

is *C. involucrata* (Nutt.) Gray (PL. 25), readily told by the 3 linear bracts which subtend each flower. The cherry-red flowers are borne on long stalks from the leaf axils of the widely spreading vinelike stems, and continue to appear over a fairly long period, from April to late June or early July. It ranges from Van Zandt, Limestone, and Brazoria counties in the east, to Pecos and Nolan counties in the west, southward to the Rio Grande, and sparingly northward into the Panhandle. The center flower of the Wine-cup group (PL. 25) is *C. leiocarpa* Martin.

TURK'S-CAP   *Malvaviscus drummondii* Torr. & Gray   (PL. 25)

> Shrub 3 to 9 ft. tall or, when cultivated in areas where frost is severe, a perennial herb to 3 ft. Stems erect, commonly widely branched. Leaves alternate; petioles 1½ to 4 in. long; blades suborbicular in outline, usually shallowly 3-lobed, harshly short-pubescent above, rather velvety beneath, 3 to 5 in. long, margins crenate, base cordate. Flowers perfect, solitary in the axils, on peduncles about as long as subtending petioles, with 7 to 12 narrowly spatulate bractlets; sepals 5, partially united; petals 5, bright crimson, *ca.* 1 in. long; stamens ∞; pistil of 5 carpels, the 5 2-parted styles emerging from the elongate cylinder of united filaments. Fruit berrylike by the union of fleshy carpels, *ca.* ⅓ in. in diameter, subglobose, maturing red, the carpels eventually separating. Distribution: Florida to Texas and Mexico.

Turk's-cap, also called Red Mallow and Mexican-apple, commonly forms clumps in the shade of East Texas woods, and is rather frequently encountered in cultivation where it is suited for low hedgework. The flowers, which never open fully, are borne all summer and are followed by edible fruit. *M. grandiflorus* H. B. K. is a larger flowering but less hardy species of Mexico, commonly grown for ornament in the Rio Grande Valley.

The Mallow Family includes, in addition to the above, several other well-known ornamentals, including Hollyhock, Rose-of-Sharon, and Rose Mallow, and a few commercially important species, especially Cotton and Okra. Rather closely related are the Basswood (Linden Family); Chinese-parasol-tree, Cacao, and Cola (Sterculia Family); Silk-cotton-tree (Bombax Family).

CANDLEWOOD FAMILY   Fouquieriaceae

26 OCOTILLO   *Fouquieria splendens* Engelm.   (PL. 26)

> Soft-wooded shrub, branched at base, the wandlike stems sometimes reaching 20 ft., armed with stout spines. Leaves alternate, usually clustered; blades leathery, entire, oblong to spatulate, ½ to ⅝ in. long,

apex obtuse, soon falling but leaving the petioles, which become spines. Flowers in dense terminal racemes or panicles, short-pedicelled; sepals 5, unequal; petals 5, united below, distinct and reflexed above, scarlet to brick-red, *ca.* ⅝ in. long; stamens 10 to 17, the filaments each bearing a spur; pistil of 3 united carpels. Fruit a 3-valved capsule, containing several winged or marginally hairy seeds. Distribution: West Texas to southern California, south into Mexico.

Ocotillo is not a cactus but is well suited as an ornamental plant in arid areas. Common on rocky hills and slopes west of the Pecos River, plantings have been made along roads by the Texas Highway Department. The resinous stems, when cut and stuck into the ground, soon strike root, and are used in Mexico for "living fences." The conspicuous flowers are most commonly seen between April and June but occur sporadically after rains until late fall.

VIOLET FAMILY   Violaceae

BIRD'S-FOOT VIOLET   *Viola pedata* L.   (PL. 26)

Glabrous perennial herb from a short vertical rootstock. Leaves alternate; petioles 4 to 6 in. long; blades nearly circular in outline, ¾ to 1½ in. across, dissected into 5 to 11 linear lobes, those of the lower leaves often fewer, broader, and round-toothed. Flowers ¾ to 1½ in. across, on peduncles as long as or slightly exceeding length of the leaves; sepals 5, finely pubescent; petals 5, pale lilac or white, the two upper ones commonly deep violet; stamens 5, the anthers conspicuously orange; pistil of 3 united carpels. Fruit a prism-shaped 3-valved capsule ⅓ to ½ in. long. Distribution: Maine to Ontario, south to Florida and Texas.

One of the most beautiful native violets, the Bird's-foot Violet is found in Texas only in the southeastern portion, from Newton County west to Walker County. Unlike most species, this one has fertile showy flowers and does not produce the peculiar cleistogamous type. It prefers acid soils in fields, roadsides, and woodland borders.

At least a dozen other species of *Viola* have been reported from Texas, with flowers ranging in color from violet-purple and rose-violet to yellow and white. Most are found in sandy soils in the eastern half of the state.

MISSOURI VIOLET   *Viola missouriensis* Greene   (PL. 26)

Glabrous stemless perennial herb. Leaves all basal, long-petioled; those of the spring flowering period narrowly cordate-deltoid and usually acuminate; summer leaves broader, with rounded basal lobes

(155)

and pointed apices, rather coarsely crenate-serrate. Flowers axillary, solitary; sepals 5, narrowly white-margined, finely ciliolate; petals 5, the lowest swollen at the base and prolonged backward into a spur, deep to pale violet (rarely white), with a deep violet band beyond the white base, lateral petals bearded; stamens 5, the anthers forming a sheath around the ovary; pistils of 3 united carpels. Fruit a capsule ¼ to ⅓ in. long, splitting 3 ways and forcibly ejecting the many hard shiny seeds. Distribution: Missouri to East Texas and Louisiana.

Although it displays considerable vegetative variation, the genus *Viola*, which includes the cultivated Pansy among its nearly 400 species, shows little departure from the basic floral plan. The anthers form a close ring around the ovary, just below the usually swollen style, in a sunken hollow of which lies the pollen-receptive stigma. The large lower petal is a landing place for visiting bees and butter-flies, its spur a reservoir for nectar secreted by projections of the two lowest stamens. The nectar-seeking visitor must lift the style to gain access to the spur. In doing so he dusts the style and perhaps the stigma with pollen from a previously visited flower, and then re-ceives a shower of pollen from the dislodged anthers of the present flower. Thus, self-pollination is prevented, but, although the mech-anism for cross-pollination seems efficient enough, it is a fact that few of the showy flowers produce seed. Some students of *Viola* believe that insects rarely visit the flowers. In most species seed is produced by a second type of flower borne on the same plant. These are the unopening, budlike, short-stalked cleistogamous flowers, usually appearing after the showy flowers have finished. In these peculiar structures, which never open to admit insects, the pollen grains germinate right inside of the anthers and grow to fertilize the ovules in the neighboring ovary. Thus, self-fertilization is assured. The capsules which may be seen in late spring or early summer are nearly always the products of cleistogamous flowers.

In Texas the Missouri Violet blooms in March and April, and is found in moist, partly shaded places from Lamar, Gregg, and Harris counties, west to Grayson, Erath, and Kerr counties, and sparingly southward to Victoria County.

WILD PANSY   *Viola bicolor* Pursh [= *V. rafinesquii* Greene]
(PL. 26)

Caulescent annual herb to 1 ft., the usually branched stems inconspic-uously pubescent. Leaves alternate, ½ to 1¼ in. long, ovate to spatu-late at least above, with large leafy deeply lobed stipules up to 1 in. long. Flowers axillary, on petioles exceeding the leaves; sepals 5, acute; petals 5, deep violet to pale lavender, the larger lower spurred one usually paler but with violet veins; stamens 5, the anthers forming a ring around the ovary; pistil of 3 united carpels. Fruit (from

(156)

cleistogamous flowers) a light brown 3-valved capsule *ca.* ¼ in. long. Distribution: Maine to Michigan, south to Georgia and Texas.

Blooming from early March to mid-April, the Wild Pansy is found often in great numbers in fields, roadsides, and waste places, usually on sandy soils, in northeastern Texas from Cass and Angelina counties west to Wichita and Erath counties. As with the Missouri Violet, cleistogamous flowers follow the conspicuous ones, the entire reproductive cycle finishing by late April, after which the plants waste away. The Garden Pansy, *V. wittrockiana* Gams., a hybrid probably derived from several Old World species, is similar in vegetative features but is, of course, readily distinguished by the large 3-colored flowers. Also vegetatively similar is the Johnny-jump-up, *V. tricolor* L., a native of Europe commonly cultivated in gardens of the eastern United States but seldom seen in Texas. It has flowers up to 1 in. across in various combinations of yellow, red-violet, blue, and white.

PASSION-FLOWER FAMILY   Passifloraceae

MAY-POP   *Passiflora incarnata* L.   (PL. 27)   **27**

Low-growing perennial vine to 15 or 20 ft., the twigs villous or hirsute, ascending by means of coiling axillary tendrils. Leaves simple, alternate; petioles 1 to 2 in. long, bearing a pair of oblong glands; blades 1½ to 5 in. long, palmately 3-lobed and finely serrate, each tooth tipped with a minute gland, pubescent at least beneath. Flowers perfect, axillary, solitary on bracteate peduncles 1½ to 4 in. long; sepals 5, the united bases forming a shallow cup; petals 5, pale lavender, 1 to 1½ in. long, opening in the morning, the numerous filamentous nectar guides (corona) lavender and purple; stamens purple, their filaments united; pistil 1. Fruit an oval to oblong glabrous berry 1½ to 3 in. long. Distribution: Virginia to Missouri, south to Texas and Florida.

Although much symbolism has been attached to the flowers of the *Passifloras*, they may well be considered as miracles in themselves. Because of their size and showiness, they are attractive to numerous insects, which are guided to the bases of the radiating filaments where, disposed as a ring, a nectar reservoir lies protected by an overhanging flap. The waxy surfaces of the filaments help to keep rain from entering, but are spaced so as to admit the tongues of the nectar-seeking visitors. In newly opened flowers the anthers droop so that pollen is brushed onto the insects' backs. Later, the styles bend down and are dusted with pollen brought from other flowers.

(157)

The fruit, introduced to early settlers by the Indians, is still used in making jellies.

May-pop blooms from May to August and is widely distributed over the eastern half of the state, west to Grayson, Erath, Travis, and Kleberg counties. Among the other species of *Passiflora* in Texas is *P. lutea* L., var. *glabriflora* Fern., a slender vine with 3-lobed leaves which are generally broader than long, and small yellowish flowers less than 1 in. in diameter. It is found in northeastern Texas southwestward to Hays County. *P. affinis* Engelm. is similar but has larger flowers, usually over 1 in. across, also with yellowish petals, and is found in valleys and on hillsides in open woods from Travis and Hays counties west to Llano and Kerr counties. *P. foetida* L., var. *gossypiifolia* (Desv.) Mast., has velvety 3-lobed leaves, the middle lobe far the largest, and white flowers enclosed by 3 much-dissected sticky bracts. It ranges from Calhoun and McMullen counties southward to the Rio Grande.

LOASA FAMILY   Loasaceae

STICK-LEAF   *Mentzelia nuda* (Pursh) Torr. & Gray [= *Nuttallia nuda* (Pursh) Greene]   (PL. 27)

Perennial or biennial herb 1 to 3 ft. tall with 1 to several erect rigid ashy-white stems, mostly unbranched below the middle. Leaves simple, alternate, mostly sessile; blades narrowly ovate or lanceolate, irregularly dentate, 1 to 2 in. long, on both sides beset with stiff hooked hairs. Flowers perfect, in corymbs; sepals 5, united below to form a cylindrical tube; petals 10, greenish yellow to yellowish white, ⅓ to ⅔ in. long; stamens in bundles opposite the petals; pistil 1, the ovary inferior. Fruit an erect cylindrical hispid capsule, the five sepal tips persisting at the top. Distribution: Nebraska to Colorado, Oklahoma, and Texas.

Most abundantly represented in South America west of the Andes, the Loasa Family comprises some 15 genera and 250 species, of which 2 genera and a dozen rather imperfectly distinguished species are found in Texas. *M. nuda,* like the other Texas members of *Mentzelia,* has leaves which feel sandpapery to the touch and which become firmly attached to the clothes of those who brush against them. It is not surprising that sheep ranchers look unkindly on the *Mentzelias,* for the herbage sometimes becomes so enmeshed in the fleece as to lower its market value. *M. nuda* prefers sandy soil in open places in the Trans-Pecos and Panhandle but occurs as far east as Dallas, Travis, and Bexar counties. The flowers, which open in late afternoon and close the following morning, appear from late May to September.

STICK-LEAF   *Mentzelia oligosperma* Nutt. [= *M. monosperma* Woot. & Standl.]   (PL. 27)

Perennial herb to 1½ ft., scabrous with barbed hairs, from a tough fusiform root. Stems often much branched and spreading, straw-colored to ashy white, rough-hirsute. Leaves alternate ovate or ovate-lanceolate, sometimes rhombic, coarsely dentate, often somewhat lobed, ½ to 2½ in. long. Flowers perfect, solitary; sepals 5, persistent, united below to form a tube; petals 5, ¼ to ⅓ in. long, yellow-orange; stamens 20 to 30, forming a ring by union at their bases; pistil 1, the ovary inferior. Fruit a capsule ¼ to ⅓ in. long and *ca.* ⅛ in. thick, containing 1 to 4 seeds. Distribution: Illinois to North Dakota, south to Louisiana, Texas, New Mexico, and Mexico.

This species differs from the preceding not only in its bushier habit but also in that the smaller flowers are diurnal, opening with the morning sun and gradually closing with the intense heat of afternoon. It is found chiefly in limestone soils, most abundantly in the hilly region of Central Texas, west of Navarro, Bell, and Guadalupe counties, to the Trans-Pecos and northward through the Panhandle. *M. texana* Urb. & Gilg., a small-flowered spreading perennial with irregularly lobed and toothed leaves rather triangular in outline, is found infrequently in Brooks, Kenedy, and Medina counties. Much commoner is *M. decapetala* (Pursh) Urb. & Gilg., an attractive species with creamy white 10-petalled flowers 3 to 4½ in. across. It grows in the Panhandle northwestward from Mitchell County. Similar but for smaller flowers, usually less than 2½ in. across, is *M. stricta* (Osterhout) Stevens, an erect perennial ranging from Kleberg and Webb counties northward to Wichita County and through the Panhandle.

CACTUS FAMILY   Cactaceae

TEXAS PRICKLY-PEAR   *Opuntia lindheimeri* Engelm.   (PL. 27)

Erect with a more or less definite trunk to 10 ft. or, more commonly, lower and spreading. Joints (pads) green to blue-green, somewhat glaucous, orbicular to obovate, 4 to 10 in. long. Leaves (on young growth only) fleshy, subulate, ⅕ to ¼ in. long, somewhat flattened, apiculate, soon falling. Areoles (spine patches) distant, 1½ to 2½ in. apart; spines 1 to 6, one 4½ in. long or longer, other(s) shorter, spreading, pale yellow to ashy white, sometimes darkened at base;

occasional plants spineless. Glochids (minute tufted barbed spines) yellow to brown, usually prominent. Flowers perfect, solitary but often crowded, 2 to 5 in. across; sepals several, greenish yellow, grading gradually into the petals, the latter varying from yellow to yellow-orange or red; stamens many, yellow; pistil 1, the ovary inferior. Fruit a fleshy berry, maturing purple, containing numerous seeds. Distribution: South and Central Texas to Tamaulipas, Mexico, and east possibly as far as southwestern Louisiana.

Although there is much dissension among botanists as to the number of genera (21 to 120) to be recognized in the Cactus Family, it can be said with certainty that its 1200 to 1800 species display the most pronounced degrees of desert adaptation. If one considers the general differences between cacti and other plants, he finds that nearly every cactus trait is directed toward conservation of water. Among the more conspicuous characteristics are: reduction or total absence of leaves (few exceptions); presence of spines, variously interpreted as to origin; thick waxy impermeable cuticle; thick stems with much water storage tissue; mucilaginous sap.

The distributional center for the family seems to be southwestern United States and northern Mexico, but of the several species native in the northern United States, at least one ranges well into Manitoba and Saskatchewan, while others in South America ascend to high elevations in the Andes, and still others are epiphytes on trees in the Amazonian rain forests.

Current records show *O. lindheimeri* is found from Travis and Burnet counties west to Brewster County, and south to the Rio Grande. It commonly grows in clumps over wide areas, the monotonous gray-green being brightened in April and May by the flower display. In periods of drought cattle ranchers burn off the spines and glochids to afford their animals forage.

28 TASAJILLO *Opuntia leptocaulis* DC. (PL. 28)

Shrub to 5 ft. with a few to numerous erect or ascending stems. Joints cylindrical, *ca.* ¼ in. in diameter, with rather indistinct tubercles, each bearing 1 or a few spines 1 to 3 in. long. Flowers perfect, solitary but usually crowded, ⅔ to ¾ in. across; sepals several, light green, grading into the greenish-yellow petals; stamens ∞; pistil 1, the ovary inferior. Fruit an ovoid or pear-shaped berry, maturing scarlet, ½ to ⅔ in. long. Distribution: West Texas to southern Arizona and adjacent Mexico.

The Tasajillo, Rat-tail Cactus, or Pencil Cactus, is one of the slenderest cacti known, often forming thickets with its curving spiny stems. It occurs in Texas from McLennan and Hays counties to the Trans-Pecos, south to the Rio Grande. The flowers appear in April and May. Although this species is not so highly prized in cultivation, there are numerous species of West Texas and of regions further west to California which are much favored by fanciers. Ordinarily such interest in the native flora would be praiseworthy, but in the case of cacti a note of concern must be sounded. Not content to raise these plants from seed, dealers and individuals have annihilated entire populations of certain forms in their native habitats, to the extent that recolonization, if at all possible, will be very slow indeed. The fate of many wild orchids, now decimated to the point of extinction, should serve to show what can happen to our cacti unless measures are taken to curb the irresponsible urge to possess, no matter what the consequences.

CHOLLA   *Opuntia arborescens* Engelm. [= *O. imbricata* (Haw.) DC.]   (PL. 28)

> Shrubby, 3 to 12 ft. tall, with few to numerous vertical to horizontal stems, often much branched near their tips. Joints verticillate, cylindrical, with prominent crested tubercles, each bearing a patch of 8 to 30 divergent spines averaging 1 in. in length. Flowers perfect, solitary; sepals several, purplish green, grading into the conspicuous reddish-purple petals; stamens ∞; pistil 1, the ovary inferior. Fruit a dry yellow unarmed berry *ca.* 1 in. across. Distribution: southwestern Colorado through West Texas to Mexico.

When freed of fleshy tissue, the long reticulate cylinders of conductive tissue are used for ornamental furniture, walking sticks, fences, etc. Cuttings, when placed in rows in the ground, eventually become attractive impenetrable hedges. Cholla is a familiar cactus in West Texas and occurs from Howard County west to El Paso County and south to the Rio Grande. It is known well east of this range in cultivation. The blooming period extends from April to early June.

DEVIL'S-HEAD   *Echinocactus texensis* Hopf. [= *Homolecephala texensis* (Hopf.) Britt. & Rose]   (PL. 28)

> Plant usually globose, up to 8 in. high and 1 ft. across, with 13 to 27 prominent ribs. Spines rigid, in patches of 7 on the ribs, spreading or recurved, more or less flattened, unequal, ½ to 1½ in. long, conspicuously annulate. Flowers perfect, solitary, 1½ to 2½ in. across, in a circle at the top of the plant; sepals several, greenish white, grading into the many petals; petals deep pink to red-orange below, pink to nearly white at their tips; stamens ∞; pistil 1, with a 10-lobed stigma, ovary inferior. Fruit a globular berry ½ to 1½ in. across, maturing scarlet. Distribution: Central Texas to New Mexico, south to Mexico.

Also known, rather less fittingly, as the Devil's–pin-cushion, this cactus, though often more below the ground than above, is regarded as a menace in pastures where unsuspecting stock animals can be badly injured by the very strong down-curved spines. The scarlet fruits are more conspicuous than the flowers and often persist for most of the summer, or at least until consumed by birds. Like most Texas cacti, Devil's-head blooms in late spring, the individual flowers lasting but one day. It is found chiefly in sandy fields from Palo Pinto County west to the Trans-Pecos and south to the Rio Grande.

MEADOW-BEAUTY FAMILY   Melastomaceae

MEADOW-BEAUTY   *Rhexia virginica* L.   (PL. 28)

> Erect perennial herb 1 to 3 ft. tall. Stems 4-angled, narrowly winged, pilose. Leaves simple, opposite, the petiole bases of each pair connected by torn ringlike stipules; blade 3-nerved, oblong-elliptic to lanceolate, 1½ to 3 in. long, margin with fine bristle-tipped teeth. Flowers perfect, in terminal corymbs; sepals 4, almost wholly united to form an urnlike cup; petals 4, broad, ½ to ⅔ in. long, rose-violet to pale pink; stamens 8, with long curved yellow anthers; pistil 1. Fruit a 4-chambered capsule containing numerous curved seeds. Distribution: Maine to Florida and East Texas.

Meadow-beauty is the most northerly representative of the large predominantly woody tropical American family, *Melastomaceae*. It is found in low swampy ground in East Texas from Van Zandt and Leon counties east to the Louisiana border. *R. mariana* L., similar but with somewhat flattened 4-angled (not winged) stems, is commoner and occurs in wet places from Gonzales, Milam, and Titus counties eastward. *R. ciliosa* Michx. [= *R. petiolata* Walt.] of extreme southeastern Texas west to Tyler and Hardin counties, is distinguished by its ovate leaves less than 1 in. long. *R. lutea* Walt. has yellow flowers and narrow leaves and occurs rather sparingly from Houston and Walker counties east to Newton and Orange counties. All species flower from late May to September.

EVENING-PRIMROSE FAMILY   Onagraceae

29   CUT-LEAVED EVENING-PRIMROSE   *Oenothera laciniata* Hill (PL. 29)

> Low pubescent annual herb with branched decumbent or ascending stems up to 1½ ft. tall. Leaves alternate, simple but variable, entire to pinnatifid, 1 to 2 in. long, apex acute or nearly so. Flowers perfect,

solitary in leaf axils, ½ to 1 in. across; sepals 4, reflexed, pinkish, united below to form a tube; petals 4, light yellow; stamens 8; pistil 1, the ovary inferior. Fruit a narrowly cylindrical or somewhat tapering capsule containing many seeds. Distribution: Vermont to Nebraska, south to Florida, Texas, and into tropical South America.

This rather inconspicuous Evening-primrose inhabits disturbed ground, in places to the near exclusion of everything else, throughout the eastern half of the state, west to Maverick, Taylor, and Childress counties, sparingly further westward to the Trans-Pecos and northward into the Panhandle. A larger flowered form, var. *grandiflora* (Wats.) Robins., with corollas up to 2 in. across, is common in South and Central Texas, extending northward to Dallas, Archer, and Hardeman counties, and westward to the Trans-Pecos. In both, the flowers, borne from April to July, open in the late afternoon and close the following morning.

BUTTERCUP   *Oenothera triloba* Nutt. [= *Lavauxia triloba* (Nutt.) Spach]   (PL. 29)

Acaulescent winter annual with numerous rosetted basal leaves 5 to 10 in. long; blades entire to deeply and irregularly lobed. Flowers perfect, sessile, usually borne one or two at a time, 1½ to 3 in. across; sepals 4, narrow, basally united from a stalklike tube 1½ to 4 in. long; petals 4, broad and showy, yellow, sometimes lightly 3-lobed; stamens 8; pistil 1, the ovary inferior. Fruit a 4-winged capsule, not opening until after the plant dies, then freeing the many closely packed angular seeds. Distribution: Kentucky to Wyoming, south to Mississippi, Texas, California, and Mexico.

Commonly seen adorning lawns, fields, and roadside ditches on spring evenings, the flowers of Buttercup wither and droop to the ground the next morning. Toward the end of the flowering period, i.e., in late April or early May, the flowers become progressively smaller, the last sometimes measuring less than ½ in. across. Within a month the leaves waste away, leaving only a tight cluster of fruit, the whole rather resembling a pine cone. The seeds sprout with the fall rains and by March the young plants have reached flowering size. Hence the term "winter annual."

Buttercup, not to be confused with the true buttercups of the genus *Ranunculus*, prefers damp limestone soils from Grayson, Navarro, and Goliad counties west to the Trans-Pecos.

PINK EVENING-PRIMROSE   *Oenothera speciosa* Nutt. [= *Hartmannia speciosa* (Nutt.) Small]   (PL. 29)

Low perennial herb from a slender rhizome with tough slender ascending or decumbent stems 8 to 18 in. high. Leaves alternate, simple,

(163)

lanceolate or oblong, rarely linear, 1 to 4 in. long, distantly toothed or pinnatifid. Flowers perfect, in terminal few-flowered spicate clusters, the buds drooping; sepals 4; petals 4, broad and showy, overlapping, rose-pink with reddish veins, yellowish white at base, sometimes entirely white; stamens 8; pistil 1, the inferior ovary topped by the 4-lobed style. Fruit a winged capsule, oblong or elliptic in form, ⅓ to ½ in. long. Distribution: Illinois to Missouri and Kansas, south to South Carolina, Texas, Arizona, and Mexico.

The Pink Evening-primrose commonly colonizes extensive areas along highways and in fields, producing a profusion of flowers from April to June. It grows in East Texas from Orange and Gregg counties west along the Red River to the lower Panhandle and into the Trans-Pecos, south to the Rio Grande. The flowers open in late afternoon, persisting until the next morning, or later on cloudy days, and are favorites of bees, moths, and hummingbirds. The seeds are ripe in June, and if spread about in the garden in late summer, will bring forth some flowering plants the following year and many more in years to come.

FLUTTER-MILL   *Oenothera missouriensis* Sims [= *Megapterium missouriense* (Sims) Spach]   (PL. 29)

Perennial herb from a deep root with gray-pubescent trailing or ascending stems 6 to 24 in. long. Leaves simple, alternate; blades entire, rather thick, silvery gray with copious appressed pubescence, linear-lanceolate to oblong, 1½ to 2½ in. long. Flowers perfect, axillary, 2 to 4 in. across; sepals 4, united below to form a tube 3 to 6 in. long; petals 4, broad and showy, yellow; stamens 8; pistil 1, the inferior ovary deeply 4-angled. Fruit a nearly orbicular capsule 1½ to 3 in. long with 4 very broad wings. Distribution: Missouri and Nebraska south to Texas.

A very drought-resistant plant preferring exposed positions in rocky limestone soils, the Flutter-mill, known also as Ozark-sundrop, Missouri-primrose, or Buttercup, is found from Grayson, McLennan, and Bexar counties northwestward through the Panhandle. The flowers appear in late spring from April to June and, as with many other Evening-primroses, open face upward in late afternoon, drooping closed when struck by the sun's rays the next morning, or remaining open longer in cloudy weather. One of our most beautiful wildflowers, its noctural blooming habits notwithstanding, Flutter-mill would probably brighten more gardens were it not so difficult to transplant. However, if the large seed capsules are picked when dry and papery, the seeds can be shaken out directly where the plants are wanted.

(164)

Low brittle-stemmed perennial, usually with many branches from the
base, 6 to 18 in. high. Leaves simple, alternate, linear or linear-
spatulate, troughlike, sharply toothed, ¾ to 2 in. long, silvery-
canescent, at least when young. Flowers perfect, solitary in upper
axils, ¾ to 1¼ in. across; sepals 4, united below to form a tube; petals
4, obovate, the margins crenulate; stamens 8; pistil 1, with inferior
ovary, the stigma disc-shaped. Fruit a linear-cylindric capsule ½ to
¾ in. long. Distribution: Manitoba and Minnesota to Texas, New
Mexico, and Mexico.

This species of *Oenothera* may be distinguished from our others by
the flowers which, though lasting only a day, remain open during
the daylight hours. It ranges in Texas from Grayson, Brazos, Calhoun, and Cameron counties westward to the Pecos River, and
northward through the Panhandle. Its habitat preference is dry
rocky limestone soil in exposed places. The flowers appear from
April to June. *O. spinulosa* Torr. & Gray is similar but usually of
more erect, slender habit, bearing leaves 1½ to 3½ in. long and
flowers 1½ to 2¼ in. across. It is found in similar habitats over much
the same range as *O. serrulata,* extending a little farther eastward
(Walker County) and westward (Culberson County), but not so
far south (Kenedy County).

WILD-HONEYSUCKLE   *Gaura suffulta* Engelm.   (PL. 30)

Erect hairy-stemmed winter annual 1 to 3 ft. tall, commonly with
numerous ascending branches from the base. Leaves simple, entire,
or sometimes toothed or lobed, linear to spatulate, 1 to 3 in. long.
Flowers in wandlike spikes above the foliage; sepals 4, glabrous beneath, united below to form a tube; petals 4, white, aging deep pink
or red, all directed to upper side of flower, ¼ to ⅓ in. long; stamens 8,
pointing down, the exserted red anthers conspicuous; pistil 1, the
ovary inferior. Fruit an ovoid capsule *ca.* ¼ in. long, 4-winged near
the top. Distribution: Texas and northern Mexico.

The *Gauras* are a distinctive group of plants, mainly because of the
upswept petals and downswept stamens with colored anthers. Wild-
honeysuckle, also known as Bee-blossom and Kisses, grows mainly
in limestone soils, often in patches, from Dallas, Travis, and Frio
counties (occasionally farther eastward) west to the Trans-Pecos
and north into the Panhandle. The flowers are nocturnal, opening
in the late afternoon, the white petals turning rosy pink or nearly
red by the time they wither the next morning. The flowering period
extends from March to May. *G. brachycarpa* Small (PL. 30) is very

(165)

similar but usually has more or less spreading, copiously branched stems, and the undersurfaces of the sepals are pubescent. Its range is similar, although it extends farther south (to Hidalgo County) but not so far west (Uvalde County). Since both of these species hybridize, distinction may in some cases be difficult.

Other *Gauras* known from Texas include Lizard-tail, *G. parviflora* Dougl., our tallest, sometimes reaching 8 ft., but least attractive species, the white flowers borne in slender spikes and bearing petals less than ⅕ in. long. It is found nearly throughout the state west of the East Texas pine forests. At the other extreme is *G. lindheimeri* Engelm. & Gray, with petals ¾ to ⅞ in. long. It resembles Lizard-tail in most respects but is restricted to the extreme southeastern corner of the state, from Newton and Orange counties west to Harris and Brazoria counties.

Gaura coccinea Pursh has very narrow leaves, 5 or more times longer than wide, and white flowers with petals of moderate size, turning deep pink before withering. A perennial to 3 ft., usually much branched, this plant is common west of Wichita, Parker, Travis, and Maverick counties.

FALSE-GAURA   *Stenosiphon linifolium* (Nutt.) Heynh.   (PL. 30)

> Erect short-lived perennial herb, the slender glabrous branched stems reaching 5 to 10 ft. Leaves alternate, sessile; blades entire, linear to lanceolate, 1 to 2½ in. long. Flowers perfect, densely clustered in long spikes; sepals 4, united below to form a filamentous tube ¼ to ½ in. long; petals 4, upswept, white; stamens 8, the anthers yellowish white; pistil 1, the inferior ovary becoming a 1-seeded indehiscent fruit 1/10 in. long. Distribution: Nebraska to Texas.

The distribution of this, the only species of *Stenosiphon*, is, when mapped, rather curious in that it takes the form of a narrow north-south strip. In Texas, False-gaura prefers limestone soils from the eastern Panhandle along the Red River to Grayson County, south to Bexar County. During dry summer weather all but the youngest leaves drop off. The individual flowers are very similar to those of the true *Gauras* but for the hairlike calyx tube and uncolored anthers.

DOGWOOD FAMILY   Cornaceae

EASTERN DOGWOOD   *Cornus florida* L. [= *Cynoxylon floridum* (L.) Raf.]   (PL. 30)

> Shrub or small often wide-spreading tree to 30 ft., with black bark in high ridges. Leaves simple, opposite; blades predominantly several-

(166)

nerved, entire, elliptic to oval, 2 to 6 in. long, acute or short-acuminate at both ends, pubescent beneath, short-petioled. Flowers perfect, in dense headlike clusters subtended by 4 white (rarely pink) petal-like bracts; sepals 4, erect, persistent; petals 4, greenish or yellow-green; stamens 4, exserted; pistil 1. Fruit an elongate red drupe with a 1-seeded stone. Distribution: Massachusetts to Ontario, south to Florida, Texas, and Mexico.

Eastern Dogwood, or Flowering Dogwood as it is known in horticulture, is one of some 60 species of the genus *Cornus:* trees, shrubs, and a few diminutive herbs, widely distributed in north-temperate regions and in tropical mountains. Several species, including the Cornelian-cherry, *C. mas* L., of Europe, Japanese Dogwood, *C. kousa* Bung., and Pacific Dogwood, *C. nuttallii* Audub., as well as the Eastern Dogwood, have the ornamental white, yellowish, or pinkish bracts which have made these plants popular in gardens in much of the United States, especially the East and Pacific Northwest. Our native species seems to be ignored in Texas, at least until the bracts unfold and expand in March and April. Then begins the shameful breaking of branches, if not whole trees, and the carrying of the short-lived blooms to the vase. Indeed, it is uncommon to find in woods near populated areas a roadside dogwood that has not suffered from such ravages. Eastern Dogwood prefers semishade in sandy pine and oak woods from Bastrop, Robertson, and Upshur counties eastward.

Rough-leaf Dogwood, *C. drummondii* G. Mey., a twiggy shrub or low round-headed tree to 15 ft., appears, when flowering in April and May, very different from the preceding species because of the lack of the conspicuous bracts. However, the flowers themselves are very much those of a dogwood, and the creamy white true petals, massed in clusters 3 to 5 in. across, help atone for the loss. This species grows in open woods on a variety of soils, and extends from Liberty, Trinity, and Grayson counties north to Wichita, Brown, and Kerr counties. Two or three close relatives also occur in Texas, chiefly in the northeast corner. Aucuba or Spotted-laurel, *Aucuba japonica* Thunb., a shrub of eastern Asia rather commonly cultivated in the South, is also a member of the Dogwood Family.

CARROT FAMILY   Umbelliferae

WILD CARROT   *Daucus pusillus* Michx.   (PL. 31)   **31**

Hispid-pubescent annual or biennial herb to 3 ft. tall. Leaves alternate, the largest ones basal; petioles with clasping bases; blades finely

31
(Cont.)

pinnately decompound, the ultimate divisions narrowly lanceolate. Flowers perfect, in flat-topped terminal umbels subtended by leafy bracts which exceed the flowering umbel; outermost pedicels ¾ to 1¼ in. long, lengthening and exceeding the bracts in fruit; sepals united to form a minute tube; petals 5, white; stamens 5; pistil 1, the ovary inferior, topped by 2 styles. Fruit 2-celled, ribbed and prickly. Distribution: Virginia to British Columbia, south to Florida and California.

A common weedy plant of roadsides and waste places, the Wild Carrot, or Seed-ticks, is nonetheless possessed of singular delicacy of structure, especially when a single plant is examined. The small white flowers, densely arranged in flat clusters, appear from April to June. When the flowers have passed, the pedicels turn upward, giving the umbel the familiar "bird nest" form, but when the prickly fruits are ripe, the umbel spreads open once again, facilitating adhesion of the fruits to passing animals. Wild Carrot is found over most of Texas, excepting perhaps the northern Panhandle and the middle and upper Rio Grande Valley.

Queen-Anne's-lace, *D. carota* L., larger in most respects, can be readily told from the preceding species by its involucral bracts, shorter than the outermost flowering pedicels, and by the central flower of each umbel, usually a deep purple. Flowering in June and July, this species, an introduction from Europe, is rather infrequent in Texas, being restricted to the north-central portion.

Several other plants of the Carrot Family, most of them smaller and native to the state, are also known as Queen-Anne's-lace. The Garden Carrot, *D. carota* var. *sativa* Hoffm., has been derived from the wild type by a long-term process of selection. However, it does not take long for the domesticated carrot to revert to the wild condition once it has escaped cultivation. Other plants of economic importance in this family include parsnip, *Pastinaca sativa* L., parsley, *Petroselinum sativum* Hoffm., dill, *Peucedanum graveolens* Benth. & Hook., and caraway, *Carum carvi* L. Also well known is the Poison-hemlock of Europe, *Conium maculatum* L., now well established in North America.

ERYNGO   *Eryngium leavenworthii* Torr. & Gray   (PL. 31)

Rigid glabrous perennial herb 1 to 4 ft. tall, branching above. Leaves simple, the lower ones oblanceolate and spiny-toothed, 1½ to 4 in. long, gradually passing into palmately cleft or parted ones on the upper part of the stem, uppermost segments incised-pinnatifid, spiny, about as long as the flower heads. Bractlets 3- to 7-toothed, the terminal ones elongate, resembling the bracts. Fruit 1/16 in. long, crowned by the 3- to 5-toothed sepals. Distribution: Kansas to Central Texas.

This plant, locally common on limestone soils in Central Texas, has an almost bizarre appearance in August and September, when its metallic coloring and iridescence become conspicuous. Not a thistle, as is often thought, but a carrot, it has few rivals for its own peculiar kind of beauty in its late summer flowering period. In some places whole fields take on a violescent cast. Although the rigid plants are easily dried for winter bouquets, the color soon fades. Eryngo is very difficult to transplant successfully, but if seeds are sown as soon as ripe, a colony may be established in the garden, with the expectation of flowers two years later. Eryngo is found from Fannin, Bell, and Comal counties west to Archer, Taylor, and Crockett counties.

Button-snakeroot, *E. yuccaefolium* Michx., is of markedly different appearance, bearing a rosette of linear-lanceolate, bristly-margined leaves, and stems to 2 ft. topped with globose heads of white flowers in July and August. It grows in sandy soils in the eastern third of the state from Grayson, Bastrop, and San Patricio counties to the Louisiana border.

O L I V E   F A M I L Y   Oleaceae

MENODORA   *Menodora longiflora* Gray [= *Menodoropsis longiflora* (Gray) Small]   (PL. 31)

Shrubby herb 10 to 15 in. tall, with erect or ascending usually branched stems. Leaves simple, opposite, or the uppermost sometimes subopposite, mostly sessile; blades ⅓ to 1 in. long, linear-lanceolate, acute, margins entire, or the lower leaves sometimes 3-cleft, revolute. Flowers perfect, few together in terminal corymbs. Sepals 10, basally united to form a tube; petals 5 or 6, yellow, wide-spreading, united below to form a tube 1¼ to 2 in. long; stamens 4, the anthers nearly sessile within the corolla tube; pistil 1. Fruit a capsule ½ to ⅜ in. across, dehiscent by loss of its top.

This species, differing from the following by its yellow buds, hidden stamens, and generally larger size, is locally common in fields, pastures, and roadsides in South Central and Trans-Pecos Texas, more specifically from Travis and Hays counties to Culberson and Presidio counties. Other species in Texas include: *M. scabra* Gray, a low tufted perennial of the Trans-Pecos with linear leaves and bright yellow flowers; *M. laevis* Woot. & Standl., of similar habit and range, but with ovate leaves; *M. ramosissima* (Steyerm.) Tharp, a taller, branched species with elliptic to oblong-lanceolate leaves, found in the upper Rio Grande Valley; *M. longifolia* (Steyerm.) Tharp, similar to the preceding but with linear-lanceolate leaves, restricted to the foothills of the Chisos Mountains in Brewster County.

The Olive Family is best known to us through its woody, mostly cultivated members, among which are Privet (*Ligustrum*), Lilac (*Syringa*), Golden-bells (*Forsythia*), Ash (*Fraxinus*), Jasmine (*Jasminum*), Fringe-tree (*Chionanthus*), and of course the Olive (*Olea*). Spring-herald, or Devil's-elbow, *Forestiera acuminata* (Michx.) Poir. and other species, is a native shrub of this family.

REDBUD *Menodora heterophylla* Moric. [= *Bolivaria grisebachii* Scheele] (PL. 31)

Small mostly glabrous perennial 2 to 6 in. tall, forming patches from creeping rootstocks. Leaves simple, opposite, sessile or nearly so; blades pinnately 3- to 7-cleft or -parted, ¼ to ¾ in. long, the segments mostly linear-oblong and acute, uppermost leaves often entire. Flowers perfect, solitary; sepals 5 to 15, united to form a tube, persistent; petals 5 or 6, yellow, commonly red or red-violet on outer surfaces, united below to form a tube shorter than the sepal lobes; stamens 2 or 3, the anthers exserted from the corolla tube on long filaments. Pistil 1, the ovary 2-celled. Fruit a membranous capsule ⅖ to ½ in. broad, with 2 seeds in each cavity. Distribution: Texas and adjacent Mexico.

Common in the Rio Grande Valley and extending northward through Central Texas is the low, spreading plant known as Redbud, an unfortunate duplication of the name more fittingly applied to the well-known shrubs and trees of the genus *Cercis* in the Pea Family. But vernacular names are conceived and used without regard to subsequent confusion, and we must accept them as the names by which wildflowers are known to most people. In this case the buds are indeed reddish, but the inner surfaces of the petals, revealed when the flowers open, are clear yellow. The blooms measure about ¾ in. in diameter and first appear as early as Christmas time in the lower Rio Grande Valley, as late as July in North Central Texas and sporadically until early fall throughout its range. Redbud tolerates a variety of soils, and has Mitchell, Stephens, and Taylor counties as its northern limits.

GENTIAN FAMILY Gentianaceae

32 MEADOW-PINK *Sabatia campestris* Nutt. (PL. 32)

Glabrous annual with erect stems 4 to 15 in. tall, dichotomously and more or less widely branched. Leaves simple, opposite, blades ovate to ovate-lanceolate, often wider toward the base of the stem, ½ to 1½ in. long, acute or apiculate. Flowers perfect, in dichotomously corymbose cymes; sepals 4, 2 of them narrow, deep green, prominently ribbed, united below, ¾ to 1¼ in. long; petals 4, lilac, purplish rose, or pink, oval or obovate, united below, the free ends as long as or shorter than the calyx lobes; stamens 5, joined to the short corolla tube; pistil 1. Fruit a capsule ¼ to ⅜ in. long, 2-valved, much-enclosed by the persistent calyx tube.

In the flowers of Meadow-pink, also called Texas-star or Rose-pink, we find a remarkable exhibition of protandry, a phenomenon in which the anthers shed their pollen before the stigmas of the same flower are ready to receive it. When a flower opens, the anthers stand erect on 5 short filaments where insects, mostly short-tongued bees, have ready access to the pollen. But the visitor cannot effect self-pollination because at this time the style lies flat, its two long slender branches twisted together, with their stigmatic lines concealed. In a few days, as the filaments wither and the empty anthers gradually sink down to the petals, the style assumes an erect position, its branches untwisting and straightening, to expose the pollen-receptive stigmatic lines. Pollen-dusted insects, seeking young flowers, inadvertently stumble into older ones and in probing about quite accidentally dust the stigmas. Meadow-pink is found in the eastern half of Texas, from the western edge of the pine forests to Childress, Taylor, and Medina counties. The flowers appear from May to July.

BLUE-BELL   *Eustoma grandiflorum* (Raf.) Shinners [= *E. russellianum* (Hook.) G. Don]   (PL. 32)

Glaucous annual herb with stems 1 to 3½ ft. tall, more or less branched. Leaves opposite, the blades sessile or clasping, 1 to 3 in. long, ovate or oblong, acute or apiculate. Flowers solitary or a few together; calyx glabrous, ½ to ¾ in. long, the 5 or 6 lobes subulate, usually erose-denticulate; petals 5 or 6, lavender-purple, cuneate to obovate, joined at the base to form a tube, the tube and lobes 1½ to 2¼ in. long; stamens 5 or 6, joined to throat of the corolla tube; pistil 1. Fruit an oblong capsule, ½ to ⅔ in. long, pointed. Distribution: Nebraska and Colorado south to Texas and New Mexico.

The flowers of the Blue-bell resemble those of the Meadow-pink in general plan, and have the same pollination mechanism, although the behavior of the stamens and styles is a little different. Blue-bell flowers from June to September and prefers low places in the limestone soils of Central Texas, but occurs in nearly all parts of the state except the pine forests of the east and the mountains of the west. *E. exaltatum* (L.) Salisb., with blue flowers and oval-elliptic capsules about 1 in. long, is found in the southern half of the state from Jefferson, Calhoun, and Cameron counties west to the Trans-Pecos. The Mountain-pink, *Erythraea beyrichii* T. & G., appearing as pink

(171)

mounds in June and July on the gravelly roadsides of Central Texas, is another member of the Gentian Family. All these plants are destined to become scarce in years ahead unless the ravages of florists and selfish people are curtailed. They are already uncommon in some places, virtually extinct in others.

MILKWEED FAMILY   Asclepiadaceae

BUTTERFLY-WEED   *Asclepias tuberosa* L.   (PL. 32)

Perennial herb with one to several, erect to ascending stems 1 to 3 ft. tall, the sap watery. Leaves simple, all or most alternate; blades lanceolate to nearly linear, 1½ to 3½ in. long, the margins entire and narrowly revolute. Flowers perfect, in many-flowered, terminal, or lateral umbels corymbosely arranged at stem ends; sepals 5; petals 5, united below, the lobes narrowly oblong, obtuse, ½ to ¾ in. long, greenish to reddish orange; stamens 5, each bearing a bright orange or yellowish petal-like corona; pistils 2. Fruit a follicle 2½ to 4 in. long, minutely pubescent, usually only a few together. Distribution: Maine to Minnesota, south to Florida and Texas.

PURPLE MILKWEED   *Asclepias brachystephana* Engelm.   (PL. 32)

Perennial herb with erect or ascending stems 6 to 15 in. tall, usually very leafy, lightly pubescent when young, the sap milky. Leaves simple, alternate, lanceolate or linear, glabrous in age, entire. Flowers perfect, arranged in 3 to 9 few-flowered umbels; sepals 5; petals 5, united below, the lobes *ca.* ¼ in. long, lavender-purple to greenish violet; stamens 5, the coronas shorter than the anthers, obtuse; pistils 2. Fruit a follicle 2¼ to 2¾ in. long, ovate, long-pointed, canescent when young. Distribution: Wyoming and Kansas south to western Texas, Arizona, and northern Mexico.

33   GREEN MILKWEED   *Asclepias oenotheroides* Cham. & Schlecht. [= *A. lindheimeri* Engelm. & Gray]   (PL. 33)

Perennial herb with simple or branched, decumbent or ascending stems 1 to 1½ ft. tall, with milky sap. Leaves simple, alternate; petiole flat, ⅓ to ¾ in. long, blades broadly oval or oblong, the upper ones often narrower, 2 to 3½ in. long, obtuse or rounded at apex. Flowers perfect, arranged in umbels, the lower ones pedunculate, the upper nearly or quite sessile; sepals 5; petals 5, united below, the lobes *ca.* ⅓ in. long, greenish white; stamens 5, each bearing a white corona about twice as long as the stamen; pistils 2. Fruit a follicle, ovate to lanceolate, long-pointed, 2½ to 4 in. long, erect on a recurving stalk. Distribution: Texas to New Mexico and northern Mexico.

The Milkweeds are a genus of about 200 species, mostly of warmer

(172)

regions of the United States and Mexico, well known for their milky juice and silky-appendaged air-borne seeds. What is not so well known is the curious means by which the flowers are pollinated. The pollen grains are united in masses, each mass called a pollinium. Each anther produces just two pollinia. In addition, each anther produces an inverted Y-shaped structure, the translator, which hangs downward. At the foot of the Y is a sticky gland, and the end of each arm is linked to a pollinium by a thread. The translator is so placed that when a nectar-seeking insect catches one of its legs between two of the closely placed anthers, considerable effort must be exerted to draw it back, and in the process the translator with its two attached pollinia is pulled out. The whole structure dries very quickly and tightly clasps the insect's leg. Inevitably the insect will fall into the same trap in the next flower, where these pollen masses are caught and torn off on the receptive style, while simultaneously a new translator and pollinia are pulled from the subtending anthers. The petals of milkweeds appear superficially to be in two sets, but the inner set, known as the corona, arises from the stamens. The exact nature of the corona seems to be a matter of some dispute.

The Butterfly-weed, also called Pleurisy-root in reference to the presumed medicinal value of the enlarged taproot, is common in fields and open woods in East Texas, less so in Central Texas and the Panhandle, and bears its bright red-orange flowers from May to July. Green Milkweed usually has several ascending stems growing from a stout root and produces its flowers in early summer. It commonly occurs scattered over hills and along highways in Central, South, and West Texas. The many stems of the Purple Milkweed or Short-crowned Milkweed bear crowded narrow leaves and small clusters of purplish flowers in the upper axils. It is a species of the Trans-Pecos region. Another Green Milkweed, *A. viridis* Walt., of East and Central Texas, has low-lying stems radiating from the root-crown. The greenish flowers with violet nectar receptacles appear from April, sometimes through the summer, and are distinctive because of the spreading, not reflexed, sepals. About 25 other species of Milkweed occur in the state.

MORNING-GLORY FAMILY   Convolvulaceae

SHAGGY EVOLVULUS   *Evolvulus nuttallianus* Roem. & Schult.
(PL. 33)

Densely silky perennial herb from a stout root, with much-branched ascending or spreading stems 6 to 12 in. long. Leaves simple, alternate, sessile or short-petioled; blades oval or oblong, ⅓ to ⅔ in. long, entire, densely pubescent on both sides, acute at the apex. Flowers perfect, solitary on very short pedicels in the leaf axils; sepals 5, united at the base, ⅕ to ¼ in. long; petals 5, united to form a funnel, *ca.* ⅓ in. across, pale to deep lavender. Fruit a capsule *ca.* ⅛ in. long. Seeds 1 to 4. Distribution: North Central Texas from Grayson to Bexar counties and westward.

This plant, sometimes called the Dwarf Morning-glory, is most commonly found on poor, dry soil in open positions, and occurs from Fannin and Travis counties westward to the Trans-Pecos and Panhandle. Rather similar but with leaves glabrous above and flowers white is *E. sericeus* Sw. This species grows in similar situations from Chambers and Tarrant counties west to the Trans-Pecos. *E. alsinoides* L. var. *hirticaulis* Torr. has ovate leaves, pedicels to 1 in. long, and white flowers, and is found in Aransas and Llano counties west to the Trans-Pecos. All species flower from early spring to fall and would appear well suited to rock gardens.

Pony-foot or Dichondra, *Dichondra repens* Forst. var. *carolinensis* (Choisy) Michx., is the familiar lawn plant, a prostrate, node-rooting perennial, also of this family, found wild in damp places from Tarrant, Blanco, and Calhoun counties eastward to the Louisiana border. Four additional species are known in Texas; of these *D. argentea* Willd., a silvery pubescent plant of the Trans-Pecos, is most distinctive. Dichondras have small inconspicuous flowers and globular two-chambered capsules.

TEXAS BINDWEED   *Convolvulus hermannioides* Gray   (PL. 33)

Silky-tomentose perennial twining herb. Stems commonly branched at base, the branches often procumbent, 3 to 8 ft. long. Leaves simple, alternate; blades ovate, oblong, or oblanceolate, ¾ to 3½ in. long, sinuate or incised-toothed, cordate at base; petioles half as long as blades or shorter. Flowers perfect, axillary on peduncles shorter than the subtending leaves; sepals 5, united at base, *ca.* ⅓ in. long; petals 5, united to form a 5-pointed funnel, white or pale pink, with a deep red throat, ¾ to 1 in. long and ⅔ to ¾ in. across; stamens 5; pistil 1. Fruit a rounded or depressed long-beaked capsule ¼ to ⅓ in. long. Seeds usually 4. Distribution: Central Texas.

WILD MORNING-GLORY   *Ipomoea trichocarpa* Ell.   (PL. 33)

Perennial twining herb, commonly flowering the first year, with stems usually somewhat branched, sometimes trailing, up to 15 ft. or more in length. Leaves simple, alternate; petioles as long as the blades or shorter; blades ovate in outline, cordate, entire or with indented or lobed margins, 1½ to 5 in. long. Flowers 1 to 3 in axillary clusters, perfect; sepals 5, hirsute at least near the tip, oblong or oblong-lanceolate, ⅓ to ½ in. long; petals 5, united to form a funnel, pink, deep purple at base of throat, 1 to 1⅔ in. long, 1½ to 2¼ in. broad. Fruit a subglobose capsule *ca.* ⅓ in. across, more or less pubescent. Distribution: South Carolina to Florida and Texas.

Few families have as high a proportion of ornamental plants as the Morning-glory Family. Most members are twining or creeping herbs with brightly colored, often large, funnelform flowers. Texas Bindweed is a slender trailing or twining plant with gray-green foliage and white or pink, red-centered flowers from May to September, and is almost restricted to open places on limestone soils from Dallas and Eastland counties south to Karnes County. *C. incanus* Vahl is similar but lacks the red throat in its white or pink flowers. It is found throughout most of the state west of Denton, Brazos, and Matagorda counties. *C. arvensis* L., a weedy tuberous-rooted creeper or twiner from Europe with green, entire, sparsely pubescent leaves and white or pale pink flowers up to 2 in. across, occurs in the northern half of the state and in the Trans-Pecos.

The Wild Morning-glory or Purple Morning-glory is an abundant perennial in Central and South Texas, becoming a troublesome weed in cultivated land. Eradication is difficult owing to the long horizontal tuberous roots, any piece of which can produce shoots. The flowers are borne in summer. *I. trichocarpa* var. *torreyana* (Gray) Shinners differs only in having entirely glabrous sepals, and is found in South Texas, less commonly in the central area. Indian-potato, *I. pandurata* (L.) G. Mey., is a milky-juiced perennial trailing and twining vine of sandy pine woods in East Texas, growing from an enormously thickened starchy root which in old plants may weigh as much as 25 lbs. This species too is a troublesome weed in fields, although when allowed to twine on a fence or arbor, its prolifically produced white, purple-throated flowers are indeed handsome.

GOAT-FOOT–CREEPER   *Ipomoea pes-caprae* (L.) Sweet   (PL. 33)

Glabrous succulent perennial herb with prostrate, creeping, sparingly branched stems up to 30 ft. long. Leaves simple, alternate; petioles approaching blades in length; blades sub-orbicular, 2 to 4 in. broad, usually notched at the apex, rounded or cordate at the base. Flowers perfect, 1 to several on stout axillary peduncles; sepals 5, oval or sub-orbicular, glabrous, *ca.* ⅓ in. long; petals 5, united to form a funnel 1½ to 2¼ in. long and 2 to 3¼ in. broad, the rim unevenly wavy, pale to rosy violet with a deeper violet throat. Fruit a capsule ½ to ⅔ in. high. Distribution: littoral regions from Georgia to Florida and Texas, and throughout most of the tropics and subtropics.

While hardly a roadside wildflower, the Goat-foot–creeper is unquestionably worthy of notice as one of our most attractive wild Morning-glories, in this case adorning the coastal dunes, often in the company of the Beach Morning-glory, *I. stolonifera* (Cyrill) J. F. Gmel., a white-flowered species of more slender habit.

Other species of *Ipomoea* include *I. purpurea* (L.) Voight, an annual of tropical America, often cultivated for ornament, but now widely escaped in much of eastern North America; the Cypressvine, *I. quamoclit* L., with leaves divided into filiform segments and red flowers less than 1 in. across, a native of tropical America north to southern United States; Bush Morning-glory, *I. leptophylla* Torr., an erect often much-branched nontwining perennial herb to 4 ft. with linear leaves, pink or purplish flowers, and an enormous thickened root, occurring in the Panhandle and northward.

34 DODDER *Cuscuta* spp. (PL. 34)

> Herbaceous parasitic herbs with white, yellow, or orange stems and minute scalelike alternate leaves. Seeds germinating in the soil but stems soon dying from the base, thence attached to host plant(s) by suckers and weakly dextrorsely twining. Flowers perfect, small, numerous, arranged in cymes; sepals 3 to 5, united; petals 3 to 5, united, usually white, the flower ⅕ to ¼ in. across; stamens usually 5, arising from corolla throat; pistil 1, with 2 styles. Fruit a subglobose capsule, 1 to 4-seeded. A genus of *ca.* 170 species of temperate and tropical regions throughout most of the world.

Seemingly very unlike Morning-glories but in fact closely related to them, the Dodders or Love-vines are represented in Texas by about 25 species. All are total parasites, having no true leaves or green pigment, ranging in color from white to brown-orange, and produce numerous small white flowers. The stems, often suggestive of tangles of rusty threads, are sensitive to contact and, somewhat in the manner of tendrils, clasp their supports tightly. A Dodder stem rarely makes more than three turns around any one host branch. At the points in closest contact, a stem produces suckers which penetrate the tissues of the host, establishing organic union with them, and drawing off the food materials it requires. Success of the Dodder's methods depends not only on the physiology of the union, but also on the germination of the Dodder's seeds after those of the host. Dodder seedlings develop short anchorage roots and the rapidly elongating stem swings about like a wand in search of a host. Up to this point all growth is supported by food reserves in the seed. When contact is established with a host, the Dodder's root and lower stem die. The species are rather difficult to distinguish, most confining themselves to one or a few kinds of host plants.

(176)

WATERLEAF FAMILY   Hydrophyllaceae

TEXAS BABY-BLUE-EYES   *Nemophila phacelioides* Nutt.   (PL. 34)

Annual herb 3 to 24 in. tall, usually much branched from the base, the young parts hirsute. Leaves simple or pinnately compound, alternate; petioles shorter than the blades; blades pinnately divided, the 5 to 9 segments entire or sometimes incised, the upper ones confluent. Flowers perfect, solitary in the axils of the upper leaves, on slender peduncles ¼ to ½ in. long; sepals 5, united, the lanceolate lobes bristly, *ca.* ⅓ in. long, acute, accompanied by ovate or oblanceolate appendages *ca.* ¼ in. long; petals 5, united, blue-lavender with a paler center, the lobes obovate to cuneate, often notched at the apex, the corolla ⅔ to 1 in. across; stamens 5, arising from the corolla; pistil 1. Fruit a globular capsule *ca.* ¼ in. across. Distribution: Arkansas and Central and southeastern Texas.

Nemophila is a genus of 25 or 30 species of southern, central, and western North America, some commonly grown as garden ornamentals. Texas Baby-blue-eyes flowers in April and May and occurs mainly on clay soils in damp places from McLennan and Kendall counties southeastward to Orange and San Patricio counties, more sparingly northward. *N. microcalyx* (Nutt.) F. & M. is a smaller plant bearing leaves with only 3 or 5 segments, and white or pale blue flowers less than ¼ in. in diameter. It is found in damp places in southeastern Texas, mainly near the coast.

BLUE-CURLS   *Phacelia congesta* Hook.   (PL. 34)

Softly hirsute or cinereous annual herb with simple or sparingly branched stems 4 to 24 in. tall. Leaves alternate, petiolate, 2 to 4½ in. long, pinnately compound with 3- to 7-toothed blunt leaflets, often with smaller leaflets interposed. Flowers perfect, arranged in terminal uncurling one-sided racemes; sepals 5, united, the lobes bristly, linear to linear-spatulate, *ca.* ¼ in. long, acute; petals 5, united, bluish purple to lavender-blue, the lobes rounded, half as long as the tube, the corolla ¼ to ⅓ in. across; stamens 5, arising from the corolla; pistil 1. Fruit an ovoid capsule less than ¼ in. long, minutely hirsute. Distribution: Central, South, and West Texas.

The *Phacelias* are a genus of 100 or more species of herbs, mostly of western North America, one of which, the California Blue-bell, *P. whitlavia* Gray, is commonly grown as a bedding plant. Of the dozen or more species in Texas, Blue-curls is the most widely distributed, often forming carpets along highways and in open woods. It ranges from Palo Pinto, Washington, and Hidalgo counties west to the Trans-Pecos. Flowers appear from April to early summer,

(177)

sometimes later with adequate moisture. *P. patuliflora* (Engelm. & Gray) Gray (PL. 34), with lower stems glabrous and the uppermost leaves sessile and simple, has larger but fewer flowers in April and May, and extends from Fort Bend, Burnet, and Tom Green counties southward to the Rio Grande. *P. strictiflora* (Engelm. & Gray) Gray of North Central Texas, with the lower leaves usually on short winged stalks and attractive bluish-purple flowers in erect elongate one-sided racemes, blooms in late March and April. *P. popei* Torr. & Gray is a Trans-Pecos species with finely divided fernlike leaves and erect densely flowered spikelike racemes of purplish flowers from April to June. Dwarf Phacelia, *P. depauperata* Woot. & Standl., also of West Texas, seldom exceeds 6 in. in height and has small blue flowers in one-sided spikes in March and April.

In the flowers of all species nectar is secreted at the bases of the ovary and corolla, but this store is shielded from ready access by little flaps at the bases of the stamens. Hence a bee must work to reach the nectar, and in doing so jars the pollen-bearing anthers. These shower the visitor by explosively turning inside-out.

PHLOX FAMILY Polemoniaceae

35 PRAIRIE PHLOX *Phlox pilosa* Michx. (PL. 35)

Erect pubescent perennial herb from a branching root, the few to several stems 8 to 20 in. tall, simple, or branched above. Leaves simple, opposite, sessile; blades linear to narrowly lanceolate, 1 to 3 in. long, long-tapered to an acute apex. Flowers perfect, in lax terminal corymbose clusters; sepals 5, united to form a tubular calyx *ca.* ⅓ in. long, each lobe terminating with a long bristle; petals 5, pale rose to bluish lavender, rarely white, united below to form a more or less pubescent tube ⅖ to ⅗ in. long, the lobes obovate, sometimes blunt-tipped; stamens 5, of differing lengths; pistil 1, 3-chambered. Fruit a broadly ovoid capsule *ca.* ⅛ in. long. Distribution: southeastern Canada to Florida and Texas.

DWARF PHLOX *Phlox nana* Nutt. (PL. 35)

Much-branched perennial herb from a somewhat woody base, the slender rather rough-pubescent and often glandular-pubescent stems erect or ascending, 3 to 12 in. tall. Leaves simple, opposite, sessile; blades linear, often narrowly so, 1 to 2 in. long, pubescent to nearly glabrous. Flowers perfect, 1 to 4 in upper axils; sepals 5, ½ to ⅔ in. long, united by pubescent papery margins below to form a tube, the long-projecting lobes linear; petals 5, usually bright pink, *ca.* 1 in.

across, united to form a tube slightly longer than the sepals, the 5 lobes broadly ovate or orbicular; stamens 5, unequal in length; pistil 1, 3-chambered. Fruit a 3-seeded capsule 1/5 to 1/4 in. long. Distribution: West Texas to southeastern Arizona and adjacent Mexico.

Prairie Phlox, sometimes called Sweet-william, is a rather common plant of open low places, especially stream borders, found from East Texas west to Young, Terrell, and Uvalde counties, and flowering in April and May. Dwarf Phlox is found in canyons and on mountain sides west of the Pecos River. The flowers are seen principally in April and May, but with adequate moisture the blooming period continues, often intermittently, to September. Moss Phlox, *P. subulata* L., a native of eastern United States, flowering in Texas in March and April, is a mat-forming perennial commonly cultivated as a bedding plant.

ANNUAL PHLOX *Phlox drummondii* Hook. (PL. 35)

Annual herb 6 to 15 in. tall, usually branched, the basal branches opposite and often ascending to the height of the main stem; upper branches alternate, obliquely ascending; viscid-pubescent with long soft hairs. Leaves simple, the lower ones opposite and oblong-spatulate, less than 7 times longer than wide, the upper alternate and oblong, often wider than the lower leaves, all 1¼ to 2½ in. long, viscid-pubescent, somewhat clasping at the base. Flowers perfect, in terminal corymbs; sepals 5, united below, 1/3 to 3/8 in. long, the lobes about as long as the tube; petals 5, united below to form a tube 5/8 to 3/4 in. long and a salverlike flare 3/4 to 1¼ in. across, the lobes obovate, bright rose-red to carmine or purple, usually with a deeper red or purple eye, but very variable in intensity, paler beneath; stamens 5, arising from and included within the corolla tube; pistil 1, 3-chambered. Fruit a pearly globose capsule *ca.* 1/8 in. across. Seeds usually 3. Distribution: southeastern Texas.

ANNUAL PHLOX *Phlox glabriflora* (Brand) Whitehouse (PL. 35)

Annual herb with widely branched stems 12 to 24 in. long, spreading or ascending, softly pubescent. Leaves simple, mostly opposite, the lower nearly glabrous, linear-lanceolate, 1¼ to 2¾ in. long, more than 7 times longer than wide, the upper shorter and proportionately broader. Flowers perfect, in loose cymes, usually 4 or 5 flowers on a peduncle; sepals 5, united below, *ca.* 1/3 in. long, long-pubescent, the linear lobes slightly longer than the tube; petals 5, united below to form a glabrous tube 3/8 to 5/8 in. long and a flare *ca.* 3/4 in. across, lobes broadly obovate-cuneate, lavender with a pair of basal white spots, throat dark bluish purple; stamens 5, within the tube; pistil 1, 3-chambered. Fruit an ovoid capsule *ca.* 3/16 in. long. Seeds mostly 3. Distribution: South Texas.

ANNUAL PHLOX   *Phlox cuspidata* Scheele   (PL. 35)

Annual herb with slender stems 4 to 9 in. tall, usually simple below and branched above, glandular-pubescent. Leaves simple, upwardly diminishing in size, the lower opposite, spatulate-oblanceolate, less than 7 times longer than wide, nearly glabrous, ⅔ to 1⅓ in. long, the upper leaves alternate, linear-lanceolate. Flowers perfect, in cymes, each with 1 to 4 pedicels and each pedicel 4-flowered; sepals 5, united below, *ca.* ¼ in. long, the lobes longer than the tube, glandular-pubescent; petals 5, united to form a tube ⅓ to ⅜ in. long and a flare ⅜ to ⅝ in. across, the lobes cubeate, pointed, lilac-purple with 2 basal maroon marks rimmed with blue; stamens 5, within the tube; pistil 1, 3-chambered. Fruit a globose capsule *ca.* ⅛ in. across. Seeds mostly 3. Distribution: East Texas.

ANNUAL PHLOX   *Phlox cuspidata* var. *humilis* Whitehouse
(PL. 35)

Similar to *P. cuspidata* but usually less than 6 in. tall, of slenderer habit, and with a smaller corolla, usually less than ⅜ in. across. Distribution: Coastal South Central Texas.

There are few better botanical ambassadors from the state of Texas than the Annual Phloxes. A rather complex assemblage of hybrids developed in Europe has been for years marketed in the horticulture trade as *P. drummondii,* the principal parent species. The distinctions among the several presently recognized wild species are in most cases rather fine details of flower color and hairiness, those illustrated representing common extremes. The wild *P. drummondii* occurs in sandy post-oak woods, often along roads, in a crescent-shaped area from Goliad County north to Brazos County and southwest to Wilson County. It is an erect or somewhat decumbent plant, usually growing in masses, with showy pink-to-deep-red flowers from April to June. A somewhat more slender, finely hairy plant is *P. cuspidata,* with bluish lavender flowers that show considerable variability in size, ranging from ¼ in. in diameter in var. *humilis* to nearly ¾ in. in var. *grandiflora* Whitehouse (not figured). Its range is similar to that of *P. drummondii* but extends south to San Patricio County and north to Navarro County, and from the Dallas-Fort Worth area north to the Red River, almost always in sandy soils. The small- and large-flowered varieties are commonest in the more southerly portion of the range. Limited to the triangle formed by Nueces, Jim Wells, and Willacy counties is *P. glabriflora,* with hairless pinkish-lavender flowers. Not too much faith can be put in flower color as a guide to the Annual Phloxes, for there seems to be considerable variability in most species, even in local populations, partly reflective of hybridization, soil, exposure, and age of the flower examined. Identification often proves very difficult in South Central Texas, where these and several other forms all grow and apparently hybridize, at least where opportunity permits. Seven species and varieties, in addition to those mentioned above, have been described from the state.

WHITE GILIA   *Gilia longiflora* (Torr.) G. Don [= *Collomia longi-*   **36**
flora Gray]   (PL. 36)

Glabrous annual or biennial herb 8 to 20 in. tall, loosely branched. Leaves alternate, the lower pinnately divided into long slender filaments, the upper undivided and filiform. Flowers perfect, arranged in more or less flat-topped corymbs; sepals 5, united below to form a tube; petals 5, white, united below to form a tube 1½ to 2 in. long and a flare ¾ to 1 in. across, lobes orbicular or ovate; stamens 5, on filaments of unequal length in the corolla tube; pistil 1, 3-chambered. Fruit a capsule. Distribution: Nebraska to Texas, west to Utah and Arizona.

BLUE GILIA   *Gilia rigidula* Benth.   (PL. 36)

Glabrous or viscid-glandular perennial herb 4 to 12 in. tall with slender, diffusely branched stems from a stout woody base. Leaves alternate, the lowermost (when present) crowded in rosettes, divided into 3 to 7 linear segments, reduced upwardly on the stem. Flowers perfect, solitary in the axils of the reduced upper leaves, on pedicels ¾ to 2 in. long; sepals 5, united below to form a tube; petals 5, blue-violet, yellow at center, united below to form a short tube, lobes ⅓ to ⅝ in. long; stamens 5, arising from the corolla tube; pistil 1, 3-chambered. Fruit an ovoid capsule *ca.* ¼ in. long, obscured by the sepals, rupturing the calyx tube when ripe. Distribution: Central Texas west to the Panhandle and New Mexico, south to northern Mexico.

STANDING-CYPRESS   *Ipomopsis rubra* (L.) Wherry [= *Gilia rubra* (L.) Heller]   (PL. 36)

Glabrous, strictly erect, usually unbranched annual or biennial herb to 6 ft. or more. Leaves alternate, copious throughout, the 11 to 17 segments and the rachis filiform or linear. Flowers perfect, in terminal spikes or a compact narrow panicle; sepals 5, united below to form a tube; petals 5, united to form a yellowish, red-speckled tube 1 to 1⅓ in. long and a scarlet (rarely yellow or white) flare ½ to ¾ in. across; stamens 5, arising from the corolla tube; pistil 1, 3-chambered. Fruit a capsule *ca.* ¾ in. long, containing numerous seeds. Distribution: South Carolina and Florida, west to Arkansas and Central Texas.

The Gilias and their close relatives are an American group of about 120 species of often showy annual, biennial, and perennial herbs, commonest in dry regions of the western half of the continent,

(181)

especially in California. Standing-cypress is certainly one of Texas' most striking wildflowers, with erect wandlike stems clothed with feathery foliage and topped from May to July with a column of scarlet trumpets, rather suggestive of those of the Cypress-vine, a member of the Morning-glory Family. A widely cultivated annual or biennial, the Standing-cypress' native Texas range is from the eastern and central portions west to Taylor and Gillespie counties. White Gilia is a lower usually much-branched plant of West Texas, from Childress County southwest to the Trans-Pecos, with long-tubed white or pale lavender phloxlike flowers from May to September or even later. Blue Gilia is a low much-branched perennial with blue, yellow-centered flowers borne from April to October. This species is found over most of the state west of Shackelford, Williamson, and Live Oak counties. Pollination in most Gilias is by butterflies, moths, and hummingbirds. The proboscis or bill of a nectar-seeking visitor is dusted with pollen from the anthers. These organs soon shrivel or drop off, and the 3-parted stigma, supported on the elongating style, is brought into position for cross-pollination by visitors from younger flowers.

NIGHTSHADE FAMILY   Solanaceae

PURPLE GROUND-CHERRY   *Quincula lobata* (Torr.) Raf. [=*Physalis lobata* Torr.]   (PL. 36)

Diffusely branched perennial herb with striate often zigzag stems usually less than 1 ft. long, spreading or ascending, whitish-granulose when young, becoming glabrous with age. Leaves simple, alternate; petioles winged or margined; blades oblanceolate to oblong or spatulate, deeply and irregularly toothed, or pinnatifid with rounded lobes, rarely subentire, tapering to the base, 1½ to 3 in. long. Flowers perfect, usually in axillary pairs, the peduncles at first erect but soon reflexing; sepals 5, united to form a bell-shaped or urn-shaped calyx which at length becomes much enlarged and encloses the fruit; petals 5, united to form a flat salver, bluish purple, the corolla ¾ to 1¼ in. across; stamens 5, the yellow anthers tinged with purple; pistil 1, 2-chambered. Fruit a greenish or yellowish ovoid berry *ca.* ¼ in. long, enveloped by the 5-angled papery calyx. Distribution: Kansas to California, south to Texas and northern Mexico.

This hardy little plant apparently thrives in the most difficult situations, seemingly unaffected by prolonged drought. The showy purple flowers and attractive hanging bladdery-inflated calyces recommend the plant for a place in the front of the garden, especially in places

(182)

where summer drought is the rule. Purple Ground-cherry, or Chinese-lantern-of-the-plains, as it is sometimes called, ranges in Texas from Wichita, Travis, and Hidalgo counties west to the Trans-Pecos and the Panhandle, flowering irregularly from March to fall.

GROUND-CHERRY   *Physalis angulata* L.   (PL. 37)   **37**

Glabrous annual herb with angular branched stems 1½ to 3 ft. tall. Leaves simple, alternate; petioles ¾ to 1½ in. long; blades ovate, more or less cuneate at the base, sharply few-toothed, 1½ to 3 in. long. Flowers solitary in leaf axils, on peduncles ¾ to 1¼ in. long, at first erect but later reflexed; sepals 5, united to form a 5-lobed, bell-shaped, membranaceous bag which becomes much enlarged and encloses the fruit; petals 5, united at their bases, yellow with purplish bases, the corolla ¼ to ½ in. across; stamens 5, joined to the fused petal bases; pistil 1, 2-celled. Fruit a yellow berry nearly 1 in. in diameter, almost filling the inflated calyx when ripe. Distribution: North Carolina to Texas, southward to Brazil and the West Indies.

GROUND-CHERRY   *Physalis viscosa* L. var. *cinerascens* (Dunal) Waterfall [= *P. mollis* Nutt. in part]   (PL. 37)

Perennial herb from horizontal rootstocks with numerous stems 1 to 2½ ft. tall, whitish- or grayish-tomentose with branched hairs. Leaves simple, alternate; petioles ¾ to 1½ in. long; blades rounded-cordate, the uppermost sometimes broadly ovate, usually coarsely and bluntly toothed, less frequently entire, 1½ to 3½ in. long. Flowers perfect, solitary in the axils, on erect but soon reflexed peduncles 1 to 2 in. long; sepals 5, united to form a 5-lobed, bell-shaped, membranaceous bag; petals 5, united at their bases, bright yellow with purple bases, the corolla ½ to ⅔ in. across, pubescent beneath; stamens 5, joined to the fused petal bases, the anthers yellow or violet-tinged; pistil 1, 2-celled. Fruit a yellow berry ⅓ to ½ in. across, enclosed by the much inflated calyx. Distribution: Arkansas and Texas west to California and south to Mexico.

The Ground-cherries are, with one or two exceptions, rather weedy plants, all of the cosmopolitan genus *Physalis*. There are about 100 species in all, of which some 10 occur in Texas. All have the distinctive, much-enlarged calyx enveloping the berry. *P. angulata* is found mainly in the eastern third of the state, from Tarrant, Bexar, and Cameron counties to the pine forests of extreme East Texas, and flowers from April to October. *P. viscosa* var. *cinerascens* has a similar blooming period but is more generally distributed, occurring throughout most of the state west of Denton, Walker, and Calhoun counties. While the ripe berries of all species are probably edible, those of the Winter-cherry, *P. alkakenji* L., a cultivated plant from Japan, are particularly suited for use in preserves. The Strawberrytomato or Cape-gooseberry, *P. peruviana* L., has bright red-orange calyces when the berries are ripe, and is sometimes grown as an ornamental.

TROMPILLO   *Solanum eleagnifolium* Cav.   (PL. 37)

> Perennial herb to about 2 ft., the stems usually more or less armed with aciculate spines, sometimes unarmed; always silvery with downy hairs. Leaves simple, alternate; petioles ⅓ to ¾ in. long; blades broadly oblong to linear-oblong, 2 to 6 in. long, undulate, the apex obtuse, often oblique at base. Flowers perfect, arranged in few-flowered axillary cymes, the pedicels only slightly enlarged beneath the calyx; sepals 5, united at their bases, persistent; petals 5, basally joined, the lobes triangular-ovate, the corolla ¾ to 1 in. across, pale violet or white; stamens 5; pistil 1, 2-celled. Fruit a subglobose berry ⅓ to ⅝ in. across, yellow, at length black. Distribution: Missouri and Kansas to Texas and Arizona.

Although August is not a month that is noted in Texas for its display of wildflowers, it is perhaps the time when the more unusual qualities of the Trompillo may be appreciated. The silvery foliage, purple corollas, yellow anthers, and touches of green, purple, yellow, and black in the pendant berries all combine to leave a pleasing impression; it is not surprising that outside of its native range, especially eastward, the Trompillo or Silverleaf Nightshade is not uncommonly seen as a garden plant. Within Texas this species occurs almost generally, but most commonly on limestone soils in the central and southern portions. It flowers from May to early fall, most freely before July except where moisture is adequate.

WHITE NIGHTSHADE   *Solanum triquetrum* Cav.   (PL. 37)

> Glabrous perennial herb, often forming clumps, with slender, branched stems 1 to 5 ft. long, sometimes twining. Leaves simple, alternate; petioles slender, usually less than ½ as long as blades; blades lanceolate to ovate, entire or irregularly few-toothed or lobed, sometimes reduced to 3 or 5 fingerlike lobes, ¾ to 2½ in. long. Flowers perfect, arranged in few-flowered cymes; pedicels club-shaped, ¼ to ⅓ in. long; sepals 5, united at the base, the lobes triangular-ovate; petals 5, united at the base, white or sometimes purplish, the corolla ½ to ⅝ in. across, the lobes marginally hairy near their ends; stamens 5, yellow; pistil 1, 2-chambered. Fruit a pea-sized red berry. Distribution: Texas and northern Mexico.

This is a rather attractive plant with deep green foliage, five-pointed white flowers, and red berries, well suited for cultivation against low fences. In regions having mild winters the leaves are more or

(184)

less evergreen, and where water is plentiful during the summer the stems will elongate and become vinelike. In the wild, White Nightshade is frequently a component of thickets, especially along fences and in hedges. It ranges from Erath, McLennan, and Chambers counties southwestward to the Rio Grande and the Trans-Pecos. The flowers are most plentiful from March to May but in damp places the flowering period extends to midsummer.

BUFFALO-BUR   *Solanum rostratum* Dunal   (PL. 38)   **38**

Hoary or yellowish-pubescent annual, usually forming a low, rounded, much-branched plant 8 to 24 in. tall. Stems and leaves copiously armed with subulate prickles of varying length. Leaves alternate, once or twice pinnatifid, 3 to 6 in. long, the segments irregular, rounded, prickly on the veins. Flowers perfect, in lateral clusters, the pedicels slightly enlarged upward; sepals 5, united, forming a flat corolla ¾ to 1¼ in. across, yellow, the lobes broadly ovate; stamens 5, yellow, one anther enlarged; pistil 1, 2-chambered. Fruit a subglobose berry ⅓ to ½ in. in diameter, invested by the copiously spiny calyx. Distribution: South Dakota and Tennessee, southwestward to Mississippi, Texas, and northern Mexico.

HORSE-NETTLE   *Solanum dimidiatum* Raf. [= *S. torreyi* Gray] (PL. 38)

Cinereous, somewhat scurfy perennial herb, with erect or ascending stems 1 to 3 ft. tall. Stems and leaves usually sparingly armed with subulate prickles; sometimes unarmed. Leaves alternate, simple; petioles stout, less than ⅓ as long as the blades; blades ovate in outline, 2½ to 6 in. long, usually sinuately lobed but sometimes nearly entire, cuneate or cordate at the base. Flowers perfect, in lateral cymes; pedicels densely pubescent and sometimes prickly; sepals 5, united, the lobes rounded and with subulate tips; petals 5, united to form a flat 5-pointed corolla 1 to 1¼ in. across, bluish purple, rarely white; stamens 5, yellow; pistil 1, 2-chambered. Fruit a subglobose yellow berry ⅓ to ⅝ in. across. Distribution: Kansas and Arkansas, south to Texas.

Solanum is a cosmopolitan genus of some 1500 species, most of them tropical and quite a few of economic importance. *S. lycopersicum* L. is the Tomato, *S. tuberosum* L. the Potato, and *S. melongena* L. the Egg-plant. Other economic plants of the Nightshade Family include *Atropa belladonna* L., the Belladonna plant; *Capsicum frutescens* L., the Sweet and Hot Peppers; *Petunia violacea* Lindl., the Garden Petunia; and *Lycium chinense* Mill., the Matrimony-vine. Buffalo-bur, a weedy plant often abundant on disturbed soils, ranges over most of the state west of the pine forests of extreme East Texas, and flowers from June to October. Horse-nettle blooms in late spring and early summer, and occurs in Central Texas from Grayson, Wichita, and Martin counties south to Uvalde and Washington counties.

MUSTARD-TREE   *Nicotiana glauca* Graham   (PL. 38)

Glabrous often glaucous shrub or small tree to 15 ft. Leaves simple, alternate; petioles slender, less than ½ as long as the blades; blades usually ovate, 2 to 6 in. long, sometimes longer, entire or irregularly undulate. Flowers perfect, arranged in loose racemes or panicles up to 9 in. long, the pedicels ⅓ to ½ in. long; sepals 5, almost entirely united, ⅜ to ⅝ in. long, the lobes lanceolate or triangular, much shorter than the tube; petals 5, united to form a narrow terminally dilated pubescent tube 1¼ to 1½ in. long and *ca.* ⅓ in. across, pale yellow, the lobes blunt; stamens 5, arising from the base of the corolla tube, not protruding; pistil 1, 2-chambered. Fruit an ovoid capsule ⅓ to ½ in. long containing numerous small seeds. Distribution: native of southern South America, widely naturalized in Mexico and southern United States.

Mustard-tree, or Coneton, or Tronadora, as it is variously called, is presently known from three widely separated regions in Texas, but undoubtedly is becoming quite general in the southern portion of the state. It occurs in the Trans-Pecos south of Pecos and Jeff Davis counties, in the lower Rio Grande Valley in Willacy, Hidalgo, and Cameron counties, and in Central Texas in Travis and Burnet counties. The plant is occasionally cultivated and flowers from April to December. Wild Tobacco, *N. repanda* Willd., is a finely pubescent annual herb to 2 ft. with clasping leaf bases and white long-tubed petunialike flowers from April to June. It occurs from Terrell, Travis, and Aransas counties south to the Rio Grande. Economically important plants in the genus *Nicotiana* include the Commercial Tobacco, *N. tabacum* L., and the Flowering Tobacco, *N. longiflora* Cav.

SMOOTH JIMSON-WEED   *Datura stramonium* L.   (PL. 38)

Glabrous or glabrate annual herb, usually with widely branching sometimes purplish stems, 1 to 4 ft. tall. Leaves simple, alternate; petioles usually shorter than the blades; blades green, ovate to oblong, 4 to 9 in. long, acute at the apex, sinuately or laciniately toothed or lobed. Flowers perfect, solitary in the leaf axils; pedicels ¼ to ½ in. long; sepals 5, united to form a tube 1 to 2 in. long, the lobes triangular lanceolate; petals 5, united to form a flaring funnel 2 to 4 in. long and 1½ to 2¼ in. across, white or lavender, opening in the late afternoon and closing by midmorning, the 5 lobes prolonged into slender tips; stamens 5, arising from the corolla tube; pistil 1, 2-chambered. Fruit a spiny subglobose capsule 1½ to 2¼ in. long. Distribution: Nova Scotia to Minnesota, south to Florida and Texas.

HAIRY JIMSON-WEED   *Datura wrightii* Regel [= *D. meteloides* DC.
of authors]   (PL. 38)

Finely and densely gray-pubescent annual herb 1 to 4 ft. tall. Leaves
simple, alternate; petioles pubescent, mostly shorter than the blades;
blades finely gray-pubescent, especially on the veins, ovate, entire or
with a few coarse teeth or lobes, 4 to 10 in. long, the broadly cuneate
or cordate base often oblique. Flowers perfect, solitary in the leaf
axils; sepals 5, united to form a tube 3 to 5 in. long, the lobes lanceolate or ovate; petals 5, united to form a funnel 6 to 9 in. long and
4½ to 6 in. across, white; stamens 5, arising from the corolla tube;
pistil 1, 2-chambered. Distribution: Texas to California and adjacent
Mexico.

The flowers of these bold annuals are adapted for cross-pollination
by nocturnal moths, although long-tongued bees and hummingbirds
may also be seen as participants. The sweetish flowers open at dusk,
exposing the store of nectar at the base of the corolla tube. On still
evenings a patch of Jimson-weeds is often swarming with hawk
moths, darting from flower to flower, never alighting, but extending
their long probosces to partake of the sugary nectar and, quite incidentally, to distribute pollen from flower to flower. The whole plant
is quite poisonous, but, owing to its unpleasant odor and taste, is
rarely consumed by stock. *D. stramonium* is known to contain the
alkaloid sedatives hyocyamine and atropine, but the plant is rarely
used as a source for these materials. The Sacred Datura of India,
D. metel L., has herbage and seeds with a higher concentration of
narcotic alkaloids. Smooth Jimson-weed is found in extreme East
Texas, sparingly westward to the Panhandle, chiefly in disturbed
soils, perhaps most frequently in barnyards, stock pens, and along
fences. Hairy Jimson-weed is commoner, occurring from Taylor and
McLennan counties, southward to the Rio Grande and west to the
Trans-Pecos. Both species flower from late May to October.

BORAGE FAMILY   Boraginaceae

PUCCOON   *Lithospermum incisum* Lehmann [= *L. linearifolium*   **39**
Goldie]   (PL. 39)

Strigose perennial herb with appressed pubescence. Stems tufted, 4 to
12 in. tall, simple or sparingly branched above, arising from a long
red taproot. Leaves simple, alternate, sessile, the lowest ones in a
rosette; basal leaves oblanceolate, pubescent, 1¾ to 2½ in. long; stem
leaves linear, becoming smaller near the flowers. Flowers perfect, in a
short leafy raceme; sepals 5, united; petals 5, united to form a 5-lobed

salver ½ to ⅔ in. across, its tube ¾ to 1¼ in. long, crested in the throat, the lobes rounded and lacerate, bright yellow; stamens 5, arising from the corolla tube; pistil 1, 4-lobed. Fruit of 4 oblong-ovoid nutlets *ca.* ⅛ in. long, each containing a hard, bony, white seed. Distribution: Manitoba to British Columbia, south to Illinois, Texas, and Arizona.

The Puccoons, or Gromwells, comprise a genus of about 50 species of hairy low perennials of temperate regions, there being 15 species in North America and 3 in Texas. *L. incisum* is found in fields and roadsides almost throughout the state, but shows a preference for the sandy soils of the eastern half. With the exception of the frilled golden yellow flowers, the plant is rather suggestive of the garden forget-me-not. *L. caroliniense* (Walt.) MacMillan, with wider leaves and yellow-orange flowers in April and May, occurs in sandy soil from Wilson County northeast to Wood and Hardin counties, and in the East Cross Timbers (Hill County northward) and West Cross Timbers (Comanche County northward). *L. matamorense* DC., an annual with small white flowers, occurs southward from La Salle and Live Oak counties.

WIDE-FLOWERED HELIOTROPE   *Heliotropium convolvulaceum*
(Nutt.) Gray [= *Euploca convolvulacea* Nutt.]   (PL. 39)

Pale strigose-hirsute annual herb, the much-branched stems 3 to 20 in. tall. Leaves alternate, simple, ½ to 1¼ in. long, short-petioled; blades oblong to narrowly lanceolate, acute at the apex, entire. Flowers perfect, in axils of leaflike bracts, on short pedicels; sepals 5, united; petals 5, united to form a white salver ⅓ to ⅔ in. across, the tube pubescent, constricted at the throat, the margins of the lobes irregular and wavy; stamens 5, arising from the corolla tube; pistil 1, 2-lobed. Fruit of 2 one-seeded nutlets ⅛ to ⅙ in. long, enclosed by the calyx tube. Distribution: Nebraska to Utah, south to Texas, Arizona, and northern Mexico.

The Heliotropes are a large genus of over 220 species of herbs and shrubs, mostly of the tropics. The Wide-flowered Heliotrope, with conspicuous white flowers from June to September, is rather well distributed over the state, but seems commonest in three regions: the Panhandle and eastward along the Red River; the Trans-Pecos; South Texas below Goliad County. The Slender Heliotrope, *H. tenellum* (Nutt.) Torr., a more delicate annual with much smaller white flowers, from May to October, is found on limestone soils, chiefly in Central Texas. The Creeping Heliotrope, *H. procumbens* Mill., usually has long, rather weak stems resting on neighboring plants and elongate one-sided spikes which appear to unroll in the manner of young fern leaves. The white flowers appear from June to October. A native of tropical America, this plant is known only from Kenedy

County southward. Salt Heliotrope, *H. curassavicum* L., a more robust plant, also from tropical America, has fleshy leaves and branched spikes of very small white flowers. It prefers moist alkaline soils, chiefly in West and South Texas. The Garden Heliotrope, *H. peruvianum* L., so popular for its fragrant purple flowers, is a native of western South America.

VERBENA FAMILY   Verbenaceae

PRAIRIE VERBENA   *Verbena bipinnatifida* Nutt.   (PL. 39)

Perennial herb, usually diffusely branched from the base, the hispid-hirsute stems prostrate or ascending, sometimes striking root, up to 1 ft. long. Leaves opposite, bipinnatifid with linear or oblong lobes, ¾ to 2¼ in. long, appressed-hirsute on both sides, margins often revolute. Flowers perfect, in bracted pedunculate spikes which elongate in fruit, the bracts linear-subulate, exceeding the sepals; sepals 5, united at the base, ¼ to ⅔ in. long, hispid-hirsute, the lobes very slender, unequal; petals 4, united, bluish purple, or reddish purple in partial shade, the corolla tube ⅜ to ⅝ in. long, pubescent outside, the flare *ca.* ½ in. across, the lobes emarginate, unequal; stamens 4, arising from the corolla tube; pistil 1, 4-lobed. Fruit of 4 cylindric nutlets. Distribution: South Dakota to Alabama, west to Arizona and northern Mexico.

The Prairie Verbena is one of the most abundant wildflowers in Texas, from the points of view of both distribution and period of flowering. While commonest on limestone soils, it is found throughout most of the state, the only exceptions being the pine forests of the East and the most desertous western regions. It flowers most freely in the spring, but in moist situations in the southern part of the state the flowers keep coming nearly throughout the year. The low matted habit suits the plant well for edge-work in the garden. Restricted to the Trans-Pecos is a plant of similar habit, Wright's Verbena, *V. wrightii* Gray, an annual with leafy erect or spreading stems and rosy or light purple flowers in spring.

LOW VERBENA   *Verbena pumila* Rydb.   (PL. 39)

Annual herb, erect or somewhat decumbent, simple or with few to several opposite branches, hirsute, 2 to 10 in. tall. Leaves opposite; petioles usually shorter than the blades; blades once or twice 3-cleft or parted, the segments broadly lanceolate to obovate, ½ to 1½ in. long. Flowers perfect, in short terminal bracted spikes which become 1½ to 2½ in. long in fruit; sepals 5, united at base, *ca.* ¼ in. long;

petals 4, united to form a tube ⅓ to ⅜ in. long and a flare ⅛ to ¼ in. across, rose-purple; stamens 4, arising from corolla tube; pistil 1, 4-lobed. Fruit of 4 nutlets enclosed by the persistent calyx. Distribution: Oklahoma to Texas and New Mexico, and southward into Mexico.

In popular parlance, the species of genus *Verbena* fall into two categories: the creeping Verbenas and the erect Vervains. Originally the latter term was restricted to *V. officinalis* L. of Europe, a garden plant sometimes escaped in Texas, formerly of great repute as a remedy in eye diseases, its "bright-eyed" corolla supposedly indicating its virtues in that direction. Of the more than 200 species of *Verbena* known, some 45 occur in Texas. Low Verbena is a rather inconspicuous plant, often locally abundant, frequenting fields, pastures, and roadsides over most of the state, but mainly west of Grayson, McLennan, Victoria, and Cameron counties. It flowers from late February to May. The Garden Verbena, *V. hybrida* Voss, is derived from several South American species. Slender Vervain, *V. halei* Small, closely resembles *V. officinalis* but occurs wild in the eastern half of the state, producing spikes of small bluish flowers from April to June and intermittently to mid-fall. Large-flowered Vervain, *V. canescens* H. B. K., is a perennial with clumps of erect stems 1 to 2 ft. tall, topped with spikes of violet-blue flowers ⅜ to ⅝ in. across. It is found from Scurry, Brown, and Bell counties south to the Rio Grande and west to the Trans-Pecos. *V. plicata* Greene is very similar but with each leaf base forming a wing on part of the petiole. Its range is that of *V. canescens* plus a northward extension to the Red River.

40   Lantana   *Lantana camara* L.   (PL. 40)

A branching shrub 3 to 5 ft. tall, the stems sometimes prickly. Leaves opposite, simple; petioles about ⅓ as long as the blades; blades ovate to oblong-ovate, 1½ to 4 in. long, acute or short-acuminate, finely crenate-serrate with 18 to 25 teeth on each side, usually rounded at the base. Flowers perfect, in dense headlike spikes arising from the leaf axils; sepals 5, united below; petals 4 or 5, united to form a tube ¼ to to ⅓ in. long, the flare *ca.* ¼ in. across, white or lavender with an orange center; stamens 4, of 2 lengths, arising from the corolla tube; pistil 1, 2-chambered. Fruit a drupe with 2 one-seeded nutlets. Distribution: tropical America; commonly cultivated and escaping in extreme southern United States.

L. camara is mainly a cultivated plant in Texas, but south of Walker, Travis, and Edwards counties it sometimes escapes and becomes naturalized in waste places. Texas Lantana, *L. horrida* H. B. K., is a commoner native species, resembling the foregoing but having 10

(190)

to 18 rather coarse teeth on each margin of a leaf and yellow or orange flowers which turn red with age. It blooms throughout most of the year in extreme southern Texas, and from April to October in the central portion. Its range is from Chambers, Travis, and Val Verde counties to the Rio Grande, but is known in cultivation and as an occasional escape northward to the Red River. *L. montevidensis* (Spreng.) Briq. is a slender trailing plant of southern South America, with deep lavender flowers, commonly cultivated throughout most of Texas south of the Panhandle. *L. macropoda* Torr. is a native aromatic shrub, usually less than 3 ft. tall, with white or pink yellow-eyed flowers in a spike which becomes longer than wide, found from El Paso to Brewster counties, east to Fort Bend and Houston counties. All species behave as perennial herbs in the northern half of Texas excepting the Panhandle, where only in exceptionally mild winters will they survive.

FROG-FRUIT   *Phyla incisa* Small   (PL. 40)

> Creeping or trailing often node-rooting perennial herb with 4-angled frequently purplish branches, often swollen at the nodes. Leaves opposite, simple; sessile or very short-petioled; blades narrowly oblong to broadly obovate, freely to sparsely spreading-dentate above the middle, entire below, base cuneate, ⅓ to 2 in. long, ⅛ to ⅔ in. broad. Flowers perfect, in short erect axillary spikes supported on peduncles ¾ to 2½ in. high, at first globose but later more elongate; sepals 4, united at base; petals 4, united to form a tube *ca.* ⅛ in. long and a flare about as wide, white with a yellow throat; stamens 4, arising from corolla tube; pistil 1, 2-chambered. Fruit of 2 one-seeded nutlets, enclosed by the calyx. Distribution: Colorado and Missouri to Texas and California and adjacent Mexico.

The genus *Phyla* embraces some 15 species and varieties, the 7 Texas representatives frequently grading one into another and therefore often difficult to identify. *P. incisa*, often a component of lawns, is found throughout most of the state south of the Panhandle and flowers from April to November. *P. cuneifolia* (Torr.) Greene is similar but the flowering heads are on peduncles about as long as the leaves. It occurs from the Panhandle to the Trans-Pecos, eastward to Dallas and Travis counties. *P. lanceolata* (Michx.) Greene, with narrow leaves broadest below the middle and toothed from below the middle to the tip, grows in East Texas from Bowie, Anderson, and Jefferson counties west to Bexar and Wise counties. *P. nodiflora* (L.) Greene is a highly variable species, often with small, appressed, forward-pointed teeth on the outer half of leaves which are usually broadest above the middle. It is found over most of Texas but most commonly southeastward from Grayson, Llano, and Val Verde counties.

(191)

MINT FAMILY Labiatae

SKULL-CAP *Scutellaria drummondii* Benth. (PL. 40)

Annual or biennial herb from a taproot, hirsute or villous-hirsute, with erect or ascending square stems 3 to 12 in. tall, often branched at the base. Leaves opposite, simple; petioles *ca.* 1/3 as long as the blades; blades ovate-oblong or oval, 1/3 to 3/4 in. long, obtuse, entire or crenate-undulate, cuneate or abruptly narrowed at the base. Flowers perfect, solitary in the axils of leaflike bracts, the peduncles shorter than the calyx, erect or ascending; sepals 5, united, at first less than 1/8 in. long, lengthening to *ca.* 1/4 in. in fruit; petals 5, united to form a 2-lipped corolla, bluish purple, pilose, the 4-lobed lower lip *ca.* 1/5 in. across, the upper much smaller; stamens 4, barely ciliate; pistil 1, 4-chambered. Fruit of 4 very small nutlets. Distribution: Kansas to Texas.

The Skull-caps comprise a large nearly world-wide genus of about 200 species, 9 or 10 of which occur in Texas. Ours are mostly perennial herbs with bluish-purple, or rarely white flowers in leafy spike-like racemes. S. *drummondii* is a clump-forming plant in prairies and fields in nearly all parts of the state, flowering in April and May. S. *parvula* Michx. has clumped stems 3 to 12 in. tall from a curious rhizome intermittently swollen and constricted, having the appearance of a string of beads. It is found in open situations in the eastern third of the state, mainly on sandy soils. S. *resinosa* Torr. is a perennial with woody lower stems and root, reaching 1 ft. Unlike the foregoing spring-flowering species, this plant flowers from April to July and again in September and October. It grows in fields and roadsides in the Panhandle southeastward to Taylor and Runnels counties.

SKULL-CAP *Scutellaria integrifolia* L. (PL. 40)

Softly or finely pubescent perennial herb with erect stems to 3 ft. tall, usually branched above. Leaves opposite, simple; sessile or short-petioled; blades variable, the lower ovate to oblong-ovate, 1/3 to 1 1/4 in. long, often coarsely toothed, the upper ones narrower, sometimes linear, up to 2 in. long, entire. Flowers perfect, in bracted racemes or panicles, each subtended by a bract; sepals 5, united, *ca.* 1/6 in. long, becoming 1/4 to 1/3 in. long in fruit; petals 5, united to form a 2-lipped corolla 2/3 to 1 in. long, blue, more or less pubescent, the tube dilated in the middle, the lower lip notched; stamens 4, the anthers ciliate; pistil 1, 4-lobed. Fruit of 4 nutlets *ca.* 1/25 in. across. Distribution: Rhode Island to Florida, west to Ohio and Texas.

Members of the Mint Family have the petals united, forming a 2-lipped corolla that restricts visiting insects to a definite position in regard to the pollen-bearing anthers and the pollen-receptive stigma while they probe for nectar at the base of the flower. The lower lip acts as an attracting flag and also as a landing place, while the upper lip serves as a hood to shelter the essential organs, these usually being situated so as to touch the visitor's back. The length of the corolla tube varies considerably among species and genera, and with it the kind of insect pollinator. The majority are bee-flowers, but others, such as the Horsemints, are suited to butterflies, and some of the Sages attract hummingbirds. The Skull-cap is found in East Texas from Cass, Robertson, and Harris counties east to the Louisiana border. The flowering period is in April and May.

RATTLESNAKE-FLOWER   *Brazoria scutellarioides* (Hook.) Engelm.   **41**
& Gray   (PL. 41)

Erect annual herb, glabrous below the inflorescence, the stems simple or paniculately branched, 3 to 15 in. tall. Leaves opposite, simple; all but the lowest sessile and somewhat clasping the stem; blades oblong or oblanceolate, serrate above the middle, acute at the apex, 1 to 2 in. long. Flowers perfect, in densely glandular-puberulent terminal racemes 1½ to 6 in. long; bracts ovate, acuminate at the apex, *ca.* ⅛ in. long; sepals 5, united to form a 2-lipped calyx, *ca.* ¼ in. long, the lobes very unequal, the tube inflated but abruptly constricted at the base; petals 5, united to form a 2-lipped corolla ⅓ to ½ in. long, rosy lavender with a paler, spotted throat, tube dilated at the middle, upper lip broader than long, the lower with 3 broad lobes, the middle one notched; stamens 4, arising from the corolla tube; pistil 1, 4-lobed. Fruit of 4 nutlets, each about ⅟₂₅ in. across. Distribution: Central and South Texas.

The Rattlesnake-flowers, or Brazos-mints, of which there are but two species, both restricted to Texas, may be distinguished from the Skull-caps, with which they are sometimes confused, by the unequally- but straight-toothed, 2-lipped calyx, that of the Skull-caps having a rounded or humped upper lip which at length bends down to close the opening and hide the nutlets within. *B. scutellarioides* is found in damp places, often on stream banks, from Dallas, Parker, and Taylor counties south to Kleberg and Val Verde counties, and flowers in April and May. *B. truncata* (Benth.) Engelm. & Gray is somewhat larger in most respects, the stems pubescent to the base, and bears purplish flowers up to 1 in. long, veined with deeper purple, in April and May. It is a gregarious plant, often forming large masses, and is found in damp, sandy places from Anderson and Atascosa counties southeast to Matagorda and Goliad counties.

LION-HEART   *Physostegia intermedia* (Nutt.) Engelm. & Gray
[= *Dracocephalum intermedium* Nutt.]   (PL. 41)

Annual herb with erect or ascending stems 1 to 3 ft. high, often unbranched. Leaves opposite, simple, relatively few; sessile, slightly clasping; blades linear or linear-lanceolate to narrowly oblong, ¾ to 2¼ in. long, acute at the apex, subentire or shallowly toothed. Flowers perfect, short-pedicellate, in spicate racemes with small bracts; bracts ovate, *ca.* ⅕ in. long; sepals 5, united to form a tube with 5 triangular teeth; petals 5, united to form a puberulent 2-lipped corolla ⅓ to ½ in. long, tube much dilated upward, the wavy upper lip nearly erect, the lower spreading, its middle lobe about twice as long as the 2 lateral ones; stamens 4, arising from the corolla tube; pistil 1, 4-lobed. Fruit of 4 ribbed or angled nutlets *ca.* ⅟₁₅ in. long. Distribution: Kentucky to Arkansas, south to Louisiana and Texas.

Most of the Texas *Physostegias* are well suited to garden culture, being easily raised from seed or transplanted. With them at hand, one may observe their pollination devices. One pair of anthers stands a little in front of the other pair, and the style poses the 2-lobed stigma between them. When one examines flowers of different ages, he sees that first the anthers split open and expose their pollen to contact with visitors—bees, some butterflies, and occasional hummingbirds—and that later the style bends downward, placing the stigma lobes, which before were pressed together but now spread apart, where visitors dusted with pollen from younger flowers will touch them. This is a common device, general in the Mint Family and in several other families. Lion-heart occurs in damp places from Lamar, Travis, and Gonzales counties east to the pine forests of extreme East Texas. *P. purpurea* Blake, of similar habit and range, has more deeply colored flowers. *P. angustifolia* Fern. has showier flowers up to 1¼ in. long and is found mainly in Northeast Texas. These 3 species flower from April to June. Dragon-head, *P. digitalis* Small, is a larger plant, sometimes reaching 6 ft., ranging from the pine forests of East Texas west to Van Zandt and Harris counties, and flowering in June and July. *P. virginiana* (L.) Greene, variously known as Lion-heart, Dragon-head, and Obedient-plant, is a perennial flowering from July to September. It is found from Hill, Blanco, and Matagorda counties eastward to the pine belt, but is frequently cultivated elsewhere.

HEAL-ALL   *Prunella vulgaris* L.   (PL. 41)

Perennial herb with erect or decumbent pilose stems 3 to 24 in. tall. Leaves opposite, simple; petioles less than half as long as the blades; blades lanceolate to ovate-oblong, entire or shallowly toothed, obtuse or acute at apex, often undulate. Flowers perfect, in dense cylindrical terminal spikes; bracts kidney-shaped, abruptly pointed; sepals 5, united to form a calyx ⅕ to ¼ in. long, dilated upward, the ribs extended into subulate tips; petals 5, united to form a 2-lipped corolla, bluish violet with a lighter portion on the lower lip, rarely all white,

½ to ⅔ in. long, upper lip notched, the lower fringed; stamens 4, arising from the corolla tube; pistil 1, 4-lobed. Fruit of 4 elliptic nutlets *ca.* ¹⁄₁₅ in. long. Distribution: rather general in moist areas in North America and Eurasia.

Heal-all or Self-heal is an attractive square-stemmed perennial, usually only a few inches high, but sometimes up to 2 ft. or more. The purplish flowers are produced from April to June, and in Texas the plant ranges from Grayson, Anderson, and Harris counties eastward. The common names allude to the employment of this species in folk medicine for the preparation of decoctions which were used to reduce external and internal inflammations.

HENBIT   *Lamium amplexicaule* L.   (PL. 41)

Sparingly pubescent winter annual with diffusely branched spreading or ascending branches 4 to 15 in. long. Leaves opposite, simple; the lowest long-petioled and triangular-ovate, those of the stem sessile, ⅓ to 1¼ in. long, crenate, truncate or cordate at the base. Flowers perfect, in dense axillary leafy-bracted whorls; bracts sessile, clasping; sepals 5, united, hirsute, ⅛ to ¼ in. long, the lobes lanceolate and somewhat shorter than the tube; petals 5, rosy purple, united to form a 2-lipped corolla ⅜ to ⅝ in. long, the tube slender and dilated into a pocket near the upper end, upper lip erect and pilose on top, lower lip cleft by a V-shaped sinus; stamens 4, arising from the corolla tube; pistil 1, 4-lobed. Fruit of 4 nutlets. Distribution: New Brunswick to Minnesota, south to Florida and Texas. Native of Europe.

Henbit is a winter annual in Texas, i.e., the seeds germinate in the fall, and the plants, after growing slowly through the winter and flowering in the spring, die when hot weather begins. The plants often are rather matted, some of the prostrate branches taking root where in contact with the soil. The flowers, borne from February to May, are rose-purple with dark blotches inside the tube. While rather an attractive plant, Henbit is unfortunately a weed of lawns and gardens, reproducing freely from October to February by a second set of smaller inconspicuous flowers which never open, fertilization being accomplished in the bud. Henbit is most frequently seen in the eastern half of Texas west to Grayson, Erath, and Bexar counties, and occurs more or less sporadically elsewhere in the state.

SCARLET SAGE   *Salvia coccinea* L.   (PL. 42)   **42**

Erect perennial herb, simple or sparingly branched, softly pubescent, 1 to 2½ ft. tall. Leaves opposite, simple; petioles slender, ½ to ¾ as long as blades; blades membranaceous, ovate or deltoid-ovate, 1¼ to 2½ in. long, acute at apex, truncate to cordate at base, crenate-serrate. Flowers perfect, in whorled clusters arranged in a raceme 2 to 9 in.

long; pedicels slender, $\frac{1}{10}$ to $\frac{1}{5}$ in. long; sepals 5, united to form a tubular calyx $\frac{1}{3}$ to $\frac{1}{2}$ in. long, the upper tooth purplish, broader than the other 4; petals 5, united to form a 2-lipped corolla, $\frac{3}{4}$ to 1 in. long, deep scarlet, the tube gradually enlarged above the contracted base, lower lip notched; stamens 2, arising from the corolla tube; pistil 1, 4-lobed. Fruit of 4 nutlets *ca.* $\frac{1}{10}$ in. long. Distribution: South Carolina to Florida, west to Texas and adjacent Mexico.

SHRUBBY RED SAGE   *Salvia greggii* Gray   (PL. 42)

Puberulent shrub or perennial herb with erect stems $1\frac{1}{2}$ to $2\frac{1}{2}$ ft. tall, usually much branched. Leaves opposite, simple; blades rather rigid, oblong or broadly ovate, $\frac{1}{3}$ to $\frac{3}{4}$ in. long, the apex rounded or broadly obtuse, the base cuneate, very short-petioled. Flowers perfect, in terminal racemes 1 to 5 in. long; pedicels $\frac{1}{8}$ to $\frac{1}{4}$ in. long; sepals 5, united to form a ribbed tubular calyx, more or less 2-lipped, the lobes *ca.* $\frac{1}{3}$ as long as the tube; petals 5, united to form a 2-lipped corolla 1 to $1\frac{1}{4}$ in. long, red, the tube distended beneath, upper lip concave, notched, pubescent on back, the lower lip with a cleft middle lobe *ca.* $\frac{1}{2}$ in. broad, the 2 segments with a tooth between; stamens 2, arising from the corolla tube; pistil 1, 4-lobed. Fruit of 4 nutlets *ca.* $\frac{1}{10}$ in. long. Distribution: South Central and West Texas, and adjacent Mexico.

BLUE SAGE   *Salvia farinacea* Benth.   (PL. 42)

Minutely pubescent perennial herb with numerous erect stems 1 to $3\frac{1}{2}$ ft. tall from a stout woody root. Leaves opposite, simple; petioles $\frac{1}{3}$ to $\frac{1}{2}$ as long as the blades; blades lanceolate or oblong-lanceolate to nearly linear, 1 to $3\frac{1}{2}$ in. long, acute at apex, entire or shallowly toothed, acuminate or cuneate at base. Flowers in terminal spikelike racemes, the flowers in rather distant whorls below, more densely aggregated above; sepals 5, united to form a bluish 2-lipped calyx $\frac{1}{3}$ to $\frac{1}{4}$ in. long, covered with whitish hairs; petals 5, united to form a 2-lipped corolla $\frac{2}{3}$ to $\frac{3}{4}$ in. long, bluish violet, tube saccate above the middle, upper lip 2-parted, bearded on the back, lower lip 3-lobed, much longer than the upper; stamens 2, arising from the corolla tube; pistil 1, 4-lobed. Fruit of 4 nutlets *ca.* $\frac{1}{15}$ in. long. Distribution: Central and West Texas.

TEXAS SAGE   *Salvia texana* (Scheele) Torr. [= *Salviastrum texanum* Scheele]   (PL. 42)

Hirsute perennial herb from a woody root, with tufted erect or ascending stems 4 to 15 in. tall. Leaves opposite, simple, mostly basal, nearly or quite sessile; blades linear or narrowly lanceolate, entire or few-toothed, $1\frac{1}{2}$ to $2\frac{1}{2}$ in. long, the stem leaves 4 or 5 pairs, progressively smaller upward. Flowers perfect, in whorled clusters arranged in a raceme 2 to 7 in. long; bracts leaflike, whorled; sepals 5, united to form an irregular tubular calyx ¼ to ⅓ in. long, densely hispid-hirsute; petals 5, united to form a 2-lipped corolla *ca.* ¾ in. long, bluish purple with a white patch inside, lips longer than the tube, the upper notched, the lower 3-lobed with the broad middle lobe notched; stamens 2, arising from the corolla tube; pistil 1, 4-lobed. Fruit of 4 nutlets *ca.* ⅛ in. long. Distribution: Central, South, and West Texas, and adjacent Mexico.

Of the many species of Sage known, over 500 in all, about 20 occur wild in Texas. Probably the most widely distributed of these is Blue Sage or Mealy Sage, with bluish-purple flowers from April to July or later, especially after rains. This species is found most abundantly in the limestone hills of Central Texas, but grows well beyond these limits: Dallas and Victoria counties west to the Trans-Pecos. *S. azurea* Lam. is similar, but has shorter petioles, spreading calyx hairs, blue flowers with a white throat, and ranges from Central Texas east-ward. Shrubby Red Sage, commonly dying back to its woody crown in severe winters, occurs from Travis and Bexar counties west to Brewster County but is cultivated over much of the state. It flowers intermittently from April to fall. Scarlet Sage or Indian-fire, with bright red flowers from April to October, grows mainly south of Travis and Harris counties, but is found in scattered localities north-ward to Grayson and Childress counties. Texas Sage differs from other native species by having floral bracts which often exceed the flowers in length and give the racemes a leafy appearance. It prefers limestone soils in Central and West Texas. *S. engelmannii* Gray is similar in habit and distribution but has lighter lavender-blue flow-ers and up to 11 pairs of leaves below the lowest flowers.

A close look at Sage flowers reveals a number of interesting mechanisms, all directed toward insuring cross-pollination. In the first place, the firm upper lip of the corolla protects the nectar from dilution by rain, and shields the two anthers and the style. The larger lower lip serves both to attract and to support insects, which then push inward to the base of the ovary for the nectar. As they do this their backs are dusted by pollen if the flower is young, or are "scratched" by the pollen-receptive stigma flaps in older flowers. Thus pollen from young flowers is transported to the stigmas of older ones as bees and other visitors work from flower to flower and from plant to plant.

The Scarlet Sage offered by seedsmen is *S. splendens* Sello, a na-tive of Brazil. The commercial source of sage seasoning is *S. offi-cinalis* L. of the Mediterranean region. Both are sometimes grown in Texas.

43   PINK HORSEMINT   *Monarda fistulosa* L. [= *M. mollis* L.]   (PL. 43)

Finely pubescent perennial herb 2 to 4½ ft. tall, usually branched above and often with purplish lines and spots. Leaves opposite, simple; petioles ⅕ to ¼ as long as blades; blades lanceolate to ovate, 1 to 4½ in. long, acute or acuminate at the apex, sharply toothed, rounded or subcordate at base. Flowers perfect, in terminal leafy-bracted heads; bracts pale green or purplish; sepals 5, united to form slightly bent cylindric calyx ⅓ to ½ in. long with prominent ribs and 5 equal lobes; petals 5, united to form a long-tubed 2-lipped corolla 1⅛ to 1⅜ in. long, lavender-pink or rarely white, minutely pilose outside, upper lip linear, slightly bent; stamens 2, arising from corolla tube; pistil 1, 4-lobed. Fruit of 4 nutlets *ca.* ⅟₁₅ in. long. Distribution: Maine to Minnesota, south to Florida and Texas.

LEMON HORSEMINT   *Monarda citriodora* Cerv. ex Lag.[= *M. dispera* Small]   (PL. 43)

Pubescent, often branched annual herb 1 to 3 ft. tall. Leaves opposite, simple; petioles ¼ to ⅓ as long as blades; blades of lower stem oblong-spatulate to oblanceolate, those of upper stem narrowly oblong to linear, ¾ to 4½ in. long, shallowly serrate. Flowers perfect, arranged in 1 to 6 successive heads; bracts leaflike, broad at apex and with a spinelike bristle, ⅔ to ¾ in. long, often purplish within; sepals 5, united to form a calyx ¼ to ⅓ in. long; petals 5, united to form a 2-lipped corolla *ca.* 1 in. long, lavender or white, with purplish spots, the upper lip broad and cupped; stamens 2, arising from corolla tube; pistil 1, 4-lobed. Fruit of 4 nutlets *ca.* ⅟₁₅ in. long. Distribution: Kansas to South Carolina, south to Florida, Texas, New Mexico, and northern Mexico.

YELLOW HORSEMINT   *Monarda punctata* L.   (PL. 43)

Freely branched annual herb 1 to 4 ft. tall with finely pubescent branches. Leaves opposite, simple; petioles ¼ to ⅓ as long as blades; blades linear-oblong or lanceolate to narrowly ovate, ¾ to 3¼ in. long, remotely and usually shallowly serrate. Flowers perfect, arranged in 1 to 6 successive heads; bracts leaflike, pale green to yellowish or pinkish, tapering to a short bristle; sepals 5, united to form a calyx *ca.* ⅓ in. long, puberulent to glabrous; petals 5, united to form a long-tubed corolla *ca.* ¾ in. long, yellow with reddish-brown dots, upper lip broad, cupped, and directed upward; stamens 2, arising from the corolla tube; pistil 1, 4-lobed. Fruit of 4 nutlets *ca.* ⅟₁₀ in. long. Distribution: New York to Wisconsin, south to Florida, Texas, and Arizona.

The clusters of Horsemint flowers are made up of many small flowers interspersed with bractlets and subtended by a whorl of bracts. The oldest flowers are in the center and each, though made up of 5 joined petals, has a distinct top and bottom lip. In the manner typical for the Mint Family, the newly opened flower has ripe anthers which shed pollen onto the backs of visiting bees. In older flowers the anthers have shriveled and their place is taken by the 2-lobed stigma which must be contacted by the backs of visitors. Some species secondarily attract butterflies; others, especially red-flowered ones, are favorites of hummingbirds.

Pink Horsemint, or Wild-bergamot, produces its terminal heads of flowers from May to July, and is found, sometimes quite abundantly, in moist sandy situations from Taylor, Gonzales, and Galveston counties northeastward to the Red River and the Louisiana border. Lemon Horsemint, *Monarda citriodora* Cerv. ex Lag., is found throughout most of Texas and blooms in May and June. Yellow Horsemint is common in East and South Texas west to Palo Pinto, Mason, and Maverick counties, and occurs rather less frequently westward. With sufficient moisture it will flower from May to September, but blooming plants are seldom seen after July. Bee-balm or Oswego-tea, *M. didyma* L., is a scarlet-flowered species of eastern North America sometimes cultivated in Texas gardens. Four or five additional wild species are known in the state.

FIGWORT FAMILY   Scrophulariaceae

GREAT MULLEIN   *Verbascum thapsus* L.   (PL. 43)

> Coarse biennial herb from a deep taproot, with felty-pubescent leaves and stems, 2 to 7 ft. tall, usually unbranched. Leaves simple, alternate; sessile or petioles winged; blades of lower stem leaves and basal leaves spatulate or elliptic-spatulate, 4 to 15 in. long, upper stem leaves oblanceolate or narrowly obovate, progressively smaller upward. Flowers in a dense spikelike raceme 6 to 36 in. long; sepals 5, united at the base; petals 5, united at the base, yellow, the lobes nearly equal, ½ to ⅝ in. long; stamens 5, unequal, the anthers reddish; pistil 1, 2-chambered. Fruit an ovoid capsule *ca.* ⅛ in. long, containing many seeds. Distribution: Nova Scotia to Minnesota, south to Florida and Texas. Native of Europe.

The Mulleins comprise a large Old World genus of about 150 species, of which 4 or 5 are now naturalized in North America, 2 of them occurring in Texas. As a group they differ from other members of the Figwort Family in having a nearly rotate or wheel-like corolla instead of an irregular one. The Great Mullein produces in its first year a rosette of successively larger leaves and a deep taproot system. In the following spring a stiffly erect leafy stem arises from the crown terminating in a wandlike raceme of crowded yellow or rarely white flowers. The stamens produce abundant pollen, which a variety of bees come to gather. In doing so they effect cross-pollination, although the pollen-bearing anthers lie so close to the stigma that much self-pollination probably takes place. Great Mullein is found on sandy soils in neglected fields, roadsides, and waste places, chiefly in the eastern one-third of the state. Much less common but having the same approximate range is the Moth Mullein, *V. blattaria* L., a slender, smooth biennial to 3 or 4 ft., with pale yellow or white petals and violet anthers.

CENIZO   *Leucophyllum frutescens* (Berland.) I. M. Johnst. [= *L. texanum* Benth.]   (PL. 43)

Much-branched spreading shrub 2 to 8 ft. tall with scurfy-pubescent foliage. Leaves simple, alternate, often crowded, sessile; blades entire, lanceolate to elliptic-obovate, gray, semi-persistent in winter. Flowers perfect, solitary in the leaf axils; sepals 5, united at base, the lobes linear; petals 5, united to form a funnel-shaped somewhat 2-lipped corolla, red-purple with dark spots in the throat, villous within, ¾ to 1 in. across; stamens 4, arising from corolla tube; pistil 1, 2-chambered. Fruit a 2-valved capsule *ca.* ⅛ in. long containing numerous wrinkled seeds. Distribution: South and West Texas and adjacent Mexico.

The Cenizos are three species of *Leucophyllum,* all growing wild in Texas. *L. frutescens,* the commonest of them, produces an abundance of flowers from June to September. Ranging from Brewster and Pecos counties east to Travis County and south to the Rio Grande, this species is most frequent south of Nueces and Webb counties. It is commonly cultivated well outside this range. *L. minus* Gray is a twiggy shrub of lower stature, bearing leaves usually less than ⅖ in. long and flowers not more than ½ in. across. It is found in the Trans-Pecos and in a few localities along the lower Rio Grande. *L. violaceum* Penn. is known only from the Chisos Mountains of Big Bend National Park and is readily distinguished by its purple flowers.

44   WILD-FOXGLOVE   *Penstemon cobaea* Nutt.   (PL. 44)

Perennial herb, finely pubescent, with 1 to several stems 8 to 24 in. tall. Leaves opposite, simple; the lower petioled, the upper sessile; blades ovate-elliptic or obovate, sharply toothed, sometimes nearly or quite entire below, 1½ to 4½ in. long. Flowers perfect, arranged in loose few-flowered clusters in axils of the reduced upper leaves or bracts; sepals 5, united at the base, ⅓ to ½ in. long; petals 5, united to form an asymmetric (but not distinctly 2-lipped) corolla 1½ to 2¼ in. long, with 5 rounded lobes, light to deep lavender with purplish

(200)

markings within; stamens 5, 4 fertile and the fifth a prominent sparing-ly bearded staminode; pistil 1, 2-chambered. Fruit an ovoid capsule *ca.* ½ in. long, containing numerous seeds. Distribution: Kansas to Texas.

The genus *Penstemon* (sometimes spelled *Pentstemon* or *Pentaste-mon*), to which the Wild-foxglove and the other Beard-tongues belong, contains over 100 species, about 20 of them growing in Texas. This genus consists mainly of erect herbaceous perennials with stout woody roots and opposite leaves of two types: those of the basal rosette and lowermost stem with more or less definite petioles; those of the upper stem with no stalks and showing an upward reduction in size. The corolla is irregular, but scarcely as 2-lipped as it commonly is in other genera of the Figwort Family. Within its tube are the 5 stamens, one represented only by an en-larged, commonly hairy filament—the "beard-tongue." Wild-foxglove is found from Grayson, Washington, and Goliad counties west to Childress, Upton, and Uvalde counties, and flowers in April and May. *P. laxiflorus* Pennell reaches 3 ft. and is found in sandy fields and open woods from extreme East Texas west to Bexar, Bell, and Clay counties. It blooms in April and May, the corolla lavender to white and the outer half of the staminode clothed with orange hairs. *P. digitalis* Nutt. is similar but always has white flowers and the staminode is clothed with white hairs for about one-third its length. It is a species of northeastern Texas. *P. ambiguus* Torr. (PL. 44) reaches 2 ft., has linear leaves, and bears pink or reddish flowers with a pale throat and a glabrous staminode. This species, distinct with its "beardless tongue," ranges from the Panhandle to the Trans-Pecos and eastward to Runnels County. *P. fendleri* Torr. & Gray is a glaucous species with lavender flowers in whorls around the stem, and occurs in the Panhandle and the Trans-Pecos, and east-ward to Taylor, Travis, and De Witt counties. *P. barbatus* (Cav.) Roth. var. *torreyi* (Benth.) Gray, known only from the mountains of the Trans-Pecos, produces red or scarlet flowers from August to October. *P. murrayanus* Hook., another red-flowered species but one blooming in spring, grows in fields and open places in the pine forests of extreme East Texas and as far west as Ellis County. This, perhaps the showiest Beard-tongue in the state, is further distin-guished by having the upper leaf pairs joined by their bases.

CLIMBING SNAPDRAGON   *Maurandia antirrhiniflora* Gray [= *Antir-rhinum antirrhiniflorum* (Poir.) Small]   (PL. 44)

Perennial herb from a woody root with several or numerous stems 1 to 4 ft. long, trailing or climbing by sensitive curling petioles. Leaves simple, alternate; petioles about as long as the blades; blades triangular to ovate, with a pair of hastate basal lobes, otherwise entire, ⅓ to 1½ in. long, the apex and basal lobes apiculate. Flowers perfect, solitary in the leaf axils; pedicels about as long as petioles; sepals 5, united at the base, ⅜ to ⅝ in. long, the lobes linear or linear-lanceolate; petals 5, united to form a 2-lipped corolla ⅔ to 1 in. long, purple or sometimes partly or wholly white, the tube saccate beneath and its throat closed; stamens 4, arising from corolla tube; pistil 1, 2-chambered. Fruit a subglobose capsule ¼ to ⅓ in. across, opening by a pair of pores. Seeds numerous, corky-ridged. Distribution: South and West Texas, and adjacent New Mexico and Mexico.

Climbing Snapdragon is a low slender-stemmed vine which responds well in cultivation on wire mesh fences or in hedges, where it produces its purplish flowers throughout the summer. In the wild it is found in a variety of habitats, from the sandy islands of the Gulf Coast north to Travis County, and along the Rio Grande to most counties of the Trans-Pecos. *M. wislizenii* Engelm., found in Ward and Crane counties and doubtless growing elsewhere, is similar, but has much smaller pale blue flowers. The sepals become greatly enlarged in fruit, measuring ¾ to 1 in. long, and enclose the globose capsule, which opens by 2 slits at the base of the style. The closely related Garden Snapdragon, *Antirrhinum majus* L., a subshrub native to the Mediterranean region, but usually cultivated as an annual or short-lived perennial, is rarely encountered as an escape.

TOAD-FLAX *Linaria texana* Scheele (PL. 44)

Annual herb 6 to 40 in. tall, the smooth stems simple or few-branched, sometimes with numerous short shoots arising from the base. Leaves simple, alternate, sessile; blades thick but flat, linear to linear-spatulate, ⅓ to 1 in. long, apex acute to rather blunt. Flowers perfect, loosely arranged in racemes 5 to 12 in. long; sepals 5, united at the base, linear-lanceolate to broadly lanceolate; petals 5, united to form a 2-lipped corolla, the corolla tube spurred at the base, light blue or lavender-blue, ⅜ to ⅝ in. long (excluding spur), the lobes notched, spur slender, ¼ to ⅓ in. long; stamens 4, arising from corolla tube; pistil 1, 2-chambered. Fruit an oblong to oval capsule *ca.* ⅛ in. long containing numerous gray seeds. Distribution: Kansas to Florida, Texas, and California.

The Toad-flaxes comprise the genus *Linaria*, with about 100 species of annual and perennial herbs distributed over the northern hemisphere and in temperate South America. Of the half-dozen species in North America, 2 or 3 are wild in Texas and a few others are cultivated. *L. texana* is common in East Texas, sometimes abounding in sandy fields and open woods; beyond Young, Travis, and La Salle counties it is rather sporadic in occurrence. The lavender-blue flowers are borne in loose, often few-flowered terminal racemes from March to May. The 2-lipped corolla is closed at the mouth, the honey secreted by the nectary at the base of the ovary collecting in the backward-directed spur. The only successful visitors are the larger bees, which are able to pry the lips apart, and whose tongues are long enough to reach the honey. Occasionally an abnormal 5-spurred terminal flower is seen. *L. canadensis* (L.) Dumort. is similar but smaller in all respects, the corolla measuring less than ⅜ in. in length, and the capsules containing black seeds. This species is not known west of Erath and Llano counties. Butter-and-eggs, *L. vulgaris* Hill., a perennial native to Europe and now widely naturalized throughout eastern United States and on the Pacific Coast, has a yellow corolla with the lower lip orange. It is occasionally seen in cultivation in East Texas and may occur there as an escape. Two other cultivated species from the Old World are *L. dalmatica* (L.) Mill. with ovate, clasping leaves and yellow flowers in the spring, and *L. maroccana* Hook. with flowers of various colors in spring and early summer.

WESTERN PAINTBRUSH   *Castilleja latebracteata* Pennell   (PL. 45)   **45**

Erect perennial herb with few to several ridged pubescent stems 1 to 2 ft. tall. Leaves simple, alternate, sessile; blades lanceolate or linear-lanceolate, prominently 3-nerved, entire or wavy-margined, rarely with a few scattered teeth, 1 to 2½ in. long. Flowers perfect, in terminal racemes 2 to 6 in. long, each flower subtended by a bract; bracts ovate, rounded or shallowly 3-lobed at the apex, the outer half bright scarlet, ¾ to 1¼ in. long; sepals 5, almost completely united, yellow-green with reddened tips, nearly as long as the bracts; petals 5, united to form a strongly 2-lipped corolla, yellowish, the arched upper lip ⅔ to quite as long as the corolla tube, the lower lip very short and 3-lobed; stamens 4, of 2 sizes, arising from corolla tube; pistil 1, 2-chambered. Fruit an ovoid capsule ⅔ to ¾ in. long, opening by an apical slit. Distribution: West Texas and adjacent Mexico.

PURPLE PAINTBRUSH   *Castilleja purpurea* (Nutt.) G. Don
(PL. 45)

Gray-tomentose or finely pubescent perennial herb, usually with several stems, 4 to 15 in. tall. Leaves simple, alternate, often crowded, sessile; blades linear to linear-lanceolate, 1½ to 3 in. long, at least some with 1 to 5 long narrow lobes. Flowers perfect, in terminal racemes 2 to 9 in. long, each flower subtended by a bract; bracts lanceolate, usually with a pair of lateral fingerlike lobes, ¾ to 1¼ in. long, the outer ⅓ or ½ varying from purple or purplish red, to red-orange or brick-red [in var. *lindheimeri* (Gray) Shinners], and to yellow or yellow-green [in Yellow Paintbrush, var. *citrina* (Pennell) Shinners (PL. 45)]; sepals 5, almost completely united, the outer one-third colored like the bracts; petals, stamens, and pistil as above. Capsule ½ to ¾ in. long. Distribution: Arkansas to Texas and Arizona.

SCARLET PAINTBRUSH   *Castilleja indivisa* Engelm.   (PL. 45)

Hirsute annual herb, simple or few-branched from the base, 6 to 15 in. tall. Leaves simple, alternate, sessile; blades linear to linear-lanceolate, entire or wavy-margined, the lowest sometimes with a few fingerlike lobes, 1 to 4 in. long. Flowers perfect, in terminal racemes 2 to 7 in. long, each flower subtended by a bract; bracts broadly lanceolate to ovate, rounded and often irregularly toothed at the apex, the outer one-third to one-half red-orange to scarlet, ⅔ to ⅞ in. long; sepals 5, almost completely united, the outer one-third colored like the bracts; petals, stamens, and pistil as above. Capsule ½ to ¾ in. long. Distribution: East Texas.

The Paintbrushes are a genus of about 75 species of annual and perennial herbs, mostly of western North America, some of which are partially parasitic on the roots of other plants. They commonly occur in masses in fields and on highway shoulders where there is little or no overhead shade. The flowers are borne in terminal spikelike racemes, each lying in the axil of a leafy bract which is partly or wholly colored red, purple, orange, or yellow (rarely white). The petals themselves are usually rather inconspicuous, often being a yellow-green, but the sepals, joined to form a tube, are frequently colored, at least at the end, like the bracts. Of the 4 or 5 species found in Texas, the Scarlet Paintbrush is most widely distributed, ranging from Grayson, Bexar, and Hidalgo counties eastward to the Gulf Coast and the pine forests of extreme East Texas. It blooms from March to May. Purple Paintbrush, including its yellow and red-orange variants, occurs from Bowie and Clay counties southwestward to the Pecos River, and flowers in April and May. Western Paintbrush has a similar flowering period and is found on the Edwards Plateau and in the Trans-Pecos.

ACANTHUS FAMILY   Acanthaceae

SNAKE-HERB   *Dyschoriste linearis* (Torr. & Gray) Kuntze [=*Calophanes linearis* (Torr. & Gray) Gray]   (PL. 45)

Perennial herb, often pubescent, from a rhizome, with few to several erect or ascending stems 8 to 15 in. tall. Leaves simple, opposite, sessile; blades linear-oblanceolate to oblong-spatulate, ¾ to 2¾ in. long, entire, pubescent on midrib, ciliate on margins. Flowers perfect, solitary, in leaf axils, sessile; sepals 5, united at the base, ⅔ to ⅞ in. long, terminating in long bristlelike tips; petals 5, united to form a flaring tubular corolla 1 to 1¼ in. long, pubescent outside, bluish purple or lavender, spotted in the throat; stamens 4, of 2 different sizes; pistil 1, 2-chambered. Fruit an oblong capsule ⅜ to ½ in. long, enclosed by the persistent calyx, containing numerous lens-shaped seeds. Distribution: Central Texas to New Mexico and adjacent Mexico.

Snake-herb, an attractive, low, branched perennial, is one of 40 or 50 species included in the predominantly tropical genus *Dyschoriste*. The flowers, usually pale lavender with purplish spots in two rows in the throat, are most abundant from April to late June, but, with sufficient moisture, continue to appear until early fall. This species is most commonly seen on limestone soils, and ranges from Denton, Bell, Lavaca, and Kleberg counties west to the Trans-Pecos.

FALSE-MINT *Dicliptera brachiata* Spreng. [= *Diapedium brachi-*   **46**
atum (Pursh) Kuntze] (PL. 46)

Perennial herb with widely branched stems, often somewhat swollen at the nodes, 1 to 2½ ft. tall. Leaves simple, opposite; petioles slender, ¼ to ⅓ as long as blades; blades ovate to oblong-ovate, 1 to 4 in. long, glabrous or sparingly pubescent, entire or wavy-margined, acute or acuminate at the apex, cuneate or rounded at the base. Flowers perfect, in bracted spikes; bracts obovate to oblong-spatulate, mucronate, ¼ to ⅓ in. long; sepals 5, united at base, *ca.* ⅕ in. long, the lobes bristlelike; petals 5, united to form a flaring 2-lipped tubular corolla ⅝ to ¾ in. long, pinkish purple to lavender, the lips about as long as the straight tube; stamens 2; pistil 1, 2-chambered. Fruit a capsule *ca.* ⅕ in. long, containing numerous flattened seeds. Distribution: North Carolina to Florida and Central Texas.

Although the Acanthus Family is not rich with ornamental plants suitable for cultivation in Texas, there are a few worthy of note. High on the list is the Flame Acanthus, *Anisacanthus wrightii* Gray, an orange-flowered shrub of dry mountainous regions of West Texas, widely cultivated, especially in regions having alkaline soils. Water-willow, *Dianthera americana* L., a creeping perennial herb of wet places in Central and East Texas, produces long leafy shoots and short dense spikes of white, purple-dotted flowers in late spring. The Shrimp-plant, *Drejella guttata* (Brandeg.) Bremekamp, [= *Bele-perone guttata* Brandeg.], is commonly seen in gardens, grown as much for the reddish overlapping bracts as for the white, purple-spotted flowers. Spiny Acanthus, *Acanthus spinosus* L., of southern Europe, furnished, it is believed, the pattern for the decoration of the capitals of Corinthian columns. False-mint is found in at least partially shaded situations in open woods from Grayson, Bell, and Bexar counties eastward to the pine belt, and the flowers appear from July to October.

(205)

WILD-PETUNIA   *Ruellia occidentalis* (Gray) Tharp & Barkley
(PL. 46)

Perennial herb from a cluster of thickened fusiform roots, with few
to several erect or ascending, pubescent, 4-angled stems 1 to 2½ ft.
tall. Leaves simple, opposite; petioles ½ to 2 in. long, pubescent;
blades ovate to broadly ovate, 1½ to 4 in. long, usually rounded at
apex and rounded or subcordate at base, copiously puberulent, margins wavy or entire. Flowers perfect, in bracted terminal compound
clusters; sepals 5, united at base, with long narrow tips; petals 5,
united to form a flaring tubular corolla 2¼ to 2¾ in. long and 1⅓ to
1½ in. across, bluish purple; stamens 4, of 2 sizes, arising from corolla
tube; pistil 1, 2-chambered. Fruit an oblong capsule ½ to ¾ in. long,
each cavity containing 5 or fewer seeds. Distribution: West and
South Texas, and adjacent Mexico.

WILD-PETUNIA   *Ruellia caroliniensis* (Walt.) Steud. var. *semicalva*
Fern.   (PL. 46)

Perennial herb with erect or ascending sparsely pubescent usually
unbranched stems 8 to 24 in. tall. Leaves simple, opposite; petioles of
lowest leaves up to ⅔ in. long, those of upper leaves ⅒ to ⅕ in. long;
blades lanceolate to ovate, 2 to 3½ in. long, acute at apex, cuneate
at base, more or less pubescent, sometimes harshly so, margins wavy
or indistinctly toothed. Flowers perfect, solitary or in small clusters in
the upper axils; with bracts resembling small leaves; sepals 5, united
at base, ½ to 1 in. long, the lobes linear; petals 5, united to form a
flaring tubular corolla 1¼ to 2 in. long and ¾ to 1¼ in. across, lavender, dotted on one side within; stamens 4, of 2 sizes; pistil 1, 2-
chambered. Fruit an oblong capsule, somewhat narrowed below, *ca.*
½ in. long. Distribution: Virginia to Florida, west to Texas.

In the United States the native members of the genus *Ruellia* are
called Wild-petunias. This is rather confusing, for in fact the *Ruellias*
belong to the predominantly tropical Acanthus Family, whereas the
true Petunias are close relatives of the tomato, potato, and tobacco,
all in the Solanaceae. As a group, the *Ruellias* are typified as being
perennial herbs with large purplish flowers, usually opening in the
morning and dropping off in the afternoon, and leaving explosive
capsules which disperse minute hair-covered seeds, the hairs becoming sticky on contact with wet soil and adhering to it. About 35 species
and varieties of *Ruellia* occur wild in Texas. *R. caroliniensis* is found
in scattered localities in East Texas west to Dallas, Brazos, and
Matagorda counties, flowering from April to September. *R. occidentalis* occurs along the Rio Grande from Cameron to Val Verde
counties, northeastward to Bexar and San Patricio counties. It blooms
from May to September. *R. nudiflora* (Engelm. & Gray) Urb. has
large terminal clusters of stalked lavender flowers in spring and

sometimes in late summer, and occurs quite commonly, often in abundance, in fields and open woods from Dallas and Jefferson counties southwest to the Rio Grande. *R. pedunculata* Torr., a tall perennial with 4-angled stems and stalked lavender flowers borne in the upper leaf axils in April and May, grows in fields and open woods in extreme East Texas west to Fannin, Anderson, and Harris counties. *R. metzae* Tharp, chiefly in limestone soils from Grayson, Travis, and Wilson counties west to Val Verde County and the lower Panhandle, has terminal clusters of white flowers about ⅕ in. long. *R. malacosperma* Greenm. with large deep purple flowers, a tall species of northeastern Mexico, is commonly grown in gardens.

TRUMPET-CREEPER FAMILY Bignoniaceae

TRUMPET-CREEPER *Campsis radicans* (L.) Seem. [= *Tecoma radicans* (L.) DC.] (PL. 46)

Shrubby vine trailing or climbing to 30 ft. or more by means of aerial holdfast rootlets arising at the nodes. Leaves opposite, pinnately compound; leaflets 7 to 13, arranged on a common rachis 6 to 13 in. long; blades oval to elliptic, ¾ to 2½ in. long, acute or acuminate at the apex, coarsely serrate, on short petiolules. Flowers perfect, in few-flowered corymbs, on stout pedicels ⅓ to ¾ in. long; sepals 5, united to form a cylindrical or narrowly campanulate calyx, the 5 teeth about ⅕ as long as the tube; petals 5, united to form a tubular-funnelform corolla 2 to 3½ in. long and 1¼ to 2 in. across, red and orange, usually yellow within, oblique, the 5 lobes suborbicular or reniform; stamens 4, of 2 different sizes; pistil 1, 2-chambered. Fruit a narrowly linear capsule 4 to 8 in. long, splitting to liberate the many seeds, each *ca.* ⅔ in. long and bearded at both ends. Distribution: Pennsylvania to Missouri, south to Florida and Texas.

The flowers of the Trumpet-creeper are strictly protandrous, the anthers discharging their pollen before the style has fully elongated and the two lobes of the stigma have separated to reveal their pollen-receptive surfaces. In time the style does lengthen and the stigma lobes spread apart well beyond the shriveling anthers, where they are certain to receive pollen from younger flowers, principally by hummingbirds and long-tongued bees. Trumpet-creeper blooms from June to early September and ranges from Grayson, Karnes, and McLennan counties eastward to the pine forests of extreme East Texas. Both this species and *C. grandiflora* (Thunb.) Loisel., a larger-flowered but somewhat less hardy plant of China and Japan, lacking the aerial rootlets, are cultivated on walls and fences and in trees.

47 YELLOW-ELDER   *Tecoma stans* (L.) Juss. [= *Stenolobium stans* (L.) D. Don]   (PL. 47)

Erect shrub 5 to 12 ft. tall, sometimes grown as a perennial herb where winters kill the top. Leaves opposite, pinnately compound with 7 to 9 leaflets arranged on a common rachis 4 to 8 in. long; leaflets narrowly elliptic to nearly linear, 1½ to 4 in. long, acuminate at the apex, sharply toothed, minutely pubescent, sessile or nearly so. Flowers perfect, in many-flowered terminal racemes, each on a pedicel varying from 1/20 to 1/3 in. long; sepals 5, united to form a more or less tubular calyx *ca.* 1/5 in. long, the 5 triangular lobes nearly equal and much shorter than the tube; petals 5, united to form a funnel-like corolla 1¼ to 1¾ in. long and 1½ to 2 in. across, yellow, the lobes undulate; stamens 4, of 2 different sizes, sometimes a fifth aborted stamen present; pistil 1, 2-chambered; fruit a flat elongate linear capsule 4 to 8 in. long, splitting to release the many transversely winged seeds. Distribution: Florida and West Texas and adjacent Mexico.

Yellow-elder is an attractive shrub, well suited to cultivation in southern and western Texas, and will withstand winters in protected places as far north as Travis County. The flowers, borne from June to September, are a clear lemon yellow and are well set off against the handsome deep green foliage. This species is found in the wild in the Trans-Pecos from Brewster to Culberson counties west to the Rio Grande. Closely related is the Catalpa or Indian-bean, *Catalpa speciosa* Warder, rarely encountered as a native tree in extreme East Texas, but commonly cultivated and sometimes escaping in the eastern half of the state. The white flowers, yellow-lined and purple-dotted inside, appear in May and are followed by cylindrical bean-like capsules 10 to 20 in. long.

CROSS-VINE   *Anisostichus capreolatus* (L.) Bureau [= *Bignonia capreolata* L.]   (PL. 47)

An evergreen woody vine climbing by means of tendrils to 30 ft. or more. Leaves usually consisting of 2 leaflets and a terminal tendril, sometimes the tendril and/or 1 leaflet absent; leaflets oblong-oval or oblong-lanceolate, 2 to 6 in. long, obtuse or mucronate at apex, cordate or auriculate at base. Flowers perfect, mostly in axillary clusters on pedicels ¾ to 1½ in. long; sepals 5, united to form a cuplike calyx with an entire or wavy rim 1/5 to ¼ in. long; petals 5, united to form a more or less 2-lipped corolla 1½ to 2 in. long, dull red or red-orange outside, orange to yellow within, the 5 lobes rounded and *ca.* ¼ as long as the tube; stamens 4, of 2 different sizes, arising from corolla tube; pistil 1, 2-chambered. Fruit a narrow, flattened, elongate capsule 4 to 8 in. long, splitting by 2 valves to liberate the winged, flattened seeds. Distribution: Virginia and Illinois south to Florida and Texas.

The Cross-vine is rather frequently seen as a high-climbing shrub in trees in open woods or at forest borders in the pine forests of extreme East Texas and west to Upshur and San Jacinto counties. Elsewhere in the state it is cultivated on fences, arbors, and porches for the attractive red-and-yellow flowers which are borne from March to May, sometimes a second time in late summer. Although the Trumpet-creeper Family includes plants of widely varying habit, most are like the Cross-vine, and in the American tropics where the family is most abundantly represented, these woody vines or lianas form an important feature of the forest vegetation. Nearly all climb by tendrils—some coiling, some with adhesive discs, and some forming woody hooks—and after these temporary organs die away, the now thickened and woody lower stem hangs, supported by the widely branching top which ramifies through and over the foliage of forest trees, binding them all together and competing with them for light. These are the bush-ropes, made familiar by Tarzan and other jungle characters.

DESERT-WILLOW   *Chilopsis linearis* (Cav.) Sweet   (PL. 47)

Erect shrub or small tree to 15 ft., often of straggling habit, the twigs slender. Leaves simple, mostly alternate, numerous, short-petioled; blades linear or linear-lanceolate, 3½ to 7 in. long, acuminate at apex, gradually narrowed to the base. Flowers perfect, in terminal racemes 2½ to 4 in. long; sepals 5, united to form a villous, several-toothed cup; petals 5, united to form a 2-lipped corolla 2½ to 3½ in. long, white with a purple lower lip and yellow lines within, the suborbicular lobes ruffled; stamens 4, arising together with a staminode from the corolla tube; pistil 1, 2-chambered. Fruit a narrowly linear capsule 4 to 9 in. long, splitting to release the numerous seeds, each *ca.* ⅔ in. long and bearded at both ends. Distribution: southwestern Texas to southern California and adjacent Mexico.

Known variously as Desert-willow, Flowering-willow, Willow-leaved-catalpa, and Flor de Mimbre, this shrub is found in the wild mainly along watercourses west of the Pecos River, flowering intermittently from April to September. It is also commonly cultivated in the Trans-Pecos and further eastward in dry areas.

UNICORN-PLANT FAMILY   Martyniaceae

DEVIL'S-CLAWS   *Martynia louisianica* Mill. [= *Proboscidea louisianica* (Mill.) Van Eseltine]   (PL. 47)

Densely viscid-pubescent ill-scented annual herb, the much-branched prostrate to ascending stems 9 to 30 in. long, fleshy, often zigzag.

Leaves simple, alternate or sometimes opposite below; petioles as long as or shorter than the blades; blades suborbicular or orbicular-ovate, often oblique, 2 to 10 in. across, ciliate, subentire or indistinctly toothed, cordate at base. Flowers perfect, in short terminal racemes, the pedicels 1 to 2 in. long; sepals 5, united, the obtuse lobes unequal; petals 5, united to form a 2-lipped corolla 1½ to 2 in. long, lavender or sometimes white, spotted with purple and yellow within; stamens 4, of 2 sizes, arising together with a staminode from the corolla tube; pistil 1. Fruit a strongly curved tapering capsule, opening by 2 elastically spreading valves, the beak longer than the body. Distribution: Maine to Iowa, south to Georgia and Texas.

But for the glandular pubescence, the plants resemble diminutive Catalpa trees in foliage and flower. The peculiar fruits are adapted for transport by animal means, the spreading claws clasping the legs of deer, rabbits, etc., or becoming hooked in the wool of sheep or in the hooves of cattle. In this way seeds are dispersed over wide areas. Devil's-claws, also known as Ram's-horns or the Unicorn-plant, occurs in scattered localities over much of Texas, but most commonly in the southern and western portions. The flowers are borne from May to September. Other species in the state include *M. fragrans* Lindl., an annual with a reddish-violet to violet-purple corolla; *M. altheifolia* Benth., perennial with dull yellowish or brownish flowers; *M. parviflora* Woot., annual, the corolla about 1 in. long, dull pale yellow with a large purple blotch in the throat. These species are known from the Trans-Pecos. All are occasionally cultivated as curiosities, and sometimes for the young fruits, which are pickled.

PLANTAIN FAMILY   Plantaginaceae

48   RIBBON-GRASS   *Plantago lanceolata* L.   (PL. 48)

Stemless perennial herb with numerous fibrous roots. Leaves simple, all basal, flat on the ground or ascending; petioles indistinct from blade bases; blades linear-lanceolate to narrowly ovate, acute or acuminate at apex, 3- to 7-veined, 1½ to 12 in. long, pubescent, becoming less so in age, entire or indistinctly toothed. Flowers perfect, in dense bracted spikes ½ to 2 in. long, atop peduncles 6 to 24 in. tall; bracts ⅐ to ⅕ in. long, the apex bent; sepals 4, unequally united at base; petals 4, united to form a salver *ca.* ⅒ in. across; stamens 4, protruding; pistil 1, 2-chambered. Fruit a capsule ¹⁄₁₂ to ⅒ in. long, opening by a lid which falls away at maturity. Seeds 2. Distribution: native of Europe, naturalized throughout most of temperate North America.

ENGLISH PLANTAIN   *Plantago major* L.   (No illustration)

Stemless perennial herb with numerous fibrous roots. Leaves simple, all basal, mostly flat on the ground; petioles flat or channeled on upper surface, about as long as the blades; blades ovate or oval, 3 to 10 in. long, obtuse or broadly acute at the apex, 5- to 7-veined, entire or shallowly toothed, glabrous or sparingly pubescent. Flowers perfect, in dense bracted spikes 2 to 8 in. long, atop peduncles as long or shorter; bracts ovate, inconspicuous; sepals 4, united at base; petals 4, united at base to form a salver 1/10 to 1/8 in. across; stamens 4, protruding; pistil 1, 2-chambered. Fruit a capsule *ca.* 1/10 in. long, opening by a lid which falls away at maturity. Seeds 6 to 18. Distribution: native of Europe, widely naturalized throughout most of temperate North America.

HELLER'S PLANTAIN   *Plantago helleri* Small   (PL. 48)

Stemless annual herb with a slender taproot. Leaves simple, all basal, erect or ascending; petioles slender, 1/2 to 2 in. long, pilose; blades linear to linear-spatulate or oblanceolate, 1 to 8 in. long, acute at the apex, 3-veined, entire, pilose but usually the outer portion becoming glabrate with age. Flowers perfect, in dense bracted spikes 1 to 2 in. long, atop pilose peduncles 3 to 15 in. tall; bracts linear-subulate, 1/3 to 1/2 in. long; sepals 4, united at base; petals 4, united at base to form a salver *ca.* 1/2 in. across; stamens 4, protruding, the versatile anthers containing much powdery pollen; pistil 1, 2-chambered. Fruit a membranous capsule opening by a lid which falls away at maturity. Distribution: Texas, New Mexico, and adjacent Mexico.

Plantago is a large genus of over 200 species of weedy stemless plants found throughout most temperate and tropical regions, and represented in Texas by about a dozen kinds. Heller's Plantain is commonest on limestone soils from Dallas, Williamson, and Bexar counties west to Howard, Pecos, and Brewster counties. English Plantain is as yet known only from the Trans-Pecos, but may be expected further east. Ribbon-grass is known from scattered localities, chiefly in and near cities, from Dallas County south to Goliad County, and also in the Trans-Pecos. *P. rhodosperma* Decne. is an annual species, often superficially resembling the English Plantain, but has spreading hairs on the peduncle. It is found throughout most of the state west of Galveston, Washington, and Grayson counties, but is especially common on the Edwards Plateau and in coastal South Texas. *P. virginica* L., ranging from Grayson, Kendall, and Aransas counties eastward, closely resembles the foregoing but for its smaller floral parts and its yellowish-brown–to–black (not red–to–reddish-brown) seeds. All species flower in spring, chiefly from March to May.

MISTLETOE FAMILY   Loranthaceae

Texas Mistletoe   *Phoradendron serotinum* (Raf.) M. C. Johnston
[often referred to as *P. flavescens* (Pursh) Nutt.]   (PL. 48)

> Evergreen perennial woody-stemmed plant parasitic on branches of
> trees, usually with many brittle stems, forming a globose mass up to
> 3 ft. or more across, the whole plant yellowish green. Leaves simple,
> opposite, sessile; blades entire, 1 to 2 in. long, leathery, faintly 3- to
> 5-veined, glabrous or pubescent (at least when young). Flowers very
> small, unisexual, the sexes on different plants, in axillary, simple or
> branched spikes; staminate flowers with 2 to 4 (usually 3) petals
> and 1 stamen at the base of each; pistillate flowers with no stamens
> but with a single pistil. Fruit a subglobose, watery, translucent,
> whitish berry, the pulp albuminous. Distribution: Texas and adjacent
> Mexico.

Texas Mistletoe is found on a wide variety of host trees over most
of the state, the Panhandle excepted. The inconspicuous flowers are
borne from October to March. Some 12 to 15 additional species of
Phoradendron occur in the state, most of them limited to the Trans-
Pecos. The Mistletoe Family is large and predominantly tropical in
distribution, most of its members having the habit of the Texas
Mistletoe. Most are attached to their hosts by modified roots, the
point of contact often being swollen and structurally complex, and
within the host the nutrient-absorbing roots ramify through living
tissues. The one or few seeds within the fleshy fruits are surrounded
by a layer of viscin, a mucilaginous substance, which causes adhesion
of the seeds to the beaks and feet of fruit-eating birds. Dispersion
of the seeds is accomplished by birds as they occasionally wipe their
beaks and feet clean of the sticky seeds on nearby branches. The
seeds soon germinate and the infestation of mistletoe spreads.

COFFEE FAMILY   Rubiaceae

Button-bush   *Cephalanthus occidentalis* L.   (PL. 48)

> Shrub 3 to 10 ft. tall, usually diffusely branched. Leaves simple, op-
> posite or in whorls of 3, softly pubescent to glabrous; petioles ⅛ to ¼
> as long as the blades; blades lanceolate to narrowly ovate, 2 to 8 in.
> long, acute or somewhat acuminate at the apex, margins entire or
> wavy, base cuneate or subcordate. Flowers perfect, in terminal heads
> ¾ to 1½ in. across, on naked peduncles 1¼ to 2 in. long; heads glo-
> bose, sepals 4, accompanied by bristlelike bractlets; petals 4, united

to form a tube *ca.* ⅓ in. long, white, the tube gradually dilating, the 4 lobes ovate and obtuse; stamens 4, arising from corolla tube; pistil 1, 2-chambered. Fruit of 2 to 4 nutlets *ca.* ¼ in. long. Distribution: New Brunswick to Washington, south to Florida, Texas, and California.

The flowers of Button-bush furnish nectar to bees and butterflies of various kinds, and bee-keepers report that where Button-bush shrubs are abundant honeybees get from them a large store of honey. Although the fruits are eagerly taken by birds in winter, the leaves are poisonous to stock. Button-bush is worth planting in yards where the soil can be kept reasonably moist, particularly because of its rather late-blooming habit, from June to August or even later. It is easily propagated from seeds or cuttings taken in the fall. In the wild, Button-bush is found on stream banks, in ditches, and in damp woods throughout most of the state.

STAR-VIOLET   *Hedyotis nigricans* (Lam.) Fosb. [= *Houstonia an-*   **49**
gustifolia Michx.]   (PL. 49)

Much-branched perennial herb from a tough taproot, with erect or ascending glabrous stems 6 to 15 in. long. Leaves simple, opposite, often with smaller ones clustered in the axils; petioles ⅕ to ¼ as long as the blades; blades narrowly spatulate below, linear above, ⅓ to 1½ in. long, entire. Flowers perfect, arranged in crowded corymbs over the foliage; sepals 4, *ca.* ¹⁄₁₂ in. long; petals 4, united at base, the 4 spreading lobes ovate-oblong, white to bluish pink; stamens 4, arising from the tube of the corolla; pistil 1, 2-chambered. Fruit a capsule *ca.* ¹⁄₁₂ in. long, containing few to several roughened seeds. Distribution: Illinois to Kansas, south to Florida and Texas.

This graceful perennial shows adaptability to a wide range of conditions by its occurrence in nearly all parts of the state. It is most common on the limestone soils of Central Texas, but is as yet unknown from the lower Rio Grande Valley. The flowering period varies considerably, but in general the greatest abundance of flowers appears from March to June. With sufficient moisture flowers continue to come until early fall. Several other species are known in Texas, among them: *H. crassifolia* Raf., with lower leaves lanceolate to ovate, occurring in Texas as the var. *crassifolia* [= *H. minima* Beck] with bluish-purple–to–lilac flowers in earliest spring and ranging from Grayson and Lamar counties south to Walker and Gonzales counties, and the var. *micrantha* Shinners, with white flowers and extending from southeastern Texas to Gregg and Henderson counties; *H. rosea* Raf., a small annual with lavender-pink flowers in February and March, also with lanceolate lower leaves, found in northeastern counties; *H. humifusa* Gray, a viscid annual with purple to white flowers, found from the Pecos River east to Brazos County; *H. acerosa* Gray, a woody-based tufted perennial with sharp-pointed leaves and white flowers, growing in the lower Panhandle and from Nolan and Tom Green counties westward to the Trans-Pecos.

TROMPETILLA   *Bouvardia ternifolia* (Cav.) Schlecht. [= *B. triphylla* Salisb. var. *angustifolia* Gray]   (PL. 49)

Low shrub or subshrub to 4¼ ft. high, with shreddy bark and scabrous-puberulent branches. Leaves simple, usually in whorls of 3, on very short petioles; blades linear to lanceolate-oblong, usually hispid-scabrous, entire, the apex acute or acuminate, ¾ to 1¾ in. long. Flowers perfect, in terminal cymose clusters; sepals 4, united at base, *ca.* ⅛ in. long, persistent; petals 4, united to form a long-tubed corolla ⅞ to 1¼ in. long, scarlet, pubescent outside, with 4 (rarely 5) flaring lobes; stamens 4, arising from corolla tube; pistil 1, 2-chambered, the style protruding. Fruit a globose capsule. Seeds winged. Distribution: West Texas and adjacent New Mexico and Mexico.

While the Trompetilla and some of its 30 or more related tropical American species are popular greenhouse subjects in Europe, none seems to have found favor in Texas gardens. Trompetilla flowers from July to September and is largely restricted to the mountains of the Trans-Pecos. The Coffee Family, a very large, predominantly tropical family, abundantly represented in the American tropics, includes not only Coffee, *Coffea arabica* L., but also *Cinchona*, which yields quinine, *Uragoga*, source of ipecacuanha, and *Rubia*, from which the once-important dye alizarin was prepared. Ornamentals include the Gardenia, *Gardenia jasminoides* Ellis, Partridge-berry, *Mitchella repens* L., Bead-plant, *Nertera* spp., and Ixora, *Ixora coccinea* L.

HONEYSUCKLE FAMILY   Caprifoliaceae

WHITE HONEYSUCKLE   *Lonicera albiflora* Torr. & Gray   (PL. 49)

Low shrub with spreading or arching, eventually twining, branches, 3 to 10 ft. long. Leaves simple, opposite, evergreen; sessile or very short-petioled, the uppermost pairs (below flowers) often joined by their bases; blades glabrous, glaucous when young, broadly oval or obovate, ½ to 1½ in. long, entire, becoming rather leathery with age. Flowers perfect, terminally clustered; sepals 5, united at base; petals 5, united to form a 2-lipped corolla ½ to ⅔ in. long, glabrous outside, pubescent within, white or yellowish white, the lobes obtuse; stamens

(214)

5, arising from the corolla tube, the filaments glabrous; pistil 1, 2-chambered. Fruit a purplish-black globose berry *ca.* ⅕ in. in diameter. Distribution: Arkansas to Texas and Arizona.

JAPANESE HONEYSUCKLE   *Lonicera japonica* Thunb.   (PL. 49)

Vigorous twining woody vine to 20 ft. or more, the young stems pubescent to nearly glabrous. Leaves simple, opposite, evergreen; petioles ¼ to ⅓ in. long; blades oblong-ovate or oblong-lanceolate, 1½ to 3 in. long, those on vigorous vegetative shoots sometimes more or less pinnatifid. Flowers perfect, axillary, or axillary and terminal, commonly in pairs; sepals 5, united at base, *ca.* ¹⁄₁₀ in. long; petals 5, united to form a 2-lipped corolla 1 to 1¼ in. long, tube pubescent outside, white or creamy white, changing to yellowish brown with age; stamens, pistil, and fruit as above. Distribution: native of China and Japan, now more or less naturalized in open woods and thickets throughout much of temperate North America.

CORAL HONEYSUCKLE   *Lonicera sempervirens* Ait.   (PL. 50)   **50**

Twining woody vine to 15 ft. or more, the stems and foliage glabrous. Leaves simple, opposite, evergreen, sessile or nearly so, the uppermost 1 to 4 pairs joined by their bases; blades lanceolate to ovate, leathery, 1¼ to 3½ in. long, apex obtuse or apiculate, glabrous and glaucous. Flowers perfect, arranged in terminal racemes of 1 to 5 whorls; sepals 5, united, very small; petals 5, united to form a 2-lipped corolla 1 to 1¾ in. long, red outside and orange inside; stamens, pistils, and fruit as above except that mature berries are red. Distribution: Connecticut to Nebraska, south to Florida and Texas.

Honeysuckle flowers are chiefly visited by nocturnal moths. The flowers open in late afternoon with the stamens extended, their anthers already dusty with free pollen, and the style depressed against the lower lip of the corolla. Later, usually during the following day, the stamens wither, and by the next night, the style, with its pollen-receptive stigma, has assumed the position previously held by the stamens. Thus the stamens and style have successively served as landing places for nectar-seeking moths which carry, quite inadvertently, pollen from young flowers to the stigmas of older ones. White Honeysuckle is a rather common shrub in the mountains of the Trans-Pecos and extends eastward to Comal, Bell, and Dallas counties, and northward into the Panhandle. It flowers in April and May. Japanese Honeysuckle is frequently cultivated on fences and trellises, and as a ground cover in most parts of the state. It is not uncommonly seen as an escape in sandy woods in East Texas, blooming mainly in late spring but intermittently until fall. Coral Honeysuckle grows in open woods from Grayson, Milam, and Jackson counties eastward to the Louisiana border and produces its attrac-

(215)

tive flowers from March to May. Several additional species, most from the Orient, are grown for ornament.

50
(Cont.) ELDERBERRY   *Sambucus canadensis* L.   (PL. 50)

> Round-headed shrub 3 to 10 ft. tall, typically with several coarse stems rising from large but shallow roots, or forming thickets by means of stolons. Leaves opposite, pinnately compound with 5 to 11 leaflets; leaflets short-stalked, broadly lanceolate to ovate, sharply serrate, the teeth directed toward the apex or somewhat incurved, mostly short-acuminate at the apex, cuneate or somewhat rounded at the base, glabrous to pubescent, 2 to 4½ in. long. Flowers perfect, arranged in large compound cymes 4 to 8 in. broad; sepals 5; petals 5 or 6, united at the base, creamy white; stamens 5 or 6; pistil 1, 2- to 6-chambered. Fruit a purplish-black berry *ca.* ⅕ in. in diameter. Distribution: New Brunswick to Manitoba, south to Florida, Texas, and Arizona.

Elderberry bears its flowers mostly in late spring, but sometimes reflowers later in the summer. It grows in damp places, commonly along streams and ditches, from Grayson, Bell, and Bexar counties eastward to the Louisiana border. *S. coerulea* Raf., a shrub or small tree to 20 ft. in the mountains of the Trans-Pecos, has spreading teeth on the leaflet margins. The making of wine from elderberries is an old custom, both in North America and in Europe. Sometimes the flower buds are used with raisins for making wine. Alone or in combination with other fruits, the berries are made into jam. Although it is no longer an important drug plant, the Elderberry was once valued as the source of many home remedies. An ornamental plant when grown in moist places, the Elderberry is easily grown from seed or cuttings, or may be transplanted when not in leaf.

VALERIAN FAMILY   Valerianceae

LAMB'S-LETTUCE   *Valerianella amarella* Krok   (PL. 50)

> Small nearly glabrous annual herb with hollow, angled, simple, or dichotomously branched stems 3 to 12 in. high. Leaves simple, opposite, all but the lowest sessile; blades oblong or obovate, obtuse, 1½ to 2¼ in. long, reduced upward, entire or with a few irregular teeth. Flowers perfect, in compact leafy-bracted corymbs; sepals indistinct, very small; petals 5, united to form a tubular corolla with a salver *ca.* ⅒ in. across, white; stamens 3, arising from corolla tube; pistil 1, 3-chambered. Fruit an achene with 1 larger and 2 smaller chambers, covered with hooked hairs. Distribution: Central Texas.

(216)

The expression "by their fruits ye shall know them" is perhaps more applicable here than among any other wildflowers, for indeed the Texas species of *Valerianella* are very difficult to distinguish anyway, and in the absence of the peculiar irregular fruits the task is virtually impossible. *V. amarella* is found in damp places from Montague, Dallas, and Houston counties southwestward to Reagan, Edwards, and Bexar counties, and blooms in April and May. The remaining species have smaller flowers, usually less than ½₂ in. across; these are frequently quite inconspicuous because only a few open at a time. *V. woodsiana* Torr. & Gray has narrow-pointed bracts and nearly globose achenes, each with two small diverging projections. It occurs mainly in damp sandy soil from Tarrant and Lee counties eastward. *V. stenocarpa* (Engelm.) Krok is similar but has columnar achenes, each with two appressed "pillars" on one side. It ranges from Grayson, Van Zandt, and Harris counties southwest to Kendall, Bexar, and De Witt counties. *V. radiata* (L.) Dufr. has upper leaves often toothed near the base, broadly pointed bracts, and irregularly 4-angled achenes. It is widely distributed in East Texas, west to Grayson, Llano, and Victoria counties. These 3 species, sometimes occurring together, bloom from March to May and are believed to hybridize.

GOURD FAMILY   Cucurbitaceae

WILD GOURD   *Cucurbita foetidissima* H. B. K.   (PL. 50)

Coarse perennial trailing or sometimes climbing vine from large fusiform roots, the angled tendril-bearing stems 8 to 20 ft. long, the gray-green foliage with a heavy unpleasant odor. Leaves alternate, simple; petioles less than ½ as long as blades; blades rather thick, triangular to triangular-ovate, more or less acute at apex, 4 to 15 in. long, margins irregularly toothed, base truncate or cordate. Flowers unisexual, the staminate and pistillate flowers on the same plant, solitary in the leaf axils, on peduncles ¾ to 2½ in. long; sepals 5, united at base; petals 5, united about halfway, 2½ to 4 in. long, orange, pubescent, especially outside; staminate flowers with 3 stamens appressed together; pistillate flowers with 3 aborted stamens, a large sticky 3-lobed stigma, and a conspicuously swollen ovary below the sepals. Fruit a globose or obovoid berry with a hard rind, green variegated with pale green or yellow, 2 to 4 in. long, containing numerous flattened seeds. Distribution: Nebraska to Texas, southern California, and Mexico.

Pumpkins, squashes, cantaloupes, watermelons, cucumbers, vegetable marrows, citron gourds, dishcloth gourds, calabash gourds, and many others are all members of the predominantly tropical Gourd Family, a large assemblage of some 100 genera and over 900 species of tendril-bearing vines. The tendrils have been variously interpreted but it is now generally agreed that they are modified leaves. In anchoring the weak fleshy stems they display two distinct actions. First the tip, on contacting a support, makes a few turns around it. Then the remainder of the tendril forms a coil spring and draws the stem to the support. In many species the tendril becomes woody in age, while in others it is merely a temporary support. Wild Gourd blooms from May to July and is found from Tarrant, McLennan, and Bexar counties west to the Trans-Pecos and northward into the Panhandle.

51 BALSAM GOURD   *Ibervillea lindheimeri* (Gray) Greene   (PL. 51)

Slender sparingly branched perennial vine from a turniplike root, climbing by means of unbranched tendrils 6 to 10 ft. high. Leaves simple, alternate; petioles ¼ to ⅓ as long as the blades; blades thick, 1½ to 3¼ in. long, deeply 3- to 5-lobed, the lobes coarsely toothed, minutely warted. Flowers unisexual, the clustered staminate and solitary pistillate flowers on different plants; sepals 5, united at base, *ca.* 1/12 in. long; petals 5, united to form a corolla tube *ca.* ½ in. long and a salver ¼ in. across, yellow striped with pale green, pubescent within. Fruit a globose berry 1 to 2 in. in diameter, maturing red, smooth, persistent. Distribution: Central and South Texas.

Balsam Gourd is found in thickets, open woods, and on fences, very locally, from Cooke, Palo Pinto, and Taylor counties south to Edwards, Bexar, and Fayette counties. The flowers are borne in May and June. *I. tenuisecta* (Gray) Small, a species of the Trans-Pecos, has leaves with linear lobes and fruit not more than ⅔ in. across. *I. tenella* (Naud.) Small ranges from Val Verde, Karnes, and Nueces counties south to the Rio Grande and bears fruit similar to that of *I. lindheimeri*, but has leaves deeply twice-lobed, rather intermediate between those of the two preceding species.

BELL-FLOWER FAMILY   Campanulaceae

VENUS' LOOKING-GLASS   *Triodanis perfoliata* (L.) Nieuwl. [= *Specularia perfoliata* (L.) A. DC.]   (PL. 51)

Rather stoutish annual herb, the stems erect, 4 to 20 in. tall, commonly unbranched, hirsute or hispid. Leaves simple, alternate, sessile; blades suborbicular or triangular-cordate, ⅓ to ¾ in. long, bluntly toothed, pilose on veins beneath, otherwise glabrous, base clasping the stem. Flowers perfect, solitary in axils, sessile; early flowers often lacking petals and with 3 or 4 short sepals; sepals of later flowers 5, united to form a flaring 5-lobed corolla ½ to ⅔ in. across, bluish purple; stamens 5, arising from corolla tube; pistil 1, 3-chambered. Fruit an oblong or obconic capsule *ca.* ¼ in. long, opening by an ovate lateral pore near the middle. Seeds numerous, roughened, with tiny points or smooth. Distribution: Ontario to British Columbia, south to Florida, Texas, and Mexico.

The early inconspicuous flowers are self-fertile, seed being set without benefit of insect pollination. Venus' Looking-glass, or Hen-and-chickens, as it is sometimes called, grows in fields and open woods, in some places abundantly, in East Texas west to Young, Mason, and Uvalde counties, and also in the Trans-Pecos. The flowers are borne in April and May. *T. leptocarpa* (Nutt.) Nieuwl., with narrower leaves that do not clasp the stem, occurs on limestone soils from Collin and Bexar counties west to McCulloch County. *T. texana* McVaugh resembles *T. perfoliata,* but the undersides of the leaves are densely pilose and the seeds are finely ridged. It is found from Dallas, Van Zandt, and Hardin counties west to Erath and Frio counties. In *T. holzingeri* McVaugh the capsule pore is a narrow slit. This species prefers open situations from Grayson, Bell, and Kleberg counties west to the Trans-Pecos and northward into the Panhandle. *T. biflora* (Ruiz & Pavon) Greene has the pore near the top of the capsule. It ranges from the western limit of the East Texas pine forests to Throckmorton, Mason, and Maverick counties, and sparingly westward to the Trans-Pecos.

CARDINAL-FLOWER   *Lobelia cardinalis* L.   (PL. 51)

Perennial herb with erect glabrous or slightly pubescent usually unbranched stems 1 to 4 ft. tall. Leaves simple, alternate, sessile or nearly so; blades lanceolate to narrowly ovate, 1½ to 6 in. long, reduced upward, tapered at both ends, serrate or dentate. Flowers perfect, arranged in racemes 4 to 15 in. long, on pedicels ¼ to ⅔ in. long; bracts linear, ⅓ to 1 in. long; sepals 5, united at the base, the lobes linear, 2 to 6 times longer than the cuplike base; petals 5, united to form a straight-tubed 2-lipped corolla 1⅔ to 2¼ in. long, deep red or, rarely, white, 2 of the 5 lobes long and narrow, the other 3 shorter and broader; stamens 5, united by their anthers; pistil 1, 2-chambered. Fruit a hemispheric capsule ¼ to ⅓ in. in diameter. Distribution: New Brunswick to Saskatchewan, south to Florida and Texas.

BLUE LOBELIA   *Lobelia appendiculata* A. DC.   (PL. 51)

Slender glabrous annual herb 1 to 3½ ft. tall, simple or few-branched. Leaves simple, alternate, relatively few; basal blades spatulate or oblong-spatulate, petioled, 1½ to 3 in. long, indistinctly toothed or sometimes serrate; upper blades sessile, lanceolate to ovate, remote. Flowers perfect, in loose, often 1-sided racemes 6 to 15 in. long, on pedicels less than ¼ in. long; sepals 5, united below, the lobes linear-lanceolate with reflexed appendages at base; petals 5, united to form a short-tubed 2-lipped corolla *ca.* ½ in. long, lavender-blue to white; stamens 5, united by their anthers; pistil 1, 2-chambered. Fruit an ovoid capsule *ca.* ⅕ in. long. Distribution: Arkansas to Louisiana and Texas.

When a Lobelia flower opens, the cylinder of stamens and the enclosed style elongate and bend downward in front of the opening to the corolla tube. Soon the style lengthens and emerges, carrying with it pollen inwardly freed by the anthers. At this stage the two stigmatic flaps terminating the style are tightly appressed and cannot be pollinated. Hummingbirds, seeking the nectar at the base of the corolla tube, receive a dusting of pollen on their beaks. In flowers a little older the stigmatic surfaces roll back and then visitors coming with pollen from younger flowers can pollinate them. In blue-flowered species, the principal pollinators are bees. Cardinal-flower blooms from August to October and ranges from East Texas south to Victoria, Bexar, and Bandera counties, sparingly westward to the Trans-Pecos and northward into the Panhandle. Blue Lobelia flowers in May and June and is commonly seen in the pine belt of extreme East Texas, westward to Fannin, Freestone, and Matagorda counties. About 4 other species, all blue-flowered, are known in the state.

DAISY FAMILY Compositae

52 IRON-WEED *Vernonia texana* (Gray) Small (PL. 52)

Clump-forming perennial herb with erect stems 1½ to 4 ft. tall, usually unbranched below the flowers. Leaves simple, alternate; sessile or short-petioled; blades linear to oblong-lanceolate, 2 to 8 in. long, reduced upward, the upper ones entire, the lower rather remotely serrate. Heads numerous, distantly arranged along slender branches; involucre cup-shaped, ⅓ to ½ in. high, with several rows of purplish-tipped phyllaries, which are progressively larger upward; rays absent; disc purple; pappus of many whitish or brownish hairs. Fruit an achene *ca.* ⅛ in. long, sparingly barbed along its ribs. Distribution: Florida to Arkansas and Texas.

IRON-WEED *Vernonia lindheimeri* Gray & Engelm. (PL. 52)

Clump-forming perennial herb with numerous very leafy gray-pubescent stems 10 to 30 in. tall, freely branched above. Leaves simple, alternate, sessile; blades linear to linear-lanceolate, 1½ to 5 in. long, rather thick, gray-green above, gray-felty below, margins entire, revolute. Heads many, on club-shaped stalks; involucre cup-shaped, ⅓ to ½ in. high, with several rows of grayish felty-tomentose phyllaries which are progressively larger upward; rays absent; disc purple; pappus of many purplish-brown hairs. Fruit an achene *ca.* ⅛ in. long, glabrous. Distribution: Central Texas.

The flowers of Iron-weeds are pollinated by various bees and flies which come for the nectar held at the bottom of the corolla tube. The mode of pollination is common to the majority of the plants in the Daisy Family. While still in the bud stage, the anthers discharge pollen over the roughened outer surface of the style. At this stage the 2 stigmatic flaps at the end of the style are tightly appressed to each other, self-pollination thus being prevented. As the flower opens the pollen-coated style elongates, carrying the pollen out beyond the corolla, where insects become dusted with it while probing for the nectar below. Later the pollen-receptive stigma flaps separate and are dusted with pollen carried on insects which have come from younger flowers. *V. texana* ranges from the pine forests of extreme East Texas west to McLennan, Travis, and De Witt counties. *V. lindheimeri* is found on limestone soils from Tarrant, Williamson, and Comal counties west to the Pecos River. Both of these species, as well as the 8 other species known from the state, flower from late May to August.

ELEPHANT-FOOT   *Elephantopus carolinianus* Willd.   (PL. 52)

Perennial herb 1 to 3 ft. tall with leafy, hirsute, freely-branched stems. Leaves simple, alternate, sessile or nearly so, the larger ones at first basal, but often becoming distributed along the elongating stem, upper leaves much reduced; blades thin, oblong, elliptic, or oval, 2 to 7 in. long, crenate-serrate, the lower ones long-tapered at the base. Heads slender-stalked, each subtended by 2 or 3 ovate bracts ⅓ to ¾ in. long; involucre rather flat, with 2 series of dry phyllaries, the outer series smaller; rays absent; disc lilac or lilac-purple. Fruit an achene, ⅛ to ¼ in. long, 10-ribbed. Distribution: Pennsylvania to Kansas, south to Florida, Texas, and Central and northern South America.

Elephantopus is a genus of about 25 species of herbs of warm regions, some of them rather troublesome weeds, especially in tropical cultivations. Elephant-foot, commonest of the 3 species occurring in Texas, ranges from the Louisiana border west to Denton, Bastrop, and Victoria counties, and flowers from August to October. *E. tomen-*

tosus L., distributed in extreme East Texas west to Wood and Walker counties, has most of its broad, rounded leaves clustered at the base of the otherwise nearly naked stem. *E. nudatus* Gray is similar to the preceding but has narrower, pointed leaves. It is found only in Orange, Jefferson, and Chambers counties.

GAY-FEATHER   *Liatris squarrosa* (L.) Michx. [= *Laciniaria squarrosa* (L.) Hill]   (PL. 52)

Perennial herb from a rounded corm *ca.* 1½ in. in diameter, the several simple or sparingly branched stems 1 to 2 ft. tall. Leaves simple, alternate, numerous, sessile; basal blades linear, 5 to 9 in. long, those of the stems 2½ to 6 in. long, gradually reduced upward, glabrous to hirsute. Heads solitary in the axils of the upper leaves, ⅔ to 1¼ in. long, 25- to 40-flowered; phyllaries leaflike, in several series but of two general types; inner ones linear, ¼ to ⅔ in. long, with acute tips; outer triangular-linear or -lanceolate, somewhat longer; rays absent; disc rosy purple, the florets ⅓ to ⅝ in. long, pubescent within. Fruit an achene ¼ to ⅓ in. long, topped with a pappus of fine branched hairs up to ½ in. long. Distribution: Ontario to Minnesota, south to Florida and Texas.

53   GAY-FEATHER   *Liatris punctata* Hook. [= *Laciniaria punctata* (Hook.) Kuntze]   (PL. 53)

Perennial herb from a branched rootstock, the stems few to several, usually simple, 1 to 3 ft. tall. Leaves simple, alternate, numerous, sessile; blades narrowly linear, 1½ to 5 in. long, firm, minutely dotted, sometimes lightly ciliate. Heads usually crowded in a partially leafy spike or short-pedicelled raceme; involucre cylindric-oblong, ⅓ to ⅔ in. long; phyllaries oblong to ovate, short-pointed, pubescent; rays absent; disc rosy purple. Fruit an achene *ca.* ¼ in. long, somewhat pubescent, topped with a pappus of fine branched hairs. Distribution: Minnesota to Montana, south to Texas and New Mexico.

The Gay-feathers, also known as Blazing-stars or Button-snakeroots, are a genus of 25 or 30 North American perennials, about ⅓ of which occur in Texas. *L. squarrosa* is found mainly in sandy soils in East Texas west to De Witt County and northwest to Wichita County. It flowers from June to August. *L. punctata* is a western species, ranging from Clay, Williamson, and Kleberg counties to the Trans-Pecos and the Panhandle, and blooming from July to October. *L. pycnostachya* Michx., a tall plant of fields in the pine forests in extreme East Texas, sometimes reaching 4 ft., flowers from June to August and bears unbranched pappus bristles. A hairy-leaved variety of this species, found in the same region, flowers from August to October.

(222)

BROOM-WEED   *Gutierrezia dracunculoides* (DC.) Blake [= *Amphiachyris dracunculoides* (DC.) Nutt.]   (PL. 53)

Glabrous annual herb 1 to 2½ ft. tall, the stems intricately branched above. Leaves alternate, simple, sessile; blades linear to linear-filiform, ⅓ to 2 in. long, entire, acute at apex, gradually reduced upward. Heads solitary at ends of slender branches; involucre hemispheric, ⅒ to ⅛ in. high; phyllaries ovate or oblong, acute at apex, lustrous; rays 3 to 10, yellow, oblong or oval, ⅛ to ⅙ in. long; disc flowers 10 to 20, yellow. Fruit an achene with a crownlike pappus. Distribution: Missouri and Kansas, south to Texas.

Broom-weed, found throughout most of the state except the pine forests of the extreme eastern portion and the driest parts of the western one-third, is a weedy plant characteristic of disturbed areas. The masses of yellow flowers are borne from September to November. Broom-weed frequently grows luxuriantly along roadways and in overgrazed pastures. While there is little doubt that this and other annual Broom-weeds are unpalatable to stock, ranchers believe the perennial species to be poisonous. *G. microcephala* (DC.) Gray, variously called Threadleaf Broom-weed, Snake-weed, Turpentine-weed, and Slink-weed, a clumped perennial otherwise similar in habit to *G. dracunculoides*, is perhaps the most troublesome.

GUM-WEED   *Grindelia squarrosa* (Pursh) Dunal   (PL. 53)

Perennial herb with glabrous stems 1 to 3 ft. tall, usually several-branched above. Leaves simple, alternate, sessile; blades lanceolate to ovate or ovate-spatulate, ¾ to 2 in. long, margins serrate, the teeth gland-tipped, base partly clasping the stem. Heads terminal, sometimes numerous; involucre ½ to ⅔ in. across; phyllaries linear-lanceolate, very glutinous, prolonged into slender leathery tips, the inner ones nearly erect, the outer spreading or recurved; rays bright yellow; disc yellow. Fruit an achene with 2 or 3 projections. Distribution: Minnesota and Illinois, south to Texas and northern Mexico.

Gum-weed ranges from Clay, Bell, and Maverick counties westward to the Trans-Pecos and northward into the Panhandle. The flowers appear from August to October. Because of its unpalatability to stock animals, Gum-weed often takes possession of run-down pastures, especially during long periods of drought. The unpleasant taste of the plant is due to tannin and several resins, these having been used by Indians and early pioneers for relief from asthma, bronchitis, and external sores. In more recent years pharmaceutical firms have prepared fluid extracts of leaves and buds for similar purposes. Beekeeping in areas where Gum-weed is common is often difficult, owing to the poor-flavored, granular honey made from Gum-weed nectar. In dry areas Gum-weed is an attractive addition to the wild garden, thriving without attention, even when the soil is poor and dry. About 10 species grow in Texas, most of them in the southern and western portions of the state.

SLEEPY DAISY   *Xanthisma texanum* DC.   (PL. 53)

Glabrous annual herb 4 to 30 in. tall, usually branched above. Leaves simple, alternate, sessile; blades narrowly oblanceolate to linear, the lower ones 1 to 2½ in. long, often pinnately lobed or pinnatifid-toothed, the upper mostly less than 1 in. long, entire or nearly so. Heads terminal, rather few; involucre ⅖ to ⅗ in. high; phyllaries elliptic, acute or acuminate; rays lemon-yellow; disc yellow. Fruit a pubescent achene *ca.* ⅒ in. long. Distribution: Central and South Texas.

Sleepy Daisy is so called because the rays do not expand until late morning, and then close again in late afternoon. When they are open the flowers are very attractive, witness the cultivation of this Texas plant in gardens well outside its native range. In the wild it is found from Navarro, Washington, Calhoun, and Willacy counties northwest to the lower Panhandle. It blooms from May to September.

54   SAW-LEAF DAISY   *Prionopsis ciliata* Nutt.   (PL. 54)

Annual or biennial herb 3 to 5 ft. tall, usually with a few short branches near the top. Leaves simple, alternate, sessile or very short-petioled; blades obovate to oblong or oval, coarsely dentate-serrate, spiny-toothed, ¾ to 3 in. long, firm, the apex acute to rounded. Heads few, terminal; involucre broadly hemispheric, ¾ to 1 in. across; phyllaries linear-lanceolate or linear, rigid, acuminate at the apex; rays numerous, yellow, ⅖ to ⅗ in. long. Fruit an achene ⅒ to ⅛ in. long, with a few soon-falling pappus bristles. Distribution: Missouri and Kansas south to Texas.

Saw-leaf Daisy, or Golden-weed, as it is sometimes called, is a drought-resistant plant with stiff, rather stout upright stems, found in waste places and fields and on prairies, from Gregg, Harris, and Matagorda counties northwestward to the Panhandle. The heads, borne on well-defined side branches, or nearly sessile to the main stem, appear from July to October.

GOLDENROD   *Solidago radula* Nutt.   (PL. 54)

Perennial herb with few to several stems 1½ to 4 ft. tall, rough-pubescent, branched or nearly simple. Leaves simple, alternate; sessile or the petioles less than ⅒ as long as the blades; blades variable in shape, those of the lower stem and base spatulate to oblong-spatulate or obovate, 2 to 4 in. long, remotely toothed, upper ones gradually or sometimes abruptly smaller, entire, all harsh-pubescent, prominently veined. Heads numerous, arranged in reflexed or recurved one-sided racemes or panicles at the ends of the main stem and branches; involucre narrowly cup-shaped, *ca.* ⅛ in. high; phyllaries mainly linear, thickish, blunt-ended; rays in 1 series, yellow; disc yellow. Fruit a pubescent achene topped with numerous slender bristles. Distribution: Illinois and Missouri to Louisiana and Texas.

GOLDENROD   *Solidago nemoralis* Ait.   (PL. 54)

Perennial herb, the few to numerous pubescent or puberulent stems 1 to 3½ ft. tall, more or less branched above. Leaves simple, alternate, sessile or nearly so; blades rough-pubescent, rather thick, becoming firm in age, those of the lower stem and base 2½ to 6 in. long, narrowly spatulate, apparently entire but in fact very finely saw-toothed, apex acute or abruptly pointed, gradually narrowed to the base, upper blades smaller, often less than 1 in. long. Heads numerous, in one-sided panicles at the ends of arching branches; involucre narrowly cup-shaped, ⅛ to ⅙ in. long; phyllaries mostly linear, flat, obtuse at the apex; rays in a single series, yellow; disc yellow. Fruit a finely pubescent achene topped with numerous slender bristles. Distribution: southeastern Canada, south to Florida and Texas.

GOLDENROD   *Solidago altissima* L.   (PL. 54)

Perennial herb from a horizontal rootstock with densely puberulent grooved stems 2½ to 5 ft. tall. Leaves simple, alternate, sessile or nearly so; blades lanceolate, 2 to 6 in. long, very finely serrate, finely harsh-pubescent, apex acute, base long-tapered. Heads in crowded one-sided panicles on few to numerous arching branches, the entire floral mass commonly pyramidal or broadly conical; involucre narrowly cup-shaped, ⅛ to ⅙ in. high; phyllaries linear-lanceolate, acute at the apex; rays in a single series, yellow; disc yellow. Fruit a sparingly hirsute achene. Distribution: Maine to Minnesota, south to West Virginia, Tennessee, and Texas.

The Goldenrods are a genus of well over 100 species of herbs, most of them erect perennials with yellow flowers in late summer and fall, all but a few native to North America. Over one-third of the known species occur in Texas. The 3 species described here range from Bowie, Harris, and De Witt counties westward to the limestone hills on the eastern edge of the Edwards Plateau, and then recur in scattered localities in the Trans-Pecos. In most species the flower heads are borne in rows along the upper side of the somewhat recurved branches. Each ray is in fact the united petals, swept to one side, of an outer pistillate flower. The disc flowers have smaller corollas and both stamens and pistils. All are snugly bound together by the closely applied phyllaries or bracts of the involucre. When the rays first spread open, the inner disc flowers are still closed.

Within each the two narrow anthers are joined into a tube around the 2-branched style. As a floret opens, its style elongates, the hairy portion behind the tip picking up pollen which has been discharged by the inwardly opening anthers. When it has protruded, the style's pollen-receptive surfaces on the inner sides of the 2 branches remain closely pressed to each other, the outer surfaces being coated with pollen. Bees, butterflies, and flies thrust their proboscises down into the tubular corollas in search for nectar, and in doing so inevitably brush against the pollen-coated style column. After a time the 2 style branches separate and visitors from younger flowers bring pollen which has adhered to them, accidentally depositing some of it on the stigmatic surfaces. Pollen grains thus placed soon produce tubular projections which grow down to the ovary and fertilize the ovules, which then enlarge to become seeds. The ovary itself becomes the dry, often papery, wall of the achene fruit.

55 Lazy Daisy   *Aphanostephus skirrhobasis* (DC.) Trel.   (pl. 55)

Gray-pubescent annual herb, simple or the stems little to diffusely branched, especially at the base, 6 to 24 in. tall. Leaves simple, alternate, sessile; blades linear to oblong, usually spatulate, ½ to 2½ in. long, reduced upward, the lower ones sharply incised or toothed, the upper entire. Heads solitary, nodding in bud, long-peduncled; involucre *ca.* ⅕ in. high, hemispheric; phyllaries linear or narrowly linear-lanceolate, pubescent; rays 20 to 44, linear, white to pink, often deeper red on underside; disc yellow. Fruit a pubescent achene with several lobes or teeth on top. Distribution: Kansas to Florida and Texas.

The rays of the Lazy Daisy behave like those of the Sleepy Daisy, opening in late morning to about 1½ in. across, and becoming erect in late afternoon. *A. skirrhobasis* flowers from April to June and ranges from the Gulf Coast northwestward to Grayson County and the lower Panhandle, and occurs sparingly in the Trans-Pecos. *A. ramosissimus* DC. (pl. 55) is often more or less prostrate or decumbent, bears 16- to 32-rayed heads from April to July, and has achenes with a ring of tiny hairs on top. It is found from Tarrant, De Witt, and Hidalgo counties west to the Pecos River, and north into the Panhandle. *A. riddellii* Torr. & Gray is a perennial with larger 30- to 85-rayed heads from April to June, often a second crop of smaller ones later in the summer, and achenes like those of the preceding species. It grows mainly on limestone soils from Taylor, Travis, and Kenedy counties west to the Rio Grande and Pecos rivers, and north into the Panhandle. Two or 3 additional species are known from the state.

SMOOTH ASTER   *Aster laevis* L.   (PL. 55)

Erect perennial herb 2 to 4 ft. tall, with glabrous, often glaucous, simple to widely branched stems. Leaves simple, alternate, sessile; blades lanceolate to narrowly ovate, often rather leathery, smooth, 1 to 5 in. long, reduced upward, entire or irregularly toothed, bases of lower ones gradually narrowed, those of the upper cuneate or rounded, the uppermost often scalelike. Heads numerous, *ca.* 1 in. across; involucre cup-shaped; phyllaries in several series, whitish with green tips, rigid, sharp-pointed; rays 15 to 30, bluish violet to purple; disc yellow. Fruit a glabrous achene. Distribution: Maine to North Dakota, south to Georgia and Texas.

NARROW-LEAVED ASTER   *Aster prealtus* Poir. [= A. *salicifolius* Ait.]   (PL. 55)

Erect perennial herb 2 to 5 ft. tall, the stems usually slender, glabrous or puberulent above, with numerous short lateral branches. Leaves simple, alternate, often with rosettes of smaller ones in the axils, sessile or barely clasping; blades lanceolate or linear-lanceolate, rather firm, 2 to 5 in. long, reduced upward, entire or irregularly and sparingly dentate, glabrous or nearly so. Heads usually numerous, ⅔ to 1 in. across; involucre broadly cup-shaped; phyllaries linear-oblong, in 4 or 5 series, their green tips acute, sometimes broadly so; rays numerous, violet to violet-purple, rarely white, ¼ to ⅓ in. long; disc yellow. Fruit a minutely pubescent achene. Distribution: Maine to Ontario, south to Florida and Texas.

SMALL-LEAVED ASTER   *Aster oblongifolius* Nutt.   (PL. 55)

Several-stemmed perennial herb 1 to 2½ ft. tall, usually much branched, pubescent when young, becoming glabrous with age. Leaves simple, alternate, sessile, the lower often falling early; blades oblong or oblong-lanceolate, ¾ to 2 in. long, reduced upward, apex broadly acute, often short-pointed, base narrowed or in lower leaves slightly clasping, roughened on both surfaces. Heads solitary on branch ends, *ca.* 1 in. across; involucre hemispheric; phyllaries in several series, the green tips spreading; rays 20 to 30, violet-purple, rarely pinkish; disc yellow. Fruit an ashy-pubescent achene. Distribution: Pennsylvania to Minnesota, south to South Carolina and Texas.

ANNUAL ASTER   *Aster subulatus* Michx. var. *ligulatus* Shinners   **56**
[= A. *exilis* Ell.]   (PL. 56)

Annual or biennial herb with 1 to several erect glabrous stems 6 to 40 in. tall, usually much branched, the branches slender and often somewhat zigzag. Leaves simple, alternate, sessile or somewhat clasping; blades linear-lanceolate or linear, entire, ¾ to 3½ in. long, reduced upward, those of the ultimate branches minute. Heads solitary at the ends of branches, numerous, ⅖ to ½ in. across; involucre cup-shaped, *ca.* ¼ in. high; phyllaries linear-subulate, in 3 or 4 series; rays numerous, ¼ to ⅓ in. long, lavender to purplish; disc yellow. Fruit a lightly pubescent achene. Distribution: Oklahoma to Alabama, south to Louisiana, Texas, and adjacent Mexico.

BROAD-LEAVED ASTER   *Aster sagittifolius* Wedemeyer   (PL. 56)

Erect perennial herb 2 to 4½ ft. tall, the few to several stems glabrous or lightly pubescent above, with numerous lateral branches forming a rounded or conical crown. Leaves simple, alternate; petioles ⅓ to ½ as long as the blades, narrowly winged; blades thin, somewhat roughened, lower ones lanceolate to ovate, 2 to 5 in. long, margins coarsely serrate, base rounded or cordate, upper blades lanceolate, nearly or quite sessile, those of ultimate branchlets much smaller, often less than ¼ in. long, crowded, linear-subulate, glabrous or nearly so, their green tips spreading; rays 10 to 15, light blue to purple, ¼ to ⅓ in. long; disc yellow. Distribution: Maine to North Dakota, south to South Carolina and Texas.

The Asters comprise a very large genus, there being more than 650 species described from nearly all parts of the world except Australia. Out of this enormous assemblage some 45 species occur in Texas, about ⅓ of them commonly. Smooth Aster is found in fields, roadsides, and open woods mainly in East Texas, but extends as far west as Kerr and Erath counties. Narrow-leaved Aster occurs principally on limestone soils in Central Texas from Bexar County northward. Small-leaved Aster has a similar range, but is known from scattered localities as far east as Walker County and as far west as Eastland and Wichita counties. Annual Aster or Blackweed is the commonest of our native species, found throughout most of the state, though rather sparingly in the Trans-Pecos. It thrives in low places, as along streams, but readily survives in lawns and in cracks in pavement. While most of our Texas Asters bloom from September to November, Annual Aster flowers intermittently throughout most of the year, but most abundantly in the cool weather of autumn. Broad-leaved Aster is a fall-flowering species ranging from Harris, Navarro, and Grayson counties southwest to Kerr County. Several species are cultivated in gardens, providing welcome color at a time when most garden flowers are past their prime. The China-aster, *Callistephus hortensis* Cass., a closely related annual of China and Japan, is frequently grown for its large multiradiate heads of purple, pink, or white flowers.

TANSY-ASTER   *Machaeranthera tanacetifolia* (H. B. K.) Nees
(PL. 56)

Annual herb from a taproot, usually much branched and bushy, to
15 in. tall, glandular-pubescent and often viscid. Leaves alternate,
pinnatifid, the lower blades twice divided, the upper once or merely
toothed, 1 to 3 in. long, reduced upward. Heads terminal at branch
ends, 1¼ to 2 in. across, showy; involucre hemispheric, ⅓ to ½ in.
high; phyllaries mainly linear, glandular, with long, narrow, green,
spreading tips; rays 15 to 25, ⅖ to ⅗ in. long, red-violet to purple;
disc yellow. Fruit a pubescent achene. Distribution: Nebraska to
Texas, California, and adjacent Mexico.

Tansy-aster is gaining in favor as a garden annual, despite the fact
that its large asterlike heads are seldom produced in profusion, and
is sold by seedsmen under the name "Tahoka Daisy." In the wild
it is restricted to the Panhandle and the Trans-Pecos, extending as
far east as Dickens, Reagan, and Mitchell counties. Several additional
species, some of them perennials, occur in Texas, all in the Trans-
Pecos.

CUDWEED   *Gnaphalium wrightii* Gray   (PL. 56)

White wooly tufted perennial herb 6 to 20 in. tall, often diffusely
branched. Leaves simple, alternate, sessile; blades linear-spatulate to
lanceolate, 1 to 3 in. long, both surfaces copiously wooly. Heads
numerous, in open corymbose clusters at the ends of the branches;
involucre oblong or ovoid, *ca.* ⅕ in. high, very wooly at the base;
phyllaries bone-white to grayish, elliptic-spatulate to linear-spatulate,
acute, the inner ones apiculate; rays absent; disc whitish. Fruit a cylindrical achene *ca.* ½ in. long. Distribution: Colorado to West Texas
and California.

The Cudweeds are a cosmopolitan group of more than 125 species
of herbs which, taken as a whole, are rather distinctive in appearance, but seldom truly striking. They are most common in dry open
places, their characteristic wooly indument helping to check water
loss from aerial parts. *G. wrightii* is common on dry slopes and flats
in the Trans-Pecos and ranges eastward to Llano County. The silvery
flower heads appear from August to November. *G. purpureum* L., a
wide-ranging species found in East Texas and as far west as Erath
and Llano counties, has oblanceolate to obovate leaves, felty beneath but gray-green and merely pubescent above. *G. peregrinum*
Fern. has leaves gray-green on both sides, loosely pubescent beneath,
greener and less hairy above. It is a native of southern South America
now well established and common from Brazos and Travis counties
south to Cameron County, and sparingly encountered in scattered

localities north and east. *G. falcatum* Lam., also introduced from South America, ranging from Llano, Houston, and Galveston counties south to Kleberg County and locally northward to the Red River, has linear to oblanceolate leaves, usually less than ⅕ in. wide, about equally gray-pubescent on both sides. Several additional species are found in the state.

57   COCKLEBUR   *Xanthium speciosum* Kearney   (PL. 57)

Coarse somewhat pubescent annual herb with erect 4-angled stems 3 to 5 ft. tall, much branched, rigid, zigzag above. Leaves simple, alternate; petioles relatively slender, 3½ to 6 in. long, shorter above, pubescent along the upper groove; blades broadly triangular-ovate, sometimes broader than long, 5 to 10 in. across, reduced upward, shallowly 3- to 5-lobed, rough-pubescent on both sides, strongly veined, especially beneath, base cordate. Heads rayless, of two sorts: those with staminate flowers in small terminal racemes, each head surrounded by a row of staggered phyllaries, the numerous florets each with a pair of slightly protruding stamens; and pistillate heads in clusters in the upper leaf axils, each with 2 florets enclosed by the involucre which is covered with hooked bristles. Fruit an achene ¾ to 1¼ in. long, long-beaked, enclosed by the spiny involucre. Distribution: North Dakota to Tennessee and Texas.

So widely spread are the 4 or 5 species of Cocklebur that it is hard to determine their native place. It is presumed to be in the Mediterranean region, but longtime unintentional transport of the spiny fruits in agricultural produce has led to their introduction in nearly all parts of the world. In addition to lowering the quality of wool, a situation which has led to local and usually unsuccessful attempts at extermination, Cockleburs are mechanically injurious when consumed and also contain a toxic glucoside. The young seedlings are even more poisonous and may prove fatal to hogs, cattle, and sheep. *X. speciosum* is known in scattered localities from Tarrant County south to the lower Rio Grande. *X. saccharatum* Wallr., with nearly straight spines on the achenes, is found from Taylor and Tarrant counties south to Bandera and Wharton counties, and no doubt elsewhere. *X. spinosum* L., the commonest species in West Texas, often abounding in waste places, ranges from Real and Edwards counties west to the Trans-Pecos, and is distinct with its much longer than broad leaf blades and its spiny leaf bases. All species flower in summer and early fall.

MOUNTAIN DAISY   *Melampodium cinereum* DC.   (PL. 57)

Perennial herb with tufted stems 4 to 12 in. long, commonly diffusely branched, the branches usually spreading, gray-pubescent, often

(230)

roughly so. Leaves opposite, simple, sessile; blades linear to linear-spatulate, ¾ to 2¼ in. long, entire or remotely blunt-toothed, somewhat reduced upward, rough-pubescent on both sides. Heads solitary; involucre cup-shaped or saucer-shaped; phyllaries 4, ovate, *ca.* ⅕ in. long, united to about halfway from the base; rays 7 to 11, white, often with purplish lines beneath, ⅓ to ⅖ in. long; disc yellow. Fruit an achene, broadened upward and somewhat incurved. Distribution: Kansas and Arkansas, south to Texas, Arizona, and adjacent Mexico.

Mountain Daisy also has the common names Blackfoot Daisy, Prairie Daisy, and Rock Daisy, and is found throughout Texas west of Wilbarger, Bell, and Jim Wells counties, most abundantly on limestone soils in the central portion. The flowering period extends from April to October. It is frequently a handsome plant, the spreading branches covered with heads, strongly resistant to drought and thriving in the most barren situations. *M. cinereum* var. *ramosissimum* (DC.) Gray has lobed leaves, and rays not more than ¼ in. long. It is found on plains from Frio, Zavala, and Maverick counties southeast to Cameron County. *M. hispidum* H. B. K., a slender-stemmed branching annual with rather inconspicuous heads, grows in the Davis Mountains of Jeff Davis County.

TEXAS-STAR *Lindheimera texana* Engelm. & Gray (PL. 57)

Pubescent annual herb 6 to 24 in. tall, ultimately with numerous branches. Leaves simple, alternate below, opposite above, sessile; blades variable, the lower spatulate to obovate, long-tapered at the base, the upper ones oblong-lanceolate to ovate, all pubescent, entire or coarsely toothed. Heads solitary or few in a cluster; involucre cup-shaped, ⅖ to ⅔ in. high; phyllaries in 2 rows, linear-lanceolate to ovate, with a few gland-tipped and many glandless hairs on the margin; rays usually 5, bright yellow, *ca.* ⅗ in. long; disc yellow, with few florets. Fruit an incurved achene *ca.* ¼ in. long, prolonged at the top into 2 hornlike teeth. Distribution: Central Texas.

Texas-star, also known as Star Daisy or Lindheimer's Daisy, occurs mainly on limestone soils from Grayson, Leon, and Calhoun counties westward to Childress, Nolan, and Val Verde counties. The heads appear in March and continue to May, or later with rains.

The Daisy Family is the largest family of flowering plants, embracing about 1,000 genera and 20,000 species, found in most parts of the earth in nearly all habitats. The family is readily recognized by the inflorescence, a head subtended by or invested in an involucre of usually numerous bracts or phyllaries, the modification of the sepals into hairs, bristles, or bumps (the pappus), the single-ovuled ovary, the 5 stamens usually cohering by their anthers, and the 2-seeded achene fruit. As might be expected in a family of these proportions, there are numerous economic plants, among them: Lettuce, *Lactuca;* Endive and Chicory, *Cichorium;* Salsify, *Trago-pogon;* Pyrethrum, *Chrysanthemum;* Safflower, *Carthamnus.* Ragweed, *Ambrosia,* is an important cause of hay fever.

CUT-LEAVED DAISY   *Engelmannia pinnatifida* Gray   (PL. 57)

Perennial herb from a thick root, 1 to 3 ft. tall, usually with several stiffly pubescent, erect to spreading stems forming a rounded crown. Leaves simple, alternate; lower leaves with petioles ½ to ¾ as long as the blades, becoming progressively shorter upward, the uppermost leaves sessile; blades deeply pinnatifid ¾ to ⅞ of the way to the midrib, the lobes again lobed or round-toothed, 3 to 6 in. long, reduced upward, the uppermost blades with a few coarse teeth or entire, harshly pubescent. Heads long-stalked, solitary or in corymbs; involucre hemispheric or cup-shaped, *ca.* ¼ in. high; phyllaries in 2 or 3 series, the outer linear, the inner broad but with linear tips, all ciliate; rays 8 to 10, yellow, *ca.* ⅖ in. long; disc yellow. Fruit a ciliate oblong-ovate achene *ca.* 3⁄16 in. long. Distribution: Kansas to Louisiana, Texas, and Arizona.

A very common plant of plains and prairies, the Cut-leaved Daisy is found over most of the state west of Fannin, Waller, and Kleberg counties, and flowers from March to June. The rays expand in late afternoon and fold under the following morning in intense sunlight. A member of the Sunflower Tribe of the Daisy Family, this plant has among its near relatives such well-known garden plants as the Zinnia, *Zinnia elegans* Jacq., Cosmos, *Cosmos bipinnatus* Cav., and Dahlia, *Dahlia variabilis* Desf., all natives of Mexico. The genus *Engelmannia* is named for George Engelmann, botanist of St. Louis who played a most important role in discovering and describing new plants in the West during the middle and late 1800's.

58   BLACK-EYED–SUSAN   *Rudbeckia   serotina*   Nutt.   [= *R.   bicolor* Nutt. = *R. hirta* L. var. *serotina* (Moore) Perdue]   (PL. 58)

Annual or perennial herb with coarse roots, stems usually branched, 1 to 2½ ft. tall, bristly-pubescent. Leaves simple, alternate, sessile or the basal ones (usually withered by flowering time) short-petioled; blades elliptic to oblong or oblong-ovate, 1 to 4½ in. long, not more than 5 times longer than wide, firmly pubescent, entire or sparingly and shallowly toothed, mostly acute at the apex. Heads solitary at branch ends, on peduncles 1½ to 8 in. long; involucre hemispheric; phyllaries linear to linear-oblong, ⅓ to ¾ in. long; rays 12 to 20, yellow or orange, ¾ to 1⅓ in. long; disc ovoid or conical, brown. Fruit a 4-angled achene. Distribution: South Carolina to Florida and Texas.

CONE-FLOWER   *Rudbeckia amplexicaulis* Vahl [= *Dracopis am-plexicaulis* (Vahl) Cass.]   (PL. 58)

Annual herb, usually few-branched, 1 to 2½ ft. tall, with smooth striate stems. Leaves simple, alternate, the lower with petioles *ca.* ⅓ as long as the blades, the upper sessile and clasping the stem; blades spatulate to oblong or ovate, the lower ones usually deeply lobed, the lobes blunt-toothed, progressively less lobed and toothed upward, the uppermost entire or with a few shallow teeth, 1¼ to 4 in. long. Heads solitary, long-peduncled; involucre cup-shaped; phyllaries lanceolate to linear-lanceolate, ¼ to ⅓ in. long, rays 5 to 10, yellow, sometimes red-brown at the base, ⅖ to 1 in. long; disc brown, ovoid or conical. Fruit a cylindrical striate achene *ca.* 1/12 in. long. Distribution: Georgia to Texas.

Rudbeckia is an American genus of some 35 species, several of which have found favor as garden plants. A large variety of insects find in the disc flowers, according to their needs, nectar or pollen or both, the takers including honeybees and numerous wild bees, as well as bugs, flies, butterflies, and beetles. *R. serotina* ranges from Wichita, Grayson, and Anderson counties south to Wilson and Goliad counties, and flowers from May to July. The very similar *R. divergens* Moore [= *R. hirta* L. var. *divergens* (Moore) Perdue], differing by having stem leaves 5 to 9 times longer than wide and peduncles 2½ to 12 in. long, is common in southeastern Texas east of Harris County, and extends northward to Henderson and Red River counties. It flowers from May to midsummer, or, with adequate moisture, to September. *R. amplexicaulis* extends from Grayson, Van Zandt, Brazos, and Gonzales counties northwestward to Taylor and Childress counties. It blooms from mid-spring to early summer. Several additional species occur in the state.

MEXICAN-HAT   *Ratibida columnaris* (Pursh) Raf.   (PL. 58)

Perennial herb 1½ to 3½ ft. tall, minutely pubescent, often flowering the first year. Leaves alternate, pinnately compound or deeply lobed into 5 to 9 narrow segments, 2 to 4½ in. long. Heads solitary on peduncles 2 to 10 in. long; involucre cup-shaped; phyllaries few, loosely arranged; rays yellow-orange, commonly with a deep reddish-brown base, sometimes only the tip yellow; disc at first hemispheric, finally columnar, changing from grayish brown to yellowish brown with age. Fruit an angled wing-margined achene. Distribution: Minnesota south to Tennessee, Texas, and Arizona.

Long cultivated in the gardens of Europe, the Mexican-hat rightfully deserves a place in Texas plantings, though as yet it is seldom seen there. The flowers are produced, often in profusion, from May to

(233)

July, even later if there is plenty of water and if the old heads are picked off. In the wild this species is found in fields and open woods over most of Texas west of Grayson, McLennan, and Galveston counties. *R. tagetes* (James) Barnhart is usually lower, rarely taller than 2 ft., and has peduncles ¾ to 2 in. long bearing heads with mainly brownish-purple soon-drooping rays and globose or ovoid discs. It occurs in the Panhandle and the Trans-Pecos. *R. peduncularis* (Torr. & Gray) Barnhart is a slender gray-pubescent annual to 3 ft. with most of the leaves crowded at the base and long-stalked heads with yellow rays and fingerlike discs. While found most commonly near the coast from Calhoun County southward, this species extends inland as far as Bexar County.

PURPLE CONE-FLOWER   *Echinacea angustifolia* DC. [= *Brauneria angustifolia* (DC.) Heller]   (PL. 58)

Perennial herb with a thick black root, the slender rough-pubescent stem 1 to 3 ft. tall, simple or few-branched. Leaves simple, alternate, the lower ones long-petioled, the upper sessile; blades lanceolate or linear-lanceolate, hirsute, 3 to 8 in. long, acute at the apex, narrowed at the base, 3- or 5-veined, entire. Heads solitary at the ends of long peduncles; involucre saucer-shaped; phyllaries narrow, in 2 to 4 series; rays 10 to 12, ¾ to 1½ in. long, not more than 1½ times longer than the breadth of the disc, rosy-lavender or occasionally white; disc ¾ to 1¼ in. high, hemispheric, with stiff, sharp-pointed, brownish or purplish scales. Fruit an acutely 4-angled achene. Distribution: Kansas and Tennessee to Arkansas and Texas.

Purple Cone-flower, or Black-sampson as it is sometimes called, is found east from Randall, Garza, Kerr, and De Witt counties to the Louisiana border, most commonly in fields and open woods in limestone or gravelly soils. *E. pallida* Nutt. is similar but has a smaller disc and rays 1½ to 2½ times longer than the breadth of the disc. It is found on sandy soils in East Texas, west to Parker and Gillespie counties. Both species flower in May and June. Indians used the roots of both for a variety of ailments. Juice was applied to burns and superficial wounds; pieces of root were placed around an aching tooth. Even today an alcoholic tincture of Echinacea root is used in the healing of wounds and curing of sore throat.

SUNFLOWER   *Helianthus annuus* L.   (PL. 58)

Strongly pubescent annual herb from a taproot, usually 3 to 8 ft. tall but showing much variation in height. Leaves simple, alternate; petioles ⅓ to about as long as the blades; blades triangular-ovate to broadly lanceolate, 2½ to 12 in. long, usually reduced upward, acute or acuminate at the apex, toothed, at least near the apex, base cordate in lower leaves to cuneate in upper ones. Heads solitary on distinct peduncles; involucre cup- or basin-shaped; phyllaries ovate to narrowly oblong, overlapping in several rows, sharp-pointed; rays yellow, 1 to 2 in. long; disc brown, up to 1½ in. or more across. Fruit a flattened achene ⅕ to ¼ in. long. Distribution: south-central Canada to Texas and Mexico.

SUNFLOWER   *Helianthus maximiliani* Schrad.   (PL. 59)   **59**

Rough-pubescent perennial herb with few to numerous stems 3 to 8 ft. tall. Leaves simple, mostly alternate, sessile or very short-petioled; blades firm, lanceolate or linear-lanceolate, 3 to 7 in. long, acute, harshly pubescent, entire or indistinctly toothed. Heads numerous, terminal, and on short axillary peduncles; involucre cup-shaped; phyllaries linear-lanceolate, gray-pubescent, ⅓ to ½ in. long, long-pointed; rays 15 to 30, yellow, 1 to 1⅓ in. long; disc yellow, ⅗ to ¾ in. across, the anthers brown. Fruit a flattened achene. Distribution: Minnesota and Montana south to Texas.

Helianthus is a genus of 75 or more species of herbs, most of them from central and western North America, about ¼ of them known in Texas. *H. annuus* is the common Sunflower of fields, roadsides, and waste places west of Dallas, Washington, Calhoun, and Cameron counties. There has been much speculation regarding the origin of the cultivated Sunflower from this species. Most recent evidence suggests that wild Sunflowers were first brought into domestication in pre-Columbian times by Indians of Central North America, who then carried their gradually improving crop eastward. Early explorers visiting the Atlantic coastal region returned with seeds to Europe, where, for a time, Sunflowers were grown merely as curiosities. Sometime before 1800 the Sunflower reached Russia, where its potentialities as a food crop were rapidly exploited, and, as a result of selection and breeding the giant one-headed large-seeded plants were developed. Thus the Sunflower is unusual as an economic plant in that it had its origin in temperate North America; the majority of American food plants (e.g., potato, tomato, corn, various beans, etc.) were originally from Central and South America. Another economic species is *H. tuberosus* L., the Jerusalem-artichoke, with edible subterranean tuberous stems resembling potatoes. *H. maximiliani*, often cultivated in gardens for its profusion of flowers in late summer, is found wild mainly in limestone soils from Dallas, McLennan, and Harris counties west to Val Verde County.

GOLDEN-WAVE   *Coreopsis grandiflora* Hogg.   (PL. 59)

Perennial herb with erect or ascending, usually branched stems 1 to 2 ft. high, glabrous throughout except for the ciliate petiolar margins.

(235)

Leaves opposite, 4 to 7 pairs, pinnately compound or deeply lobed, 3 to 6 in. long, the divisions linear-spatulate, the basal and lower stem leaves petioled. Heads terminal, 1½ to 2¼ in. across; involucre cup-shaped; phyllaries in 2 series, the outer lanceolate, ¼ to ⅓ in. long, the inner ones united, slightly longer; rays yellow, obovate, 3-lobed at the apex; disc yellowish brown. Fruit an orbicular achene *ca.* ⅒ in. long with outspread wings. Distribution: Kansas and Missouri to Georgia, Texas, and New Mexico.

Long a favorite flower-garden subject in America and Europe, Golden-wave, also called Tickseed or Coreopsis, is found as a wild-flower in East Texas west to Denton and Colorado counties. The variety *longipes* (Hook.) Torr. & Gray, with only 1 to 4 pairs of leaves below the flowers, the lobes fewer and broader or the leaves entire, is found southward from Cooke County. Both flower from April to June. Other species found in the state include: *C. nuecensis* Hell., annual, usually somewhat hairy, with bright yellow rays often marked with purplish brown at the base, and achenes with incurved thickened wings, from Burleson, Caldwell, and Frio counties south to Willacy County; *C. tinctoria* L., a glabrous annual with reddish-brown bases on the otherwise yellow rays and thin, flat, oblong, wingless achenes, Lamar, Angelina, and Orange counties west to Llano County and northwestward to the Panhandle; *C. basalis* (Dietrich) Blake, annual, with outer involucral bracts about as long as the inner ones, leaves mostly toward the base of the plant, pedun-cles 2 to 8 in. long, yellow rays with purplish-brown bases, and thick, obovate achenes, Gulf Coast north to Van Zandt County; *C. basalis* var. *wrightii* (Gray) Blake, with narrower leaflet lobes, occurs as far west as Taylor and Kerr counties; *C. cardaminaefolia* (DC.) Torr. & Gray, with simple but deeply toothed leaves, yellow rays with reddish- or purplish-brown bases, and winged achenes, south of Orange, Harris, and Burnet counties and west of Taylor and Childress counties.

BEGGAR-TICK   *Bidens bipinnata* L.   (No illustration)

Erect annual herb with a nearly or quite glabrous, 4-angled, branch-ing stem 1 to 5 ft. tall. Leaves opposite or the upper ones sometimes alternate, the blades once or twice pinnately dissected, the divisions again incised or lobed, 2 to 7 in. long, reduced upward. Heads soli-tary; involucre cup-shaped; outer phyllaries 7 to 10, linear, shorter than the acute-tipped inner ones; rays absent or few, cream-colored, seldom longer than the breadth of the disc, entire or nearly so; disc yellowish brown. Fruit a spindle-shaped achene ½ to ⅗ in. long, with a pappus of 3 or 4 barbed projections. Distribution: native of Europe; naturalized from Rhode Island to Nebraska, south to Florida, and Arizona, and from Mexico to South America.

This is a weedy annual of moist, shady places from Grayson, Bowie, and San Augustine counties, southwest to Gonzales County, usually around 2 or 3 ft. tall. The flowers make but little show, there being 4 to 6 small pale yellowish rays, or frequently none at all. The relatively few disc flowers give rise to the interesting achenes known as Spanish needles, which take on nuisance value as they tenaciously cling to clothing. Despite the absence of conspicuous flags, bees are the main visitors and the honey made from Beggar-tick nectar is said to be of high quality. Beggar-tick blooms from July to September. About 5 additional species, all yellow-rayed, occur in Texas, all but one in the eastern half.

THELESPERMA   *Thelesperma filifolium* (Hook.) Gray [erroneously listed in some works as *T. trifidum* (Poir.) Britt.]   (PL. 59)

Annual or short-lived perennial blooming the first year, with few to numerous erect loosely branched stems 8 to 30 in. tall. Leaves opposite, bipinnately divided, 1½ to 4 in. long, the filiform segments not broader than the rachis. Heads solitary, nodding in bud; involucre cup-shaped; phyllaries in 2 series, the outer linear-subulate, the inner united about half way, papery-margined, about as long as the outer ones; rays 6 to 9, yellow, ⅖ to ⅔ in. long; disc purplish brown. Fruit a narrow achene ⅛ to ⅙ in. long. Distribution: South Dakota to Texas and adjacent Mexico.

THELESPERMA   *Thelesperma simplicifolium* Gray [= *T. subsimplicifolium* Gray]   (PL. 59)

Perennial from a woody root, with numerous loosely branched striate stems 15 to 40 in. tall. Leaves opposite, 1 to 3 in. long, the lower pinnately divided with 3 to 5 linear lobes, the upper ones fewer-lobed, the uppermost simple, margins otherwise entire. Heads solitary; involucre cup-shaped; phyllaries in 2 series, the outer linear to oblong, green, the inner much larger, brown, united at base, with papery margins; rays 6 to 9, yellow, ¼ to ⅓ in. long; disc yellowish brown, darkening with age. Fruit a spindle-shaped achene *ca.* ⅕ in. long. Distribution: Texas to Arizona and adjacent Mexico.

RAYLESS THELESPERMA   *Thelesperma megapotamicum* (Spreng.)   **60**
Ktze. [= *T. gracila* (Torr.) Gray]   (PL. 60)

Perennial herb with creeping rootstocks, stems 1 to several, usually branched, 1½ to 3 ft. tall. Leaves opposite, mostly confined to the lower ⅔ of the plant, usually twice pinnately divided below with linear divisions, reduced upward to the simple filiform uppermost leaves, 1 to 3 in. long. Heads solitary, long-peduncled; involucre cup-shaped; phyllaries in 2 series, the outer 4 to 6, ovate or oblong, green, the inner much larger, partly united, papery-margined above; rays

(237)

absent; disc yellow to yellowish brown, turning darker with age. Fruit a slender achene *ca.* ¼ in. long, tipped with 2 bristles not longer than the width of the achene. Distribution: Wyoming to Nebraska, south to Texas and Arizona.

Plants of the genera *Thelesperma* and *Coreopsis* are very similar, distinguished only by characters of the minute disc flowers and by the teeth of the rays (3 in *Thelesperma*, 4 in *Coreopsis*). *T. filifolium* is by far the commonest of our Thelespermas, flowering mainly from April to June, and ranging from Grayson, Washington, Calhoun, and Kenedy counties westward to the Trans-Pecos and the Panhandle, often blanketing fields, if only for a short time, with golden yellow. The brevity of the flowering period in some areas is due to the activity of larvae which develop from eggs laid in the buds by certain insects. Later, after the larvae have matured and left, flowering resumes and may continue sporadically until September. *T. simplicifolium* grows chiefly on limestone soils from McLennan, Karnes, and Jim Hogg counties west to the Trans-Pecos, and blooms from May to September. The relatively inconspicuous *T. megapotamicum* occurs in the Trans-Pecos and the Panhandle, and eastward as far as Clay and Young counties, flowering from April to October.

OLD-PLAINSMAN   *Hymenopappus artemisiaefolius* DC.   (PL. 60)

Leafy-stemmed, taprooted biennial herb 1 to 3½ ft. tall, the stem stout, finely gray-pubescent, striate, usually branched above. Leaves simple, alternate, mainly crowded at the base, reduced upward; blades green and lightly pubescent to nearly glabrous above, dense white-tomentose beneath, the earliest (lowest) ones lanceolate and entire or nearly so, followed by deeply and irregularly lobed blades 3½ to 8 in. long, the lobes again lobed or toothed, stem leaves once or twice pinnatifid with lanceolate to linear lobes, the uppermost ones less than 1 in. long, with a few lobes or nearly entire. Heads in corymbs; involucre ⅓ to ⅖ in. broad and *ca.* ¼ in. high; phyllaries in 2 series, papery, white or pale yellow to pink, ¼ to ⅓ in. long; disc grayish white to pale pink, the florets with reflexed corolla lobes. Fruit a hirsute, striate achene *ca.* ⅛ in. long. Distribution: Texas, Oklahoma, and Louisiana.

Old-plainsman is found in Texas from Wood, Williamson, Wilson, and Hidalgo counties eastward to the Gulf Coast and the Louisiana border, and is in flower from March to July. Other species in Texas, all with phyllaries ¼ in. long or less, include: *H. scabiosaeus* L'Herit., with greenish or yellowish white disc corollas, a common plant of fields, roadsides, and waste places from Grayson, Washington, and Bee counties westward over the Edwards Plateau, more sparingly to the Trans-Pecos and the Panhandle; *H. flavescens* Gray, with deep yellow disc corollas, the flowering period extending from May to September, in sandy soils from the Panhandle to the Trans-Pecos and eastward to Runnels County; *H. tenuifolius* Pursh, a perennial with linear or filiform leaf segments and downrolled margins, from Fannin and Bexar counties northwestward to the Panhandle.

YELLOW DAISY   *Tetraneuris scaposa* (DC.) Greene [= *Actinea scaposa* (DC.) Ktze.]   (PL. 60)

Perennial herb with a woody branched caudex and ascending or creeping branches 2 to 5 in. long. Leaves alternate, crowded on the short wooly-pubescent stems, sessile or nearly so; blades linear to linear-lanceolate, sparingly long-hairy, 3 to 5 in. long, entire, the apex acute to obtuse, base gradually tapering. Heads on peduncles 3½ to 15 in. tall, densely silvery-pilose with whitish or grayish hairs, especially at the top; involucre similarly pilose, especially at the base, *ca.* ¼ in. high, ⅓ to ½ in. across; phyllaries numerous, purplish-tipped; rays 12 to 25, yellow, *ca.* ⅓ in. long, 4-nerved, 2 nerves converging at the apex of each of the 3 teeth; disc yellow. Fruit a pubescent ribbed achene topped with several scales. Distribution: Arkansas to Texas, New Mexico, and adjacent Mexico.

Yellow Daisy is a common plant, especially in coarse limestone soils, and ranges from Dallas, Travis, and Webb counties west to the Trans-Pecos and northward to the Panhandle. In unusually wet years the flowering period extends from February to October, but normally it ends in June and resumes in September. Other species include: *T. linearifolia* (Hook.) Ktze., a branched annual with leaves at first crowded at the base but later more evenly distributed along the branches, 6 to 15 yellow rays, occurring throughout the state westward from Grayson, Harris, and Kleberg counties; *T. glabra* (Nutt.) Greene, similar to *T. scaposa* but the peduncle and involucre base with grayish or yellowish hairs, involucre *ca.* ⅕ in. high, rays ⅕ to ¼ in. long, from Archer and Eastland counties westward to the northern Trans-Pecos and in the Panhandle.

POISON BITTERWEED   *Hymenoxys odorata* DC. [= *Actinea odorata* (DC.) Ktze.]   (PL. 60)

Low, usually much-branched annual herb 4 to 20 in. tall, the stems puberulent, striate. Leaves alternate, 1½ to 2½ in. long, once or twice pinnately divided into narrowly linear segments, reduced upward. Heads solitary on peduncles 1 to 2 in. long, numerous; involucre cup-shaped; phyllaries 6 to 10, lanceolate, acute, united at base, thick and convex on back, membranaceous on margins; rays yellow, oblanceolate, ¼ to ⅓ in. long, with 3 teeth at tip; disc yellow-orange. Fruit an achene *ca.* 1⁄10 in. long, densely hirsute, with a projection at the top.

Distribution: Kansas to Colorado, south to Texas, southern California, and adjacent Mexico.

A rounded plant with many yellow-rayed, orange-centered daisylike flowers, and feathery foliage that becomes aromatic when bruised—this is a general description of an attractive plant of the Edwards Plateau, the Trans-Pecos, and the Panhandle, but for sheep ranchers, it is a description of trouble, especially in late winter and early spring and in dry periods thereafter. As the common name suggests, this is a poisonous plant, sheep being the most severely affected, and its abundance on the range seems related to low rainfall and frequent, close cropping of other plants by stock. The flowering period is from April to June and sporadically later.

61 BITTERWEED *Helenium amarum* (Raf.) H. Rock [= *H. tenuifolium* Nutt.] (PL. 61)

Annual herb with 1 or few erect stems branched above, 1 to 2½ ft. tall, often forming a rounded mass of foliage. Leaves simple, alternate, numerous; blades narrowly linear, ½ to 2 in. long, very finely resin-dotted, entire or the lowest ones (usually dying away by flowering time) wavy-margined. Heads few to numerous, solitary on slender peduncles 2 to 6 in. long; involucre flat or shallowly cup-shaped; phyllaries few, linear-subulate, ⅙ to ¼ in. long, spreading or reflexed; rays few, yellow, ¼ to ⅓ in. long, with 3 or 4 terminal teeth; disc hemispherical, yellow, ¼ to ⅓ in. across. Fruit an achene *ca.* ⅛ in. long, broadest above the middle. Distribution: Virginia and Missouri to Florida and Texas.

SNEEZEWEED *Helenium latifolium* Mill. [= *H. autumnale* of authors] (PL. 61)

Perennial herb, often rather stout, the stems 1 to 3½ ft. tall, finely rough-pubescent to nearly glabrous, longitudinally winged from leaf bases, branched above. Leaves simple, alternate, sessile; blades lanceolate to narrowly elliptic, 1½ to 6 in. long, very finely glandular-dotted, remotely and shallowly serrate, or the upper blades entire. Heads numerous, solitary or in open corymbs, on peduncles 1½ to 3 in. long; involucre flat; phyllaries linear, long-pointed, ⅕ to ¼ in. long; rays several, yellow, ⅖ to ⅗ in. long, with 3 or 4 terminal teeth; disc globose or hemispheric, ⅖ to ⅗ in. in diameter. Fruit an achene *ca.* ⅒ in. long. Distribution: Connecticut to Minnesota, south to Florida and Texas.

Bitterweed, also called Bitter Sneezeweed, Eastern Bitterweed, or Fineleaf Sneezeweed, is the most common species of *Helenium* in Central and East Texas, ranging as far west as Eastland and Frio counties. It is a poisonous plant to sheep and is a problem for dairymen too, for it imparts an undesirable flavor to milk. Bitterweed flowers continuously or intermittently from May to November. Sneezeweed (*H. latifolium*) is either quite harmless or at least not sufficiently toxic to pose problems. It is found from Tarrant and Gonzales counties westward to Kerr County and northward into the Panhandle and blooms from July to October. About 10 additional species of *Helenium* are known in Texas, one of which, Purplehead Sneezeweed, *H. flexuosum* Raf. (*H. nudiflorum* Nutt.), a perennial of fields in the pine belt of extreme East Texas, with orange rays and reddish-brown discs, is reported as toxic to livestock.

FIRE-WHEEL   *Gaillardia pulchella* Foug.   (PL. 61)

Annual herb 1 to 2½ ft. tall, commonly producing numerous ascending branches from the base, the stems striate, short-hirsute with upward-directed hairs. Leaves simple, alternate, sessile or nearly so, the uppermost clasping the stem; blades of the lower leaves oblanceolate or oblong, 1½ to 4 in. long, irregularly round-toothed or -lobed, densely short-hirsute on upper surface, more sparingly so beneath, upper blades lanceolate, entire or wavy-margined, ¾ to 1½ in. long. Heads solitary on peduncles 2 to 8 in. long; involucre at first shallowly cup-shaped, later flattened; phyllaries lanceolate, whitish, and united at the base, long-pointed; rays ⅓ to ¾ in. long, red with yellow at the tip, deeply 3-cleft; disc spherical, yellowish brown to purplish brown, ⅓ to ⅔ in. across, the florets intermixed with stiff bristles. Fruit a densely hirsute achene *ca*. ¹⁄₁₀ in. long. Distribution: Missouri and Nebraska to Louisiana, Texas, and New Mexico.

PINCUSHION DAISY   *Gaillardia suavis* (Gray & Engelm.) Britt. & Rusby [= *G. trinervata* Small]   (PL. 61)

Perennial herb often forming dense stands, the stems very short, rising very little above the tough, branching roots. Leaves alternate, all basal on the short stems, petiolate, slightly fleshy; blades mostly spatulate in outline, 2 to 5 in. long, varying from entire to twice-pinnatifid, glabrous. Heads solitary on peduncles 8 to 25 in. tall; involucre flat; phyllaries several, united but not basally whitened, their tips reflexed; rays absent or if present not more than ⅓ in. long, pale orange to red-orange, deeply 3-cleft; disc spherical, ⅔ to 1 in. broad, deep reddish orange to brown, the florets heavy-scented. Fruit a 5-ribbed pubescent achene. Distribution: Missouri to Texas.

Fire-wheel or Indian-blanket is found throughout Texas except in the forested and driest parts, and should there ever be held a convention of state flowers, this plant could well deputize for the Bluebonnet. Fire-wheel covers miles of roadsides in prairie districts from April to June with rusty red and innumerable flecks of yellow. The plant does very well in cultivation and readily self-sows. Indeed,

(241)

Fire-wheel is one of the most popular garden annuals elsewhere in the country and in Europe. Pincushion Daisy makes up for lack of visual attraction by its odor, rather suggestive of that of gardenias. It is found in fields and roadsides west of Cooke, Bell, Fayette, and Kleberg counties, and flowers from April to June. With adequate moisture and removal of old heads, both species may be induced to flower until late summer.

62 PAPER DAISY   *Baileya multiradiata* Harv. & Gray   (PL. 62)

> Annual or biennial herb 8 to 18 in. high, with erect or more commonly ascending much-branched wooly stems, usually more or less leafless below at flowering time. Leaves alternate, the lower ones once or twice pinnatifid, progressively reduced upward to the linear, entire uppermost ones, ½ to 2½ in. long, densely gray-wooly. Heads solitary, long-peduncled; involucre cup-shaped; phyllaries numerous, linear, densely gray-wooly; rays 25 to 50, ⅓ to ⅗ in. long, yellow, persistent; disc yellow. Fruit an oblong-prismatic striate achene. Distribution: West Texas to Utah, southern California, and adjacent Mexico.

A common and attractive plant of hills and flats in the Trans-Pecos, Paper Daisy, or Desert Baileya, flowers intermittently throughout most of the year. Unfortunately, stock ranchers have little affection for this daisy because its aerial parts, whether fresh or dry, are quite toxic to sheep. Goats are also susceptible but do not appear to eat the plant. Horses and cattle graze Paper Daisy but seem unaffected. Poisoning becomes a problem in dry periods when the evaporation-reducing efficiency of Paper Daisy's wooly indument permits its continued existence while less well-endowed plants wither and die. A hardy plant, Paper Daisy resists 2, 4-D spray in dry weather, but can be killed by it after rains.

MILFOIL   *Achillea millefolium* L.   (PL. 62)

> Aromatic perennial herb from a creeping rootstock, the stems usually unbranched below the inflorescence, 1 to 3½ ft. tall, striate, sparingly covered with long weak hairs. Leaves alternate, bi- or tri-pinnatifid, the numerous ultimate divisions linear or filiform, lower blades oblanceolate in outline, 4 to 8 in. long, petiolate, the shorter upper ones narrowly lanceolate or linear, sessile. Heads many, in broad compound corymbs; involucre cup-shaped, *ca.* ⅕ in. high, hairy; phyllaries *ca.* 20, in 4 series; rays 20 to 25, yellowish white, rarely pink; disc similarly colored. Fruit a wing-margined achene *ca.* 1/12 in. long. Distribution: native of Europe, widely naturalized in temperate America.

Milfoil is one member of a large Old World genus of aromatic herbs, some of them, including Milfoil, having had considerable value in early medicine. The herbals of the Middle Ages attributed sweeping curative powers to Milfoil; influenza, gout, liver malfunctions, kidney ailments, and many other maladies were supposedly amenable to its effects. Today Milfoil seems generally out of favor, not only in the pharmacopoeias but also in flower and herb gardens. Still, it provides a pleasing appearance in roadsides and fields in late spring and early summer, and whether in a vase or dried and mixed with other aromatics, it imparts a pleasantly spicy fragrance. Milfoil, sometimes called Yarrow, is found in northeastern Texas west to Cooke, Erath, and Gillespie counties, and in scattered localities elsewhere. *A. lanulosa* Nutt., very similar and sometimes treated as a variety of the preceding, is somewhat more pubescent and has upturned leaf segments. It ranges westward from Grayson, Parker, and Eastland counties to the Trans-Pecos and the Panhandle.

RAGWORT   *Senecio plattensis* Nutt.   (PL. 62)

Perennial herb from a rhizome, the erect stems reaching 8 to 20 in. Leaves alternate, the basal ones with petioles 1 to 4 in. long; blades ovate or elliptic, wooly when young, becoming glabrate with age, lower stem leaves sessile and with pinnatifid oblong-lobed blades, upper leaves linear-lanceolate, pinnatifid or toothed, 1 to 2 in. long. Heads in corymbs; involucre cup-shaped, *ca.* ¼ in. high, soft-hairy at the base; phyllaries linear-lanceolate, acute, united to about halfway from the base by membranous margins; rays yellow-orange to orange, *ca.* ⅓ in. long; disc yellow-orange, *ca.* ⅓ in. broad. Fruit an achene *ca.* ¹⁄₁₂ in. long, short-bristly on the angles. Distribution: South Dakota and Wyoming to Colorado and Texas.

THREADLEAF GROUNDSEL   *Senecio longilobus* Benth. [= S. *filifolius*
Nutt.]   (PL. 62)

Perennial herb or subshrub from a stout root, 2 to 5 ft. tall, usually much branched. Leaves alternate, pinnately divided into 3 to 7 linear lobes, 2 to 4½ in. long, reduced upward, the uppermost less than 1 in. long and undivided, all gray with close felty pubescence. Heads solitary or arranged in corymbs; involucre cup-shaped, ⁵⁄₁₆ to ⅜ in. high; phyllaries numerous, linear, darkened at the base; rays several, yellow, 3- or 4-nerved; disc yellow to yellowish brown. Fruit a narrow flat-topped achene *ca.* ⅛ in. long. Distribution: Nebraska and Wyoming south to Texas, Arizona, and adjacent Mexico.

Senecio is one of the largest genera of flowering plants, some 2,000 species having been described. While the majority are perennial herbs, many are succulents, some with fleshy leaves, others with thickened stems; several are climbers and a few, such as S. *johnstoni* Oliv. of the slopes of Kilimanjaro, are trees. About 20 species, most of them perennial herbs, are found in Texas. Ragwort, or Squaw-

(243)

weed, is in flower from March to May and ranges from Fannin, Erath, and Gillespie counties eastward to Van Zandt and Victoria counties. *S. ampullaceus* Hook., a wooly-pubescent annual with entire or irregularly but shallowly toothed leaves and yellow heads from March to May, is found in open places from Anderson County south to Willacy County and west to Menard County. Butterweed, *S. glabellus* Poir., also an annual, has very deeply lobed or pinnately compound leaves, the end segment of the lower leaves much larger than the others and often broader than long. It bears yellow heads in spring and is found in damp places throughout East Texas and sparingly westward to the Trans-Pecos. Threadleaf Groundsel, ranging from the Panhandle and the Trans-Pecos eastward to Stephens and Kinney counties, and flowering from April to fall, is considered very toxic to cattle and horses. This is especially true of the young growth, the primary effect being the development of liver lesions. Butterweed is also suspected of causing trouble in dairy herds in northeastern Texas. Another West Texas species, *S. riddellii* Torr. & Gray, considered by some a form of *S. longilobus*, is greener and more definitely herbaceous but equal in toxicity to the latter.

63 TEXAS THISTLE   *Cirsium texanum* Buckl. [= *C. austrinum* (Small) E. D. Schulz]   (PL. 63)

Biennial or perennial herb from a taproot, 2 to 5 ft. tall, simple or sparingly long-branched above, wooly-pubescent. Leaves simple, alternate, numerous; blades narrowly oblong to lanceolate in outline, green above, whitish-felty beneath, 4 to 9 in. long, reduced upward, the irregular teeth or lobes spine-tipped, spines elsewhere on the margin smaller. Heads solitary; involucre cup-shaped, ⅔ to ¾ in. high, indented at the base; phyllaries many, overlapping, progressively longer upward, each tipped with a weak spine; rays absent; disc corollas deep rosy lavender. Fruit glabrous achene surmounted by a crown of pinnately branched pappus hairs united at the base. Distribution: Central and South Texas.

BULL THISTLE   *Cirsium horridulum* Michx. [= *Carduus spinosissimus* Walt.]   (PL. 63)

Biennial or winter annual, very variable in height at time of flowering, from 10 in. to 5½ ft., simple at first, later sparingly branched. Leaves simple, alternate, the basal ones petioled; blades mostly oblanceolate in outline, 8 to 24 in. long, reduced upward, irregularly lobed and toothed, the lobes and teeth ending in long rigid spines, other spines on margins usually much smaller, glabrous above, sometimes felty-pubescent beneath. Heads solitary or racemosely arranged; involucre 1½ to 2¼ in. high, subtended by a whorl of spiny-pinnatifid bracts often longer than the phyllaries; phyllaries many, hispid, the uppermost 1¼ to 2 in. long, linear, bristle-tipped; rays absent; disc corollas rosy lavender or occasionally pale yellow. Fruit an achene *ca.* ⅛ in. long. Distribution: Maine to Florida and Texas.

The thistles are a distinctive group of some 200 species of herbs of north-temperate regions, represented in Texas by about 18 species. Texas Thistle is a common plant west of Grayson, Washington, and Cameron counties, flowering in May and June. Bull Thistle is found in southeastern Texas, west to Rusk and Caldwell counties and south to Kenedy County. It flowers from February or March until May. Pasture Thistle, *C. undulatum* (Nutt.) Spreng., a clump-forming perennial species with rather shallowly lobed gray-green leaves, and phyllaries with long spiny tips, produces its lavender to white heads from May to July and ranges westward from Dallas and Bexar counties. *C. ochrocentrum* Gray is similar but has deeply pinnatifid green leaves, the bases of which are decurrent on the stem, and bears rosy-lavender flowers from May to October. It is found from Clay and Kimble counties west to Childress County and the Trans-Pecos.

STAR-THISTLE   *Centaurea americana* Nutt.   (PL. 63)

Erect annual herb 1½ to 5 ft. tall with glabrous ridged stems. Leaves simple, alternate, sessile; blades oblong or linear-lanceolate, 1 to 3½ in. long, entire or shallowly toothed. Heads solitary, showy, the peduncles dilated just below the involucre; involucre hemispheric, 1 to 2 in. in diameter; phyllaries numerous, appressed, in several series, prickly-margined; rays absent; disc rose-violet to pink around the outside, shading to white at the center, sometimes wholly white, the outermost disc florets enlarged. Fruit a hairy achene *ca.* ¼ in. long, with an oblique scar at the base. Distribution: Missouri to Louisiana, Texas, and Arizona, and in adjacent Mexico.

Star-thistle is our commonest native representative of a large genus of perennials and annuals, principally of the Mediterranean area. Flowering in June and July, it is found from Titus, Leon, Jefferson, and De Witt counties northwestward to the Trans-Pecos and the Panhandle, but is most common in East Central Texas. The Bachelor-button or Cornflower, *C. cyanus* L., a European species commonly cultivated for its blue, pink, purple, or white heads, is sometimes found as a roadside escape in populated areas. *C. melitensis* L., an annual 1 to 2 ft. tall with spiny-bracted yellow heads from April to June, grows in Central Texas from Travis and Bexar counties west to Pecos County. The pollination mechanism in *Centaurea* follows the pattern common for the Daisy Family except that in most species the stamens are touch-sensitive; on being contacted by probing insects they suddenly contract, forcing pollen out the top of the tube which is formed by their lateral fusion. In addition to *C. americana* and

C. cyanus, several species are cultivated as garden ornamentals. The closely related Burdock, *Arctium minus* Schk., a coarse weed introduced from Europe and now naturalized throughout most of temperate North America, is known from as far south as Arkansas and northern Louisiana and may be expected in northern Texas.

PEREZIA   *Perezia wrightii* Gray   (PL. 63)

> Erect perennial herb from a woody, wool-covered caudex, the 1 to several stems glabrous, 1 to 3 ft. tall. Leaves simple, alternate, sessile or with a very short thick petiole; blades oblong to ovate, 1 to 5 in. long, reduced upward, the margins sharply and unevenly toothed, the teeth tipped with weak spines, base more or less cordate or truncate. Heads numerous, in large corymbose clusters; involucre narrowly cup-shaped, ¼ to ⅓ in. long; phyllaries in 3 or 4 series, the innermost largest, all flat and obtuse or round-tipped; rays absent; disc pink to nearly white. Fruit a cylindrical achene topped with numerous hairlike bristles. Distribution: West Texas to Arizona and south into adjacent Mexico.

Perezia is a genus of 75 or more species of herbs and shrubs ranging from Texas, New Mexico, and Arizona to Argentina. Three species are of fairly common occurrence in West and South Texas. *P. wrightii,* the tallest, ranges from the Trans-Pecos eastward to Kimble and Uvalde counties. It flowers from May to August. *P. runcinata* Lagasca, a stemless plant, resembles a pink-flowered Dandelion, but has firm rather prickly-margined leaves, a cluster of long swollen roots, and up to 4 heads on a peduncle. It is found in dry fields and prairies from Travis, Karnes, and Cameron counties west to the Rio Grande and the Trans-Pecos. *P. nana* Gray is a low leafy-stemmed plant, rarely exceeding 1 ft. in height, with broadly ovate to nearly circular prickly-margined leaves ¾ to 1½ in. long. Each branch is terminated by a single pink head about 1 in. across. This species occurs on dry plains and slopes in the Trans-Pecos and eastward to Tom Green County.

64   TEXAS-DANDELION   *Pyrrhopappus multicaulis* DC. [= *Sitilias multicaulis* (DC.) Greene]   (PL. 64)

> Perennial or winter annual with milky juice, the few to several erect or ascending stems 6 to 20 in. tall. Leaves alternate and mainly basal; petioles ⅓ to ½ as long as the blades; blades 2 to 6 in. long, irregularly dentate to pinnatifid, the segments entire or toothed, upper leaves few, much reduced, the segments narrower or the blades merely toothed, the uppermost sometimes linear and entire. Heads solitary or a few together, long-peduncled; involucre ⅓ to ¾ in. long; phyllaries linear,

in 2 series, the inner whitish-margined, joined about halfway; the outer ones much smaller, subulate at the apex; rays bright yellow, oblong to linear-oblong, ⅔ to ¾ in. long. Fruit a reddish achene *ca.* ⅛ in. long, topped with a tuft of pappus hairs. Distribution: Florida to Texas and Arizona, south to Mexico.

Texas-dandelion is a common plant of grassy roadsides, pastures, and lawns, found mainly in the southern part of the state and northward to Chambers, Bastrop, Taylor, and Terrell counties. It flowers from March to May. *P. grandiflorus* Nutt. is a tuberous-rooted perennial with solitary heads on stems with very much reduced leaves, blooming in April and May, and occurring in scattered localities from Nolan, Childress, and Denton counties southeastward to Waller and Goliad counties. *P. geiseri* Shinners, an annual to 20 in. with leafy, pubescent stems, the uppermost leaves deeply several-lobed, is very common in Central Texas, ranging from Lamar, Grimes, and Waller counties west to Howard and Schleicher counties, and flowering from March to June. *P. carolinianus* (Walt.) DC. is similar to the preceding but often taller, sometimes to 3½ ft., and with glabrous leafy stems, the uppermost blades entire or with a pair of basal lobes. It is an East Texas plant, most frequent in the pine belt and extending westward to Grayson, Dallas, and Travis counties. In well-watered places most species continue to flower sporadically until early fall.

Sow-thistle   *Sonchus asper* (L.) Hill   (pl. 64)

Fibrous-rooted annual with a stout, hollow, leafy stem 2 to 5 ft. tall, usually unbranched below, exuding milky sap when bruised. Leaves alternate, simple; the lowest with margined petioles *ca.* ¼ as long as the blades; blades 4 to 12 in. long, obovate or oblanceolate, margins variable, from pinnatifid to merely toothed, the teeth with weak spine-like tips, blades of upper leaves sessile, clasping by an auricled base, the auricles rounded in outline. Heads several to many, ⅔ to 1 in. across; involucre cup-shaped, *ca.* ½ in. high; phyllaries in several series, linear, glabrous; rays pale yellow. Fruit a flat ribbed achene *ca.* 1/12 in. long, topped with a crown of pappus hairs. Distribution: native of Europe, generally naturalized throughout inhabited areas in temperate and subtropical regions.

Although almost everyone would call Sow-thistle a weed, it does nevertheless have features of interest. The milky sap has an intensely bitter taste, yet rabbits, pigs, goats, and sheep eat the whole plant with relish. In continental Europe Sow-thistle leaves are used as a component of salads and as an ingredient of soups. When mashed or cut up they are fed to ducks and geese. In Texas Sow-thistle is found most commonly on disturbed ground throughout most of the state. The flowers appear throughout most of the year on plants situated in damp places in the southern part of the state, but usually between March and June elsewhere. *S. oleraceus* L., also from Europe, is very similar but has pointed basal lobes on the clasping stem leaves, and the lower leaves usually have a triangular tip. This species is the common Sow-thistle of the lower Rio Grande Valley but is rare north of Travis and Brazos counties.

DANDELION   *Taraxacum officinale* Wiggers [= *T. taraxacum* (L.)
Karst.]   (PL. 64)

> Perennial or winter annual from a taproot, with bitter milky sap and without visible stem. Leaves simple, alternate, and all basal, usually numerous, glabrous or nearly so; petioles ¼ to ⅓ as long as blades; blades spatulate to oblong or oblanceolate in outline, irregularly dentate to runcinate-pinnatifid, 2 to 9 in. long, somewhat pubescent when young, becoming glabrous with age. Heads solitary on hollow scapes 4 to 20 in. long; involucre ⅗ to ¾ in. high; phyllaries green, the several outer rows short and reflexed, the 1 or 2 inner rows longer and erect to the spreading tips; rays bright yellow. Fruit a greenish-tan achene with a pappus of numerous persistent whitish hairs. Distribution: native of Europe; now rather generally naturalized in inhabited areas throughout most of temperate North America and elsewhere.

There is an interesting sequence of events in the development of the Dandelion's flower heads. In the bud stage the phyllaries completely cover the immature flowers within, but soon the outer rows turn back, followed by the inner rows, allowing the opening flowers, each with a strap-shaped ray, to spread apart. After pollination by various bees, flies, and butterflies, the flowers draw together in a vertical sheaf formed by the again enclosing phyllaries, now completely erect. At this point the style, anthers, and rays are shed and the top of the ovary elongates to form a neck or beak with the pappus hairs on top. The phyllaries again reflex, the achene fruits spread apart as the receptacle assumes a broad domelike form, and the feathery pappus radiates, becoming the parachute that carries the 2-seeded achene away on a breeze. The bitter principle, taraxin, notwithstanding, dandelion leaves have long been used in European dishes and as the basis for a wine. Dandelion is found principally in disturbed soils in and near towns, and is rather rare outside the northeastern part of the state. Far more common in the same region and further afield too is *T. erythrospermum* Andrz., scarcely different except for its reddish-brown achenes. Both species flower from February to June and at other times, especially in relatively cool, damp weather.

DWARF-DANDELION   *Krigia virginica* (L.) Willd. [= *Adopogon carolinianum* (Walt.) Britt.]   (PL. 64)

Small glabrous annual herb with milky juice and no stem. Leaves simple, alternate and all basal; blades spatulate to nearly linear in outline, ¾ to 4 in. long, coarsely toothed to deeply pinnatifid. Heads solitary on slender, erect or ascending peduncles 1½ to 20 in. tall, ½ to ⅔ in. across; involucre *ca.* ¼ in. high; phyllaries 8 to 18, flat, linear to lanceolate; rays yellow to yellow-orange. Fruit a 5-angled cone-shaped achene *ca.* ⅟₁₅ in. long, with pappus bristles about twice as long. Distribution: Maine to Minnesota, south to Florida and Texas.

The *Krigias* are a small group of North American herbs which resemble diminutive Dandelions. Dwarf-dandelion flowers mainly in early spring and is found in grassy fields and roadsides in East Texas as far west as Llano County. *K. occidentalis* Nutt. is similar but has 4 to 10 phyllaries, all keeled. It is commoner and ranges from Cooke and Grayson counties south to Brazoria and Kleberg counties. The flowers appear from March to May. *K. dandelion* (L.) Nutt. is a tuberous-rooted perennial with large heads up to 1 in. across in April and May, and occurs in open woods and fields in East Texas west to Grayson and Washington counties. *K. gracilis* (DC.) Shinners has 1 or more leaves or leaflike bracts on short, often branching stems and each floret measures ¼ to ⅓ in. long. This is a species of limestone soils, found from Hunt and Tarrant counties south to Comal and Gonzales counties. *K. oppositifolia* Raf. is similarly leafy-branched but has much smaller florets, each between ⅟₁₂ and ⅛ in. long, and is found mostly on sandy soils from the pine belt of extreme East Texas west to Tarrant and Blanco counties, and south to San Patricio County.

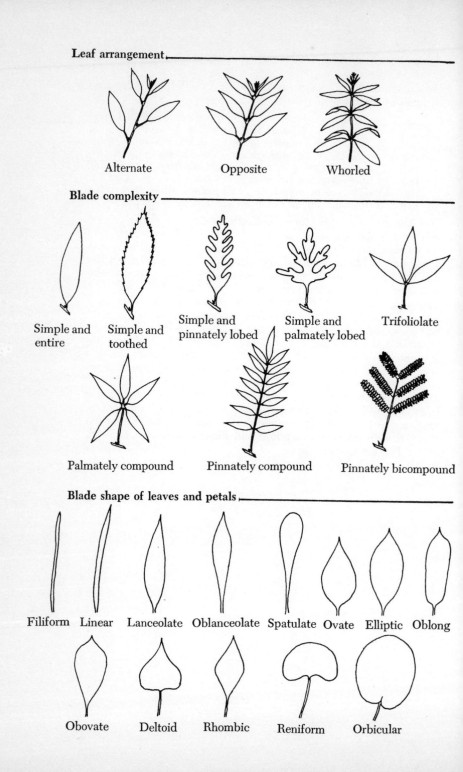

Leaf arrangement

Alternate   Opposite   Whorled

Blade complexity

Simple and entire   Simple and toothed   Simple and pinnately lobed   Simple and palmately lobed   Trifoliolate

Palmately compound   Pinnately compound   Pinnately bicompound

Blade shape of leaves and petals

Filiform   Linear   Lanceolate   Oblanceolate   Spatulate   Ovate   Elliptic   Oblong

Obovate   Deltoid   Rhombic   Reniform   Orbicular

Diagrams of the Parts of a Plant

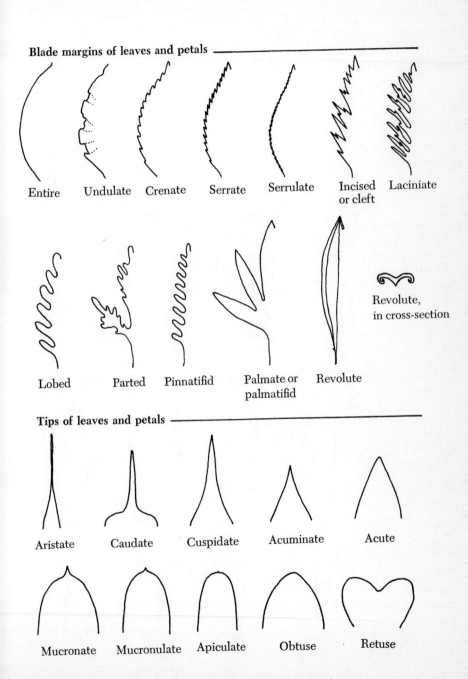

Blade margins of leaves and petals

Entire   Undulate   Crenate   Serrate   Serrulate   Incised or cleft   Laciniate

Lobed   Parted   Pinnatifid   Palmate or palmatifid   Revolute

Revolute, in cross-section

Tips of leaves and petals

Aristate   Caudate   Cuspidate   Acuminate   Acute

Mucronate   Mucronulate   Apiculate   Obtuse   Retuse

Bases of leaves and petals

Attenuate   Cuneate   Obtuse or rounded   Oblique

Truncate   Cordate   Auriculate   Sagittate

Hastate   Peltate   Perfoliate   Connate-perfoliate

Inflorescence types

Solitary   Spike (bractless)   Raceme (bracted)   Panicle

Cyme   Corymb   Umbel   Head

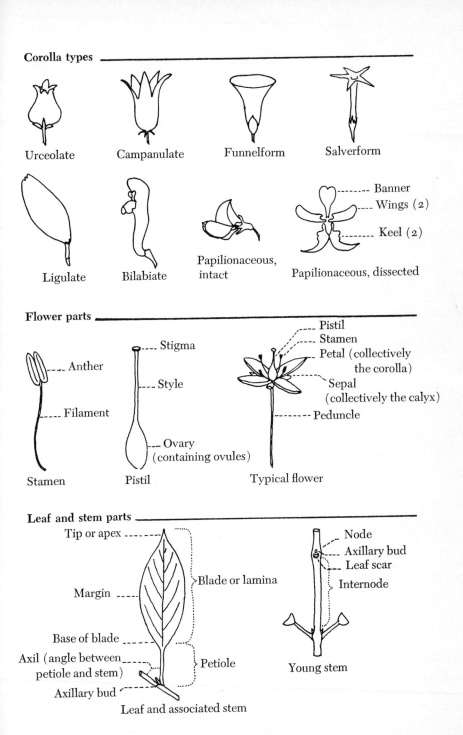

Corolla types

Urceolate   Campanulate   Funnelform   Salverform

Banner
Wings (2)
Keel (2)

Ligulate   Bilabiate   Papilionaceous, intact   Papilionaceous, dissected

Flower parts

Anther

Filament

Stamen

Stigma

Style

Ovary
(containing ovules)

Pistil

Pistil
Stamen
Petal (collectively
the corolla)
Sepal
(collectively the calyx)
Peduncle

Typical flower

Leaf and stem parts

Tip or apex

Margin

Base of blade

Axil (angle between petiole and stem)

Axillary bud

Blade or lamina

Petiole

Leaf and associated stem

Node
Axillary bud
Leaf scar
Internode

Young stem

Definition of Botanical Terms

Acaulescent. Stemless, or without visible stem

Achene. One-seeded, dry, indehiscent fruit in which the seed and ovary wall are grown together

Acuminate. Gently tapering to a point

Acute. Sharp-pointed

Alternate. Placed singly at different heights on the stem or axis

Annual. Living for 1 year or less

Anther. Pollen-bearing portion of a stamen, usually supported by the filament

Apetalous. Lacking petals

Apex. The tip or outer end

Apiculate. With a small, sharp, flexible point

Appendage. An attached subsidiary part

Appressed. Pressed against

Arborescent. Treelike

Aristate. Bearing a stiff bristle

Armed. Provided with any of a variety of sharp projections, e.g., spines, prickles, barbs, etc.

Articulate. Jointed

Ascending. Sloping upward

Attenuate. Long-tapered

Auricle. Lobe or projection extending below the base (usually of a leaf)

Awl-shaped. Narrow and tapering from the base to a sharp point

Awn. A bristlelike appendage

Axil. The upper angle between a leaf and the stem on which it is borne

Axillary. In an axil

Banner. The only unpaired and usually the largest and uppermost petal in flowers of the Pea Family (Leguminosae-Papilionoideae)

Barbed. Pertaining to bristles or other appendages provided with backward-directed hooks

Beak. A long, prominent point (especially on fruits)

Beard. A tuft or line of hairs, as on certain petals

Berry. A fleshy fruit with 1 to many seeds but no stone

Biennial. Living two years, and usually not flowering the first

Bladdery. Inflated, pouchy

Blade. The expanded, usually plane, portion of a leaf or petal

Bract. A much reduced leaf, especially one in whose axil a flower arises

Bracteole. A small bract, borne on a secondary axis of the inflorescence

(254)

Bractlet. A bracteole
Bristly. Bearing stiff, rigid, rather thick hairs
Bulb. An underground structure most closely resembling a large bud, made up of rings or layers of modified (usually fleshy) leaves and a short, centrally located stem from which the roots and aerial parts arise
Bush. A low, diffuse shrub having many stems

Caducous. Dropping early
Calyx. The outermost whorl of structures in a complete flower; the sepals in the collective sense
Campanulate. Bell-shaped
Canescent. Gray-pubescent; hoary
Cap. A convex part which falls off
Capillary. Hairlike
Capitate. Headlike; arranged in a head, i.e., in a very dense, compact cluster
Capsule. A dry fruit that opens by one or more splits or pores
Carpel. A unit of a compound pistil, formed of a highly modified, ovule-bearing leaf
Catkin. A scaly-bracted, usually pendulous spike or raceme that falls as a unit
Caudex. Stem; particularly the short, thick stem of certain low plants
Caulescent. Stem-bearing
Cauline. Belonging to or borne on the stem
Ciliate. Marginally hairy; fringed with hairs
Cinereous. Ashy-gray
Clasping. More or less surrounding the stem
Cleft. Lobed about halfway to the middle
Cleistogamous. Referring to closed, self-fertilized flowers
Coherent. Touching and sticking together, but not fused
Composite. Compound, of many parts; apparently simple but in fact composed of several distinct units
Compound. Made up of 2 or more similar parts
Compound inflorescence. One having additional degrees of branching, as in panicles; a raceme bearing smaller racemes
Compound leaf. One bearing 2 or more distinct blades from a common petiole
Compressed. Flattened
Connate. United, fused; related to the union of 2 or more similar structures to form one
Connective. The upper extension of the filament between and sometimes beyond the anther cells
Cordate. Heart-shaped; i.e., ovate in outline and with 2 rounded lobes at the base
Coriaceous. Leathery in texture
Corm. An enlarged stem base, often superficially bulblike, composed of solid tissue
Corolla. Typically, the whorl of showy flower parts, just inside the calyx; petals in the collective sense

Corona. An appendage or extension of petals or stamens, lying between the corolla and stamen whorls, and often suggesting a second set of petals

Corymb. A short, usually broad, more or less flat-topped racemose inflorescence, the outermost flowers opening first

Creeper. A plant with prostrate stems that strike root

Crenate. Shallowly round-toothed; scalloped

Crown. That portion of the stem at ground level; the corona of a flower; the leafy head of a tree

Cultivar. A variety or species that originated in cultivation and has persisted more or less unchanged

Cuneate. Wedge-shaped

Cuspidate. With an abrupt, sharp-pointed, toothlike apex

Cyathium. A type of inflorescence found in the Spurge Family typified by the aggregation of unisexual, often much reduced flowers within a modified bract, the latter sometimes bearing appendages resembling petals

Cyme. A broad, flat-topped or rounded inflorescence, each axis of which ends in a flower, the center flowers opening first

Deciduous. Dropping at the end of a growing season; falling at the completion of function; referring to a tree or shrub with deciduous leaves

Decompound. More than once compound

Decumbent. Lying on the ground, but with the tip ascending

Decurrent. Extending down and joined to the stem

Dehiscent. Opening

Deltoid. Triangular

Dentate. Toothlike; with sharp, broadly acute or blunt projections more or less perpendicular to the margin

Denticulate. Finely dentate

Dextrorse. Twining spirally upward from left to right

Dichotomous. Forked into 2 equal parts

Diffuse. Loosely branched; of open growth

Digitate. Handlike; the members (e.g., leaflets) arising from a common point

Dioecious. Having pollen-bearing (staminate) and ovule-bearing (pistillate) flowers on separate plants

Disc. The central portion of the head in the Daisy Family

Dissected. Divided into few or numerous slender segments

Distinct. Separate; not united

Divaricate. Spreading far apart

Divergent. Spreading, but less so than when divaricate

Divided. Separated nearly to the base; almost compound

Double. Referable to flowers having more than the usual complement of petals

Double-serrate. Coarsely sharp-toothed, each tooth bearing 1 or more additional smaller teeth

Downy. Covered with soft, weak hairs

Drupe. A fleshy fruit, the single seed invested by a woody coat (the "stone")

Drupelet. One of a number of small aggregated drupes (as in the raspberry)

Elliptic. Oval with rounded ends and broadest at the middle

Elongate. Lengthened; stretched out

Emarginate. Shallowly notched at the apex

Endemic. Restricted to a particular area, usually of limited extent

Entire. Unbroken; with a smooth, continuous margin, lacking teeth or lobes

Epiphyte. A plant which clings to or rests on another for support, but is not parasitic and has no soil contact

Erose. Ragged, as if gnawed

Estuarine. Of river estuaries

Even-pinnate. With paired leaflets or parts, and lacking a solitary terminal member

Evergreen. Remaining green and leafy in the dormant period

Exserted. Projecting beyond; extending out of

Eye. A conspicuous flower center; a bud on a tuber

Falls. The outermost whorl of perianth parts in an Iris flower, commonly bent down and under toward the stem

Family. A group of similar genera

Fascicle. A condensed cluster, the individuals arising from a common point

Fasciculate. In condensed clusters

Fertile. Referable to pollen-bearing anthers; to seed-bearing fruits; to seeds which are capable of germination

Fertilization. The union of pollen nucleus with ovule nucleus, resulting in the development of seed

Filament. Thread; the stalk bearing an anther

Filiform. Threadlike

Fimbriate. Fringed

Flaccid. Limp

Flexuous. Zigzag

Floret. A small flower, numbers of which make up a dense inflorescence, as in the Daisy Family

Flower. A stem, often much modified, bearing at least 1 stamen or 1 pistil, but most commonly having both, and in addition, 1 or more sepals and 1 or more petals

Foliaceous. Leaflike

Foliage. Vegetative parts

Follicle. A dry fruit opening by a single split

Free. Not joined to other organs (i.e., petals not joined to sepals)

Fruit. Ripened ovary with accessory parts

Funnelform. Having the tube gradually widened to form a flare; trumpet-shaped

Furcate. Forked

Furrowed. Longitudinally grooved

Fusiform. Spindle-shaped; swollen on the middle and tapered at both ends

Genus (plural: genera). A group of similar species

Gibbous. Swollen on one side

Glabrate. Nearly glabrous; becoming so in age

Glabrous. Without hairs

Gland. A secretory structure

Glandular. Gland-bearing

Glandular-pubescent. With glands and hairs intermixed; with gland-tipped hairs

Glaucescent. Covered with a light bloom

Glaucous. Covered with a bloom (a whitish waxy dustlike substance that rubs off, as on grapes and plums)

Glochid. A minute spine, usually in tufts and, in many cacti, easily detached

Glutinous. Sticky

Granular. Mealy; covered with small grain

Hastate. Resembling an arrowhead in shape, with the basal lobes at right angles to the blade

Head. A dense inflorescence of flowers arising from a common point

Herb. A plant which naturally dies to the ground; one lacking persistent aerial structure

Herbaceous. With little or no persistent aerial structure; soft in texture

Hirsute. Covered with coarse hairs

Hispid. Covered with stiff, bristly hairs

Hoary. Covered with a fine, close, whitish pubescence

Host. The plant on which a parasite feeds

Hyaline. Translucent

Hybrid. A plant resulting from the cross of 2 unlike parents, as one from 2 species

Incised. More or less sharply, deeply, and irregularly toothed or lobed

Included. Not protruding; within

Indehiscent. Not opening

Inferior. Below, as an ovary situated below the calyx

Inflated. Puffed up; bladdery

Inflorescence. Arrangement of flowers

Inserted. Attached

Internode. Part of stem or axis between 2 nodes

Interrupted. Discontinuous, as in a raceme with flowers grouped in bunches

Involucre. One or more whorls of bracts subtending a flower or inflorescence

Irregular flower. A flower in which the parts of the same series (e.g., the petals) are not alike; one which may be divided into equal halves along only one plane

Jointed. With prominent or exaggerated nodes; articulate

Keel. The two lower, partially united petals in flowers of the Pea Family (Leguminosae-Papilionoideae); a ridge on the underside
Keeled. Ridged on the bottom

Labiate. Lipped
Laciniate. With narrow lobes
Lamina. The blade
Lanceolate. Lance-shaped; long and narrow, broadest at the middle, and tapering more or less equally to both ends
Lateral. On, from, or at the side
Latex. Milky sap
Lax. Loose, not congested
Leaflet. A leaflike unit of a compound leaf
Legume. The fruit of members of the Pea Family, usually with 2 equal halves, typically splitting down one side (sometimes both) when ripe
Ligulate. Strap-shaped
Limb. The expanded, flat portion, especially that of a corolla whose petals are united
Linear. Long and narrow, the sides very nearly parallel, as in most grass leaves
Lip. One of usually 2 parts of certain irregular corollas, there being an upper lip and a lower one
Lobe.. Any part or segment of a structure; a deep indentation which does not break the continuity of the structure (small lobes and large teeth are not clearly distinguished)

Margin. The edge of a plane or laminal structure
Membranaceous. Parchmentlike in texture
Membranous. Parchmentlike in texture
Midrib. The main, usually central, vein of a lamina
Monoecious. Bearing staminate and pistillate flowers on the same plant, as in corn
Mucronate. Having a small, sharp, firm, abrupt tip
Multiradiate. Having many rays

Nectar. A sweetish substance secreted from nectaries
Nectary. A nectar-secreting gland, usually in a flower
Nerve. Leaf vein, especially one of the main ones
Nocturnal. Referable to flowers that open at night and close during the day
Node. The point at which a leaf, flower, or branch shoot is attached
Nut. A 1-seeded bony fruit that does not open
Nutlet. A tiny nut; especially referable to the 1-seeded sections formed by the maturing ovary in the Borage, Mint, and Verbena families

Obcordate. Ovate in general outline and deeply lobed at the apex; the reverse of cordate

Oblanceolate.   Lanceolate but broadest in the outer half
Oblique.   With unequal sides
Oblong.   Longer than broad and with nearly parallel sides
Obovate.   Ovate in outline and broadest in the outer half
Obtuse.   Blunt-tipped; with a more or less rounded indistinct apex
Odd-pinnate.   With paired leaflets or parts and, in addition, a solitary terminal member
Opposite.   In pairs, the members on opposite sides of the stem or axis
Orbicular.   Circular or disc-shaped
Ovary.   The part of the pistil bearing the ovules, usually the lower major portion, becoming the fruit after fertilization
Ovate.   Egg-shaped and broadest below the middle

Palmate.   Divided or radiating from 1 point
Panicle.   A branched raceme, the pedicellate flowers arranged on the secondary axes; a raceme of racemes
Paniculate.   Resembling a panicle
Papilionaceous.   Used in reference to a corolla whose petals are shaped and arranged in the same manner as in the sweet pea
Pappus.   In the Daisy Family, a modified calyx, commonly appearing as hairs, bristles, or bumps, and usually persisting on the fruit
Parted.   Cut not quite to the base
Pedicel.   The stalk of an individual flower in a cluster
Pedicellate.   Borne on pedicels
Peduncle.   The stalk of a solitary flower or of a flower cluster
Pedunculate.   Borne on peduncles
Peltate.   Having the stalk attached to the lower surface and not to the edge, as in leaves of the Water-lily
Pendulous.   Drooping
Perennial.   Living for several or many years
Perfect.   Referable to a flower bearing both types of essential organs (stamens and pistils) but not necessarily perianth
Perfoliate.   Referable to a leaf or bract that completely surrounds the stem
Perianth.   Calyx and corolla, in the collective sense
Persistent.   Remaining attached after apparent function is completed
Petal.   Unit of the corolla, usually colored and more or less showy
Petaloid.   Petal-like
Petiolate.   Having petioles
Petiole.   Leafstalk
Phyllary.   An involucral bract below the head, in the Daisy Family
Pilose.   With long, soft hairs; shaggy
Pinnate.   Arranged along an axis, as with veins that arise from a midrib
Pinnatifid.   Cleft or parted in a pinnate manner
Pistil.   The female reproductive structure of the flower; collectively the ovary, style, and stigma
Pistillate.   Having pistils but no fertile stamens
Pitted.   Covered with small depressions or cavities

Plumose.   Featherlike; a long hair bearing smaller branch hairs

Pod.   A general term referring to a dry dehiscent fruit, frequently used in the sense of legume, but also applied to fruits to which no other more precise term seems suited

Pollen.   Grains borne by the anther, containing male nuclei capable of fertilizing ovules

Pollination.   The transfer of pollen from anther to stigma

Pore.   A small round aperture

Prickle.   A small, weak, spinelike structure borne irregularly from the outermost covering of the stem

Procumbent.   Trailing but not rooting

Prostrate.   Lying flat on the ground

Protandry.   The phenomenon in which the anthers shed their pollen before the stigmas of the same flower are ready to receive it

Puberulent.   Minutely pubescent with soft, straight, erect hairs

Pubescent.   Soft-hairy; downy

Pulvinus.   A swollen petiole base (in most members of the Pea Family) capable of bending and changing the position of the blade according to such stimuli as light, temperature, vibrations, etc.

Punctate.   With translucent dots

Raceme.   An elongate inflorescence bearing stalked flowers

Racemose.   Racemelike

Rachis.   Axis of an inflorescence or of a compound leaf or frond

Ray.   A strap-shaped corolla, found in many members of the Daisy Family

Receptacle.   The typically swollen terminal end of a peduncle or pedicel; the expanded disclike or domelike structure bearing the florets in the Daisy Family

Recurved.   Bent or curved downward or back

Reflexed.   Abruptly curved downward or back

Reniform.   Kidney-shaped

Resinous.   Resin-bearing

Reticulate.   Netted

Rhizomatous.   Bearing rhizomes

Rhizome.   An underground stem, often rootlike in appearance, but considered a stem on the bases of internal structure, presence of buds, scale leaves, etc., as found in Iris and many grasses

Rib.   The primary vein; a prominent vein

Riparian.   Relating to river or stream banks

Rootstock.   A rhizome or rhizomelike structure

Rosette.   An arrangement of leaves radiating from the stem at a nearly common level, frequently at or just above the ground line

Rotate.   Wheel-like; saucer-shaped

Rotund.   Nearly circular

Rugose.   Covered with wrinkles

Runcinate.   Coarsely toothed or lobed, the projections pointing backward or toward the base

Runner.   A slender trailing shoot rooting at the nodes

Saccate.   Bag-shaped
Sagittate.   Resembling an arrowhead in outline or form, the basal lobes pointing downward
Salver.   The abruptly expanded flare of a corolla whose petals are fused or closely associated
Salverform.   Salver-shaped
Scabrous.   Rough to the touch
Scale.   A reduced, often colorless, dry leaf or bract
Scandent.   Climbing or rising through surrounding vegetation without aid of tendrils
Scape.   Leafless peduncle arising from the level of the ground
Scapose.   Bearing flowers on a scape
Scarious.   Thin, dry, membranous, often translucent
Seed.   Ripened ovule, usually invested by one or more coats
Segment.   One of the parts of a divided (but not compound) leaf, petal, etc.
Sepal.   The unit of the calyx, frequently green and foliaceous
Sepaloid.   Simulating a sepal or calyx
Septum.   A partition or cross-wall
Sericeous.   Silky
Serrate.   A saw-toothed margin, the teeth pointing toward the apex
Sessile.   Lacking a stalk
Sheath.   A tubular structure surrounding an organ
Shrub.   A low, woody plant, usually with several or many stems from the base
Silicle.   A silique broader than it is long
Silique.   A narrow, elongated, many-seeded capsule
Silky.   Covered with soft appressed hairs
Simple.   Referable to a leaf with a continuous blade; to an unbranched stem or inflorescence
Smooth.   Hairless; free of projections
Solitary.   Borne singly or alone
Spatulate.   Spoon-shaped
Species (used as singular and plural; abbreviations are sp. in the singular and spp. in the plural).   A kind of plant; a group of individuals resembling each other in most respects, differing from others in few to many respects
Spicate.   Spikelike
Spike.   An unbranched elongate inflorescence bearing sessile flowers
Spine.   A sharp-pointed woody projection
Spp.   Abbreviation for plural of "species"
Spur.   A tubular or saclike projection, usually from a perianth part, often containing nectar
Stalk.   Any kind of stem
Stamen.   The male organ of a flower, consisting of a stalk, the filament (sometimes absent), and the pollen-bearing anther
Staminate.   Having stamens but no pistils

Staminode. An infertile stamen, the anther aborted or absent, and the filament sometimes dilated and colored to resemble a petal

Standard. The banner of a flower of the Pea Family (Leguminosae-Papilionoideae); the erect petals of Iris flowers

Stellate. Starlike; referable to hairs with radiating branches

Stem. The main aerial axis of the plant, bearing leaves, flowers, and subsidiary axes or branches

Sterile. Lacking functional sex organs; incapable of germination

Stigma. That part of the pistil, usually located at the end of the style, which receives the pollen

Stigmatic. Pertaining to the stigma

Stipule. A basal appendage of the petiole, usually in pairs

Stolon. A shoot with reduced leaves, looping above the ground, often rooting at intervals; a horizontal stem arising from beneath the ground, its finally upturned end producing a vegetative shoot

Stone. The woody, seed-investing coat of a fleshy fruit (e.g., in cherries, peaches); a pyrene

Striate. With fine longitudinal lines or shallow grooves

Strigose. With stiff appressed hairs or bristles

Style. Portion of the pistil between the ovary and stigma, often resembling a stalk but sometimes absent

Subshrub. Low shrubby plant, woody below, the leafy shoots often dying back part way; a diminutive shrub

Subtending. Lying just below

Subulate. Awl-shaped; tapered from base to apex

Succulent. Fleshy and thickened

Sucker. A shoot arising below the ground; a new, often lush shoot from the lower stem; the modified roots of parasites which take nourishment from the host

Suture. A line or groove marking a natural union; a line of dehiscence; the longitudinal groove of a plum, peach, or other "stone fruit"

Tapering. Gradually diminishing in diameter or width

Tendril. A threadlike or hairlike, curling or twining projection of stem, leaf, or inflorescence of certain vines by which attachment is made to a support

Terete. Circular in cross-section

Terminal. At the tip

Ternate. In threes

Thorn. A stiff, pointed outgrowth of various origin; collective term including spines, prickles, etc.

Throat. The opening of a corolla where petals are fused

Tomentose. Densely wooly or pubescent, the hairs often matted

Tree. Woody plant with a single stem (the trunk or bole)

Trifoliate. Three-leaved

Trifoliolate. With leaves composed of three leaflets

Truncate. Flat-ended; cut straight across

Tuber. A short, congested root or underground stem

Tubercle. A rounded protuberance; a small tuber

Tuberous. Tuber-bearing
Twig. The current season's stem growth in a woody plant

Umbel. An often flat-topped inflorescence whose pedicels arise from a common point
Undulate. Wavy
Unilateral. One-sided
Unisexual. Of one sex, i.e., staminate or pistillate
Urceolate. Urn-shaped
Utricle. A bladdery, 1-seeded, indehiscent fruit

Valve. One half or a separable part of a pod; one of the pieces into which a dehiscent fruit breaks
Variety (abbreviation: var.). A local population of a species having one or a few minor differences from other populations
Velutinous. Clothed with straight, erect hairs, and having a velvety texture
Venation. Arrangement of veins
Versatile. Attached at the middle and often swinging freely, as with the anthers of various lilies
Vesture (or vestiture). Hairiness; anything modifying the glabrous condition
Villous. Covered with long, soft hairs
Virgate. Wandlike; straight and slender
Viscid. Sticky; viscous

Whorl. Three or more leaves, flowers, or bracts arranged in a ring or circle at a node
Wing. A thin, flat appendage; one of the 2 lateral petals in a flower of the Pea Family (Leguminosae-Papilionoideae)
Wooly. Covered with long, soft, matted hairs; resembling wool

Index

For each illustrated entry two numbers are given: (1) the number of the plate where the illustration appears and (2) the number of the page of text (in parentheses) where the discussion appears.

Low: (114)
Pine: (114)
Buttercup Family: (111)–(114)
Butterfly-weed: 32, (172), (173)
Butterweed: (244)
Button-bush: 48, (212)–(213)
Button-snakeroot: 52, 53, (169), (222)

Cacao: (154)
Cactus, Pencil: 28, (160)
  Rat-tail: 28, (160)
Cactus Family: (159)–(162)
Calabash Gourd: (217)–(218)
California Blue-bell: (177)
Caltrop Family: (144)–(145)
Camas, Death: (93)
Canaigre: 7, (103)–(104)
Candelilla: (148)
Candle-tree: (129)
Candlewood Family: (154)–(155)
Cantaloupe: (217)–(218)
Cape-gooseberry: (183)–(184)
Caper Family: (121)–(122)
Caraway: (168)
Cardinal-flower: 51, (219), (220)
Careless-weed: (104)
Carnation: (111)
Carolina
  Anemone: (112)–(113)
  Larkspur: (112)
Carrot, Garden: (168)
  Wild: 31, (167)–(168)
Carrot Family: (167)–(169)
Cassie: 15, (125)
Catalpa: (208)
-catalpa, Willow-leaved: 47, (209)
Catchfly, Sleepy: (111)
Catclaw: 15, (125), (126)
Catgut: 19, (136)–(137), (137)
Cat-tail: 1, (89)

Cat-tail Family: (89)
Cebollita: 2, (94)
Celestial: 5, (100)
Cenizo: 43, (200)
Century-plant: 5, (99)
Chaff-flower: (104)–(105)
Cherokee-bean: 20, (139)
-cherry, Cornelian: (167)
  Ground: 37, (183)–(184)
  Purple Ground: 36, (182)– (183)
  Winter: (183)
-chestnut Family, Horse: (151)
Chickweed: 10, (110)–(111)
Chicory: (231)–(232)
China-aster: (228)
Chinese-lantern-of-the-plains: 36, (183)
Chinese-parasol-tree: (154)
Cholla: 28, (161)
Citron Gourd: (217)–(218)
Clammy-weed: 13, (121)–(122)
Clammy-weed, Large-flowered: 13, (122)
Climbing Snapdragon: 44, (201)– (202)
Cloudberry: (124)
-clover, Bush: 19, (138)–(139)
  Pin: (140)–(141)
  Purple Prairie: (136)
  Sour: (135)
  White Sweet: 18, (134), (135)
  Yellow Sweet: 18, (134), (135)
Cocklebur: 57, (230)
Cock's-comb: (104)
Coffee: (214)
Coffee Family: (212)–(214)
Coffee Senna: (129)
Cola: (154)
Commercial Tobacco: (186)
Common Lespedeza: (139)
Cone-flower: 58, (233)

(267)

SCIENTIFIC NAMES

Abronia
  ameliae Lundell: (106)
  angustifolia Greene: (106)
  fragrans Nutt.: 8, (106)
  villosa Wats.: (106)

Abutilon
  incanum (Link) Sweet: 25,
    (151)–(152)
  megapotamicum St. Hil. &
    Naud.: (152)
  theophrastii Medic: (152)
  vitifolium Presl.: (152)

Acacia
  angustissima (Mill.) Ktze.:
    (125)
  berlandieri Benth.: (125)
  farnesiana (L.) Willd.: 15,
    (124)–(125)
  greggii Gray: (125)
  wrightii Benth.: (125)

Acanthaceae: (204)–(207)

Acanthus spinosus L.: (205)

Achillea
  lanulosa Nutt.: (243)
  millefolium L.: 62, (242)–(243)

Acleisanthes
  longiflora Gray: 8, (107)
  obtusa (Choisy) Standl.: (107)

Actinea
  odorata (DC.) Ktze.: 60, (239)–
    (240)
  scaposa (DC.) Ktze.: 60, (239)

Adopogon carolinianum (Walt.)
    Britt.: 64, (249)

Aesculus
  discolor Pursh, in part: 24, (151)
  glabra Willd., var. *arguta*
    (Buckl.) Robins.: (151)
  pavia L.: 24, (151)

Agaloma corollata (L.) Raf.: 23,
    (148)

Agave
  americana L.: 5, (99)
  havardiana Trel.: (99)
  lechuguilla Torr.: (99)

Alismaceae: (89)–(90)

Allionia nyctaginea Michx.: 7,
    (105)

Allium
  cepa L.: (93)–(94)
  drummondii Regel: 2, (93)–
    (94)
  helleri Small: 2, (93)–(94)
  porrum L.: (93)–(94)

Alsine media L.: 10, (110)–(111)

Alternanthera repens (L.) Ktze.:
    (104)–(105)

Amaranthaceae: (104)–(105)

Amaranthus spp.: (104)

Amaranthus
  albus L.: (104)–(105)
  hybridus L.: (104)
  hypochondriacus L.: (104)
  tamariscinus Nutt.: (104)–
    (105)
  viridis L.: (104)–(105)

Amaryllidaceae: (97)–(99)

Ambrosia: (231)–(232)

Amphiachyris dracunculoides
    (DC.) Nutt.: 53, (223)

Anacardiaceae: (148)–(150)

Anemone
  caroliniana Walt.: (112)–(113)
  decapetala Ard.: 10, (112)–
    (113)

Anisacanthus wrightii Gray: (205)

Anisostichus capreolatus (L.)
Bureau: 47, (208)–(209)

Antirrhinum
antirrhiniflorum (Poir.) Small:
44, (201)–(202)
majus L.: (202)

Aphanostephus
ramosissimus DC.: 55, (226)
riddellii Torr. & Gray: (226)
skirrhobasis (DC.) Trel.: 55,
(226)

Arctium minus Schk.: (246)

Arenaria drummondii Shinners:
(111)

Argemone
aenea G. Ownb.: 12, (118)
albiflora Hornem., var. *texana*
(G. Ownb.) Shinners: 12,
(117)–(118)
aurantiaca G. Ownb.: (117)–
(118)
chisosensis G. Ownb.: (118)
mexicana L.: (118)
polyanthemos (Fedde) G.
Ownb.: (117)
sanguinea Greene: 12, (118)
squarrosa Greene, var. *glabrata*
(G. Ownb.) Shinners: (118)

Asclepiadaceae: (172)–(173)

Asclepias
brachystephana Engelm.: 32,
(172), (173)
lindheimeri Engelm. & Gray: 33,
(172)–(173)
oenotheroides Cham. & Schlecht.:
33, (172)–(173)
tuberosa L.: 32, (172), (173)
viridis Walt.: (173)

Aster
exilis Ell.: 56, (227)–(228),
(228)
laevis L.: 55, (227), (228)
oblongifolius Nutt.: 55, (227),
(228)
prealtus Poir.: 55, (227), (228)
sagittifolius Wedemeyer: 56,
(228)

salicifolius Ait.: 55, (227),
(228)
subulatus Michx. var. *ligulatus*
Shinners: 56, (227)–(228),
(228)

Astragalus
carnosus Pursh: (138)
lindheimeri Gray: (138)
mollissimus Torr.: 19, (137)–
(138)
nuttallianus DC.: (138)

Atropa belladonna L.: (185)

Aucuba japonica Thunb.: (167)

Baileya multiradiata Harv. & Gray:
62, (242)

Baptisia
leucophaea Nutt.: 17, (132),
(132)–(133)
minor Lehmann: (132)–(133)
sphaerocarpa Nutt.: 17, (132)–
(133)

Beleperone guttata Brandeg.:
(205)

Berberidaceae: (116)–(117)

Berberis
aquifolium Pursh: (116)–(117)
haematocarpa Woot.: (116)
swaseyi Buckl.: (116)
thunbergii DC.: (117)
trifoliata Moric.: 11, (116)–
(117)
vulgaris L.: (117)

Bidens bipinnata L.: (236)–(237)

Bignonia capreolata L.: 47,
(208)–(209)

Bignoniaceae: (207)–(209)

Boerhavia
coccinea Mill.: 7, (106)
erecta L.: 7, (105)–(106)
erecta L., var. *intermedia:* (106)

Bolivaria grisebachii Scheele: 31,
(170)

Boraginaceae: (187)–(189)

Bouvardia
  ternifolia (Cav.) Schlecht.: 49,
    (214)
  triphylla Salisb. var. *angustifolia*
    Gray: 49, (214)

Brassica
  campestris L.: (121)
  campestris (L.) Rabenhorst:
    (121)
  juncea (L.) Cosson: 13, (120)–
    (121)
  kaber (DC.) L. C. Wheeler:
    (121)
  nigra (L.) Koch: (120)–(121)
  oleracea L.: (120)
  rapa L.: (121)

Brauneria angustifolia (DC.)
    Heller: 58, (234)

Brazoria
  scutellarioides (Hook.) Engelm.
    & Gray: 41, (193)
  truncata (Benth.) Engelm. &
    Gray: (193)

Bromeliaceae: (90)–(91)

Cactaceae: (159)–(162)

Caesalpinia
  gilliesii Wall.: 17, (131)–(132)
  pulcherrima Sw.: (132)

Callirhoe
  alceoides (Michx.) Gray: (153)
  digitata Nutt.: 25, (153)–
    (154)
  involucrata (Nutt.) Gray: 25,
    (153)–(154)
  leiocarpa: 25, (154)

Callistephus hortensis Cass.: (228)

Calophanes linearis (Torr. & Gray)
    Gray: 45, (204)–(205)

Campanulaceae: (218)–(220)

Campsis
  grandiflora (Thunb.) Loisel.:
    (207)
  radicans (L.) Seem.: 46, (207)

Capparidaceae: (121)–(122)

(281)

Caprifoliaceae: (214)–(216)

Capsicum frutescens L.: (185)

Carduus spinosissimus Walt.: 63,
    (244)–(245)

Carthamnus: (231)–(232)

Carum carvi L.: (168)

Caryophyllaceae: (110)–(111)

Cassia
  alata L.: (129)
  bauhinoides Gray: (129)
  corymbosa Lam.: (129)
  durangensis Rose: (129)
  fasciculata Michx.: 16, (129)–
    (130)
  fasciculata Michx., var. *ferrisiae*
    (Britt.) Turner: (130)
  fasciculata Michx., var. *rostrata*
    (Woot. & Standl.) Turner:
    (130)
  lindheimeriana Scheele: 16,
    (129)
  marilandica L.: (129)
  nictitans L.: (130)
  obtusifolia L.: (129)
  occidentalis L.: (129)
  pumilio Gray: (129)
  roemeriana Scheele: 16, (128)–
    (129)
  tora L.: (129)

Castalia
  elegans (Hook.) Greene: 11,
    (115)–(116)
  odorata (Ait.) Woodville &
    Wood: (115)

Castilleja
  indivisa Engelm.: 45, (204)
  latebracteata Pennell: 45, (203),
    (204)
  purpurea (Nutt.) G. Don: 45,
    (203), (204)

Catalpa speciosa Warder: (208)

Cathartolinum rigidum (Pursh)
    Small: 21, (142)–(143),
    (143)

Celosia argentea L., var. *cristata*
    (L.) Ktze.: (104)

Eriogonum
  annuum Nutt.: 6, (103)
  wrightii Torr.: (103)

Erodium
  cicutarium (L.) L'Her.: 20,
    (140)–(141)
  texanum (L.) L'Her.: 20,
    (140)–(141)

Eryngium
  leavenworthii Torr. & Gray:
    31, (168)–(169)
  yuccaefolium Michx.: (169)

Erythraea beyrichii T. & G.: (171)–
  (172)

Erythrina
  arboracea (Chapm.) Small:
    (140)
  crista-galli L.: (140)
  herbacea L.: 20, (139)–(140)

Erythrostemon gilliesii (Hook.)
  Link, Klotsch, & Otto: 17,
  (131)–(132)

Euphorbia
  antisyphilitica Zucc.: (148)
  bicolor Engelm. & Gray: 23,
    (147)–(148)

Euphorbiaceae: (147)–(148)

Euphorbia
  corollata L.: 23, (148)
  marginata Pursh: (147)–(148)
  pulcherrima Willd.: (148)
  splendens Boj.: (148)

Euploca convolvulacea Nutt.: 39,
  (188)–(189)

Eustoma
  exaltatum (L.) Salisb.: (171)
  grandiflorum (Raf.) Shinners:
    32, (171)–(172)
  russellianum (Hook.) G. Don:
    32, (171)–(172)

Evolvulus
  alsinoides L. var. *hirticaulis*
    Torr.: (174)
  nuttallianus Roem. & Schult.:
    33, (173)–(174)

  sericeus Sw.: (174)
Fallugia paradoxa (D. Don) Endl.:
  14, (124)
Forestiera acuminata (Michx.)
  Poir: (170)
Forsythia: (170)
Fouquieriaceae: (154)–(155)
Fouquieria splendens Engelm.: 26,
  (154)–(155)
Fraxinus: (170)
Froelichia floridana (Nutt.) Moq.:
  7, (104)–(105)

Gaillardia
  pulchella Foug.: 61, (241),
    (241)–(242)
  suavis (Gray & Engelm.) Britt. &
    Rusby: 61, (241)–(242)
  trinervata Small: 61, (241)–
    (242)

Gardenia jasminoides Ellis: (214)

Gaura
  brachycarpa Small: 30, (165)–
    (166)
  coccinea Pursh: (166)
  lindheimeri Engelm. & Gray:
    (166)
  parviflora Dougl.: (166)
  suffulta Engelm.: 30, (165)–
    (166)

Gentianaceae: (170)–(172)

Geraniaceae: (140)–(141)

Geranium carolinianum L.: (141)

Gilia
  longiflora (Torr.) G. Don: 36,
    (181), (181)–(182)
  rigidula Benth.: 36, (181),
    (181)–(182)
  rubra (L.) Heller: 36, (181)–
    (182)

Gnaphalium
  falcatum Lam.: (230)
  peregrinum Fern.: (229)–(230)
  purpureum L.: (229)
  wrightii Gray: 56, (229)–(230)

Gomphrena globosa L.: (104)
Grindelia squarrosa (Pursh) Dunal:
   53, (223)–(224)
Gutierrezia
   dracunculoides (DC.) Blake: 53,
     (223)
   microcephala (DC.) Gray:
     (223)
Gypsophila elegans L.: (111)
Gyrostachys cernua (L.) Kuntze:
   6, (102)

Hartmannia speciosa (Nutt.)
   Small: 29, (163)–(164)
Hedyotis
   acerosa Gray: (213)–(214)
   crassifolia Raf. var. *crassifolia*:
     (213)–(214)
   crassifolia Raf. var. *micrantha*
     Shinners: (213)–(214)
   humifusa Gray: (213)–(214)
   minima Beck: (213)–(214)
   nigricans (Lam.) Fosb.: 49,
     (213)–(214)
   rosea Raf.: (213)–(214)
Helenium
   amarum (Raf.) H. Rock: 61,
     (240), (240)–(241)
   autumnale of authors: 61,
     (240)–(241)
   flexuosum Raf.: (241)
   latifolium Mill.: 61, (240)–
     (241)
   nudiflorum Nutt.: (241)
   tenuifolium Nutt.: 61, (240),
     (240)–(241)
Helianthus
   annuus L.: 58, (234)–(235),
     (235)
   maximiliani Schrad.: 59, (235)
   tuberosus L.: (235)
Heliotropium
   convolvulaceum (Nutt.) Gray:
     39, (188)–(189)
   curassavicum L.: (189)
   peruvianum L.: (189)

   procumbens Mill.: (189)
   tenellum (Nutt.) Torr.: (188)
Hesperaloe
   funifera (Koch) Trel.: (96)
   parviflora (Torr.) Coult.: 3,
     (95)–(96)
Hippocastanaceae: (151)
Homolecephala texensis (Hopf.)
   Britt. & Rose: 28, (161)–
   (162)
Houstonia angustifolia Michx.: 49,
   (213)–(214)
Hydrophyllaceae: (177)–(178)
Hymenocallis
   galvestonensis (Herb.) Baker:
     5, (98)–(99)
   liriosme (Raf.) Shinners: 5,
     (98)–(99)
   occidentalis Kunth: (99)
Hymenopappus
   artemisiaefolius DC.: 60,
     (238)–(239)
   flavescens Gray: (238)–(239)
   scabiosaeus L'Herit.: (238)–
     (239)
   tenuifolius Pursh: (238)–(239)
Hymenoxys odorata DC.: 60,
   (239)–(240)
Hypoxis
   hirsuta (L.) Cov.: 4, (97)
   humilis Tharp: (97)
   juncea Smith: (97)
   rigida Chapm.: (97)

Ibervillea
   lindheimeri (Gray) Greene: 51,
     (218)
   tenella (Naud.) Small: (218)
   tenuisecta (Gray) Small: (218)
Indigofera: (132)
Ionoxalis violacea (L.) Small: 21,
   (141)–(142)
Ipomoea
   leptophylla Torr.: (176)
   pandurata (L.) G. Mey.: (175)

(285)

Medicago sativa L.: 18, (134)–
(135)
Megapterium missouriense (Sims)
Spach: 29, (164)
Melampodium
cinereum DC.: 57, (230)–(231)
cinereum DC. var. *ramosissimum*
(DC.) Gray: (231)
hispidum H. B. K.: (231)
Melastomaceae: (162)
Melilotus
albus Desv.: 18, (134), (135)
indicus All.: (135)
officinalis Lam.: 18, (134),
(135)
Menodora
heterophylla Moric.: 3, (170)
laevis Woot. & Standl.: (169)–
(170)
longiflora Gray: 31, (169)–
(170)
longifolia (Steyerm.) Tharp:
(169)–(170)
ramosissima (Steyerm.) Tharp:
(169)–(170)
scabra Gray: (169)–(170)
Menodoropsis longiflora (Gray)
Small: 31, (169)–(170)
Mentzelia
decapetala (Pursh) Urb. &
Gilg.: (159)
monosperma Woot. & Standl.:
27, (159)
nuda (Pursh) Torr. & Gray:
27, (158)–(159)
oligosperma Nutt.: 27, (159)
stricta (Osterhout) Stevens:
(159)
texana Urb. & Gilg.: (159)
Meriolix serrulata (Nutt.) Raf.: 30,
(165)
Mirabilis
jalapa L.: (105)
nyctagineus (Michx.) MacMillan: 7, (105)
repens L.: (214)

Monarda
citriodora Cerv. ex Lag.: 43,
(198), (198)–(199)
didyma L.: (199)
dispera Small: 43, (198),
(198)–(199)
fistulosa L.: 43, (198), (198)–
(199)
mollis L.: 43, (198), (198)–
(199)
punctata L.: 43, (198)–(199)
Monoxalis dichondraefolia (Gray)
Small: (142)

Nelumbo lutea (Willd.) Pers.:
(115)
Nemastylis
acuta (Bart.) Herb.: 5, (100)
geminiflora Nutt.: 5, (100)
purpurea Herb.: (100)
Nemophila
microcalyx (Nutt.) F. & M.:
(177)
phacelioides Nutt.: 34, (177)
Nertera spp.: (214)
Nicotiana
glauca Graham: 38, (186)
longiflora Cav.: (186)
repanda Willd.: (186)
tabacum L.: (186)
Nolina spp.: (96)–(97)
Nothoscordium bivalve (L.) Britt.:
3, (94)
Nuphar advena (Ait.) Ait.: (115)
Nuttallia nuda (Pursh) Greene:
27, (158)–(159)
Nyctaginaceae: (105)–(107)
Nyctaginea capitata Choisy: 8,
(107)
Nymphaea
elegans Hook.: 11, (115)–(116)
mexicana Zucc.: (115)–(116)
odorata Ait.: (115)
Nymphaeceae: (115)–(116)

(288)

Oenothera
 laciniata Hill: 29, (162)–(163)
 laciniata Hill, var. *grandiflora*
  (Wats.) Robins.: (163)
 missouriensis Sims: 29, (164)
 serrulata Nutt.: 30, (165)
 speciosa Nutt.: 29, (163)–(164)
 spinulosa Torr. & Gray: (165)
 triloba Nutt.: 29, (163)

Olea: (170)

Oleaceae: (169)–(170)

Onagraceae: (162)–(166)

Opuntia
 arborescens Engelm.: 28, (161)
 imbricata (Haw.) DC.: 28,
  (161)
 leptocaulis DC.: 28, (160)–
  (161)
 lindheimeri Engelm.: 27, (159)–
  (160)

Orchidaceae: (102)

Oxalidaceae: (141)–(142)

Oxalis
 berlandieri Torr.: (142)
 dichondraefolia Gray: (142)
 dillenii Jacq.: 20, (141), (142)
 drummondii Gray: (142)
 stricta L.: 20, (141), (142)
 violacea L.: 21, (141)–(142)

Oxybaphus nyctagineus (Michx.)
  Sweet: 7, (105)

Papaveraceae: (117)–(118)

Parkinsonia aculeata L.: 16, (131)

Parthenocissus quinquefolia (L.)
  Planch.: 24, (150)

Passiflora affinis Engelm.: (158)

Passifloraceae: (157)–(158)

Passiflora
 foetida L., var. *gossypiifolia*
  (Desv.) Mast.: (158)
 incarnata L.: 27, (157)–(158)
 lutea L., var. *glabriflora* Fern.:
  (158)

Pastinaca sativa L.: (168)

Pediomelum cuspidatum (Pursh)
  Rydb.: 18, (135)–(136)

Pelargonium: (141)

Penstemon
 ambiguus Torr.: 44, (201)
 barbatus (Cav.) Roth. var.
  torreyi (Benth.) Gray: (201)
 cobaea Nutt.: 44, (200)–(201)
 digitalis Nutt.: (201)
 fendleri Torr. & Gray: (201)
 laxiflorus Pennell: (201)
 murrayanus Hook.: (201)

Pentastemon: (201)

Pentstemon: (201)

Perezia
 nana Gray: (246)
 runcinata Lagasca: (246)
 wrightii Gray: 63, (246)

Petroselinum sativum Hoffm.:
  (168)

Petunia violacea Lindl.: (185)

Peucedanum graveolens Benth. &
  Hook.: (168)

Phacelia
 congesta Hook.: 34, (177)–
  (178)
 depauperata Woot. & Standl.:
  (178)
 patuliflora (Engelm. & Gray)
  Gray: 34, (178)
 popei Torr. & Gray: (178)
 strictiflora (Engelm. & Gray)
  Gray: (178)
 whitlavia Gray: (177)

Phlox
 cuspidata Scheele: 35, (180),
  (180)–(181)
 cuspidata Scheele var. *grandiflora* Whitehouse: (180)
 cuspidata Scheele var. *humilis*
  Whitehouse: 35, (180)–(181)
 drummondii Hook.: 35, (179),
  (180)–(181)

pedunculata Torr.: (207)
Rumex
  acetosella L.: (104)
  crispus L.: (104)
  hastatulus Baldwin: (104)
  hymenosepalus Torr.: 7, (103)–
    (104)

Sabatia campestris Nutt.: 32,
  (170)–(171)
Sagittaria
  calycina Engelm.: (90)
  graminea (Engelm.) J. G.
    Smith: (90)
  latifolia Willd.: 1, (89)–(90)
  longiloba Engelm.: (90)
  papillosa Buch.: (90)
  platyphylla (Engelm.) J. G.
    Smith: (90)
Salvia
  azurea: (197)
  coccinea L.: 42, (195)–(196),
    (197)
  engelmannii Gray: (197)
  farinacea Benth.: 42, (196),
    (197)
  greggii Gray: 42, (196), (197)
  officinalis L.: (197)
  splendens Sello: (197)
Salviastrum texanum Scheele: 42,
  (196)–(197)
Salvia texana (Scheele) Torr.: 42,
  (196)–(197)
Sambucus
  canadensis L.: 50, (216)
  coerulea Raf.: (216)
Schmaltzia
  copallina (L.) Small: 24, (148)–
    (149)
  glabra (L.) Small: 24, (149)
Schoenocaulon drummondii Gray:
  2, (93)
Schrankia
  microphylla (Dryander) Mac-
    bride: (126)
  occidentalis (Woot. & Standl.)
    Standl.: (126)

roemeriana (Scheele) Blankinship: (126)
uncinata Willd.: 15, (125)–
  (126)
Scrophulariaceae: (199)–(204)
Scutellaria
  drummondii Benth.: 40, (192)
  integrifolia L.: 40, (192)–(193)
  parvula Michx.: (192)
  resinosa Torr.: (192)
Senecio
  ampullaceus Hook.: (244)
  filifolius Nutt.: 62, (243)–(244)
  glabellus Poir.: (244)
  johnstoni Oliv.: (243)
  longilobus Benth.: 62, (243)–
    (244)
  plattensis Nutt.: 62, (243),
    (243)–(244)
  riddellii Torr. & Gray: (244)
Silene antirrhina L.: (111)
Sinapis arvensis L.: (121)
Sisyrinchium spp.: 5, 6, (100)–
  (101)
Sisyrinchium
  albidum Raf.: (101)
  ensigerum Bicknell: (101)
  longipedunculatum Bicknell:
    (101)
  micranthum Cav.: (101)
  minus Engelm. & Gray: (101)
  pruinosum Bicknell: (101)
  varians Bicknell: (101)
Sitilias multicaulis (DC.) Greene:
  64, (246)–(247)
Solanaceae: (182)–(187)
Solanum
  dimidiatum Raf.: 38, (185)–
    (186)
  eleagnifolium Cav.: 37, (184)
  lycopersicum L.: (185)
  melongena L.: (185)
  rostratum Dunal: 38, (185),
    (185)–(186)
  torreyi Gray: 38, (185)–(186)
  triquetrum Cav.: 37, (184)–
    (185)

Tribulus terrestris L.: 21, (144), (144)–(145)
Triodanis
 biflora (Ruiz & Pavon) Greene: (219)
 holzingeri McVaugh: (219)
 leptocarpa (Nutt.) Nieuwl.: (219)
 perfoliata (L.) Nieuwl.: 51, (218)–(219)
 texana McVaugh: (219)
Typhaceae: (89)
Typha
 domingensis Pers.: (89)
 latifolia L.: 1, (89)

Umbelliferae: (167)–(169)
Uragoga: (214)

Vachellia farnesiana (L.) Wight & Arn.: 15, (124)–(125)
Valerianceae: (216)–(217)
Valerianella
 amarella Krok: 50, (216)–(217)
 radiata (L.) Dufr.: (217)
 stenocarpa (Engelm.) Krok: (217)
 woodsiana Torr. & Gray: (217)
Verbascum
 blattaria L.: (200)
 thapsus L.: 43, (199)–(200)
Verbena
 bipinnatifida Nutt.: 39, (189)
 canescens H. B. K.: (190)
Verbenaceae: (189)–(191)
Verbena
 halei Small: (190)
 hybrida Voss: (190)
 officinalis L.: (190)
 plicata Greene: (190)
 pumila Rydb.: 39, (189)–(190)
 wrightii Gray: (189)
Vernonia
 lindheimeri Gray & Engelm.: 52, (220)–(221)

texana (Gray) Small: 52, (220), (221)
Victoria regia Lindl.: (116)
Viola bicolor Pursh: 26, (156)–(157)
Violaceae: (155)–(157)
Viola
 missouriensis Greene: 26, (155)–(156)
 pedata L.: 26, (155)
 rafinesquii Greene: 26, (156)–(157)
 tricolor L.: (157)
 wittrockiana Gams: (157)
Viorna: (114)
Viorna reticulata (Walt.) Small: 11, (113)–(114)

Wissadula
 amplisericea (L.) Fries: (152)
 holosericea (Scheele) Garcke: 25, (152)

Xanthisma texanum DC.: 53, (224)
Xanthium
 saccharatum Wallr.: (230)
 speciosum Kearney: 57, (230)
 spinosum L.: (230)
Xanthoxalis stricta (L.) Small: 20, (141), (142)

Yucca
 arkansana Trel.: 3, (94), (95)
 brevifolia Engelm.: (95)
 glauca Nutt.: (95)
 rupicola Scheele: (95)
 treculeana Carr.: 3, (94)–(95)

Zephyranthes
 brazosensis Traub.: 4, (98)
 drummondii D. Don: 4, (98)